MORE THAN MIRACLES

Elaine Zeidman Markovic
and the Story of The Scott Mission

ELAINE ZEIDMAN MARKOVIC
AND THE STORY OF THE SCOTT MISSION

more
THAN MIRACLES

BEN VOLMAN
FOREWORD BY THE HONOURABLE DAVID C. ONLEY

CASTLE QUAY BOOKS
WWW.CASTLEQUAYBOOKS.COM

MORE THAN MIRACLES:
ELAINE ZEIDMAN MARKOVIC AND THE STORY OF THE SCOTT MISSION

Copyright © 2015 Scott Mission
All rights reserved
Printed in Canada
International Standard Book Number 978-1-927355-74-9
ISBN 978-1-927355-75-6 EPUB

Published by:
Castle Quay Books
19-24 Laguna Pkwy, Lagoon City, Brechin, Ontario, L0K 1B0
Tel: (416) 573-3249
E-mail: info@castlequaybooks.com   www.castlequaybooks.com

Edited by Marina Hofman Willard, and Lori Mackay
Cover design by Burst Impressions
Printed at Essence Printing, Belleville, Ontario

Library and Archives Canada Cataloguing in Publication
Volman, Ben, author
        More than miracles : Elaine Zeidman Markovic and the
story of Scott Mission / Elaine Markovic, Ben Volman.

Issued in print and electronic formats.
ISBN 978-1-927355-74-9 (paperback).--ISBN 978-1-927355-75-6 (epub)

    1. Scott Mission--History. 2. Zeidman, Morris, 1894-1964.
3. Zeidman, Annie. 4. Homeless persons--Services for--Ontario--
Toronto. 5. Poor--Services for--Ontario--Toronto. 6. Jewish
Christians--Ontario--Toronto--Biography. I. Volman, Ben, author
II. Title.

BV2820.T67M37 2015   266'.0220922713541   C2015-905572-5
                                                 C2015-905573-3

CASTLE QUAY BOOKS
www.castlequaybooks.com

TABLE OF CONTENTS

FOREWORD

I f you asked the average Torontonian what they knew of the Scott Mission, the vast and overwhelming majority, young or old, long-time resident or new to the city, would have positive words to say about "a place that helps the poor and homeless."

And that is true. In fact, founded in 1941, the Mission has for 75 years developed and maintained the same core ministries that have served the poor and neediest of our city.

But what Ben Volman has achieved in this inspiring new book, *More Than Miracles: Elaine Zeidman Markovic and the Story of The Scott Mission*, goes well beyond an historic overview. It is a celebration of the achievements of the remarkable Zeidman family, a testimony of service and of generosity of supporters and, moreover, the unique story of Elaine Zeidman Markovic.

What emerges is a tapestry of overcoming adversity, of faith and love, and a clear message that one woman, through long-term ministry, has made a difference in the Scott Mission and in Toronto itself.

That great theologian and evangelist Andrew Murray wrote in his 1885 classic *With Christ in the School of Prayer*:

> It is when we give ourselves to be a blessing that we can specially count on the blessing of God. It is when we draw near to God as the friend of the poor and the perishing that we may count on his friendliness; the righteous person who is the friend of the poor, is very specially the friend of God.

In that spirit, may you be blessed by this book as you meet friends of the poor and very special friends of God.

DAVID C. ONLEY
Ontario Lieutenant Governor, 2007–2014

INTRODUCTION

Meeting Elaine

As Elaine Zeidman Markovic came downstairs from her second-floor office to the foyer of the Scott Mission, her steps were deliberate, unhurried. Each time we met, I'd experience that ethereal aura of serenity that permeated the air around her. It seemed as much a part of Elaine as her thin, elegant appearance.

In contrast, activity at "The Scott" can seem overwhelming, especially on a first visit. A dozen things are going on at once. Counsellors are directing people to different parts of the building depending on their needs. In the dining room, transient men are being fed, while colourfully dressed immigrant families go by with their arms full of groceries and bags of clothes. A women's Bible study is about to start— it's not in English. Mothers speaking some unfamiliar dialect are dropping off babies and toddlers for an hour's respite. In a time when everyone has a cellphone or an e-mail address, a homeless man is asking for mail. This is the only place where his family can reach him.

Elaine moved calmly through all of this. She'd been serving here through six decades. Many of those years were spent at the front desk, receiving people while they coped with every conceivable personal crisis. She would take the first steps: offering a meal, groceries, clothing or a handout. If the Mission couldn't help, she'd have a referral, making sure the client had the means to get there.

But over the years, Elaine had learned that the most important part of her task wasn't providing groceries or clothing, urgent as that

What mattered most took place in the first moments of meet-
[...]ether it was an elderly woman needing help to pay the rent or
a w[...]e-eyed immigrant stumbling over their English. Each client
should feel that they were heard, understood and valued and, despite
any awkwardness, a measure of their humanity was restored. With
that approach, it's not surprising that for many, Elaine was the heart
of a work known in Toronto as "the miracle on Spadina."

Since the Scott Mission was founded in 1941 by her parents,
Morris and Annie Zeidman, it has expanded exponentially; the services have grown and changed to meet the increasingly complex
needs of the downtown core and a growing city of millions. But
Elaine's greatest concerns were the spiritual and personal welfare of
the staff and clients around her. Beyond efficiencies and success rates,
she expected the Mission to sustain the values taught by her parents
decades before.

I'd follow her upstairs, where we settled into her office, a sunlit
refuge full of memories around a pleasantly disorganized desk with
stacks of projects, books and papers. Pictures of Elaine's extended
family could be seen in every direction: Morris and Annie; her husband, Mica (pronounced Mee' cha); daughters Lois and Sera; her late
older brother, Alex; a vacation picture from Greece with son-in-law
Thanasis; another showing her relaxed against the dark blue
Mediterranean.

As we cleared room for the laptop, Elaine would prepare to
recount the story of the Mission as she'd seen it unfolding over a lifetime. Annie, her mother, had long since warned her, "When I die,
don't let anybody write any books about me." But Elaine wanted a
new generation to understand Morris and Annie's legacy and to give
future ones a glimpse of the divine presence that helped them to
establish the ministry.

While the book was still in concept form, a prominent Canadian
Christian magazine featured the Mission, noting briefly that it was
founded "by a Polish immigrant." It's been about 50 years since
Elaine's father was ranked among Toronto's best-known clergy. Her
parents regularly appeared in newspapers and on the radio as models
of selfless aid to the poor during the darkest years of the Depression.

INTRODUCTION: MEETING ELAINE

Inner-city missionaries are rarely popular figures, but the Zeidmans were revered in their own city and across Canada. Their integrity and determination to meet the pressing needs of the poor, the homeless and struggling new Canadians in downtown Toronto led to the Mission's expansion over the post-war years from a Bay St. store-front into one of the city's most highly visible ministries. In 1961 Morris was named a Canadian "Citizen of the Year." Not bad for an immigrant who arrived in 1912 with no English or high school diploma.

Work began on this book in April 2008 with a series of interviews about Elaine's personal life, the Zeidman family and the Mission. (In a review of an early chapter she'd been emphatic: "'Mission' *must* always be capitalized.") Elaine was asked to choose photos or mementoes to prompt her memories and begin our conversations. At the first interview she presented a photo of Annie, hair swept up in a kerchief, emerging from an outhouse, broom in hand. It was taken around 1942 or '43, when the Scott had taken over a new camp property north of the city. The state of the outhouses was of great concern to local public health authorities, and Annie was convinced that no one else could do a better job of cleaning up after the campers. Elaine recalled how her brother Alex circulated the photo among the Mission staff after he became the director. It came with a reminder: "In case you think any job is beneath you..."

Elaine eventually showed me other treasures, including her father's passport from Czarist Russia (Poland was a subject state). She even suggested that the disorder in her office was a kind of memento. "The Zeidmans are notoriously messy, as you can see by my desk," she said. "We try, but we don't do a very good job of it." She punctuated that comment by pulling out a rusty three-hole punch, dropping it emphatically on the desk. This, she said, exemplified the Mission's true character as well as her parents' motto: "Use it up, wear it out, make it do."

Memories of her family and her Mission stories unspooled easily in our afternoon meetings, and Elaine hesitated only from an effort to be certain that details were correct. Some recollections dated back to early childhood. All of the Zeidman children helped out at the Mission, but she was the first who would choose to work there full-time after graduating from high school in 1953.

No institution, not even one identified with miracles, perseveres for so long without innumerable financial and administrative crises. Elaine knew every one of its successes and trials, some more intimately than others, because for more than half of the history of the Mission it was led by a member of the family. Leadership began with Morris, and at his passing in 1964, her brother Alex took the helm until his sudden death in 1986; afterwards, Elaine's younger brother, David, stepped into the breach as director for about a year. Since 1989, the Mission had been led by others, although family members have continued on staff and on the board. In recent decades, she'd been an interim Mission director a few times until a new one was appointed.

That close involvement through the years had engaged her in many stages of the Mission's development and transition. All this was in addition to her exhausting responsibilities of making sure that services were available for thousands each week. Add to this, her daughters reminded me, the endless duties on evenings and weekends: meeting donors and coping with any number of minor crises and unexpected problems at the various Mission sites.

The more I heard, the more I wanted to know about her personal and spiritual motivation. What kept her going? What were her aspirations? After numerous interviews, Elaine was still finding it painfully hard to reflect on her own life. She spent weeks searching for the text of Alex's poetic mission statement and made sure that I had all of Annie's published songs and poetry. She didn't once mention her own sensitive poems; I received a portfolio much later from her daughters. They also provided a sheaf of more than 25 songs with the byline "Words & Music by Elaine Markovic." Early on, she'd revealed that learning to pray for herself had been one of the greatest challenges in a life of prayer. Putting herself at the centre of a book about the Mission was going to be just as difficult.

I had to press further. How did she come into an authentic faith? What were the origins of her maturity, a turning point? At last it was revealed: a startling moment of clarity, lying in a hospital bed close to death. Having begun with good intentions and a youthful sense of duty she was destined to discover far greater treasures—"something more" that we're all seeking from God. In time, her spiritual confidence and convictions were so deeply rooted that she had a transforming effect on many who knew her. When she spoke or prayed, people sensed that she was saying the most important things for them to hear.

The original interviews were supposed to be a first round with many more details to be filled in later. She received some initial drafts but wasn't well enough to receive the edited versions. Soon, illness made it impossible for her to continue reading any of the material. We spoke only once more, briefly, while she still anticipated getting the project done. One year after we began meeting, in late April 2009, when we had hoped to have the manuscript ready, Elaine passed away.

Afterwards, her daughters, Lois and Sera, and I agreed that the book would be more comprehensive. There is no way to fully acknowledge the full array of remarkable individuals whose efforts sustained the ministry. This book will focus on some unique individuals in the Zeidman family who took part in the ministry. Each one saw the remarkable grace of God at work and gave themselves to the cause. Along the way, each one confronted tough questions: What does it mean to live by faith? When your family is committed to a mission, how do you separate their expectations from your personal calling? How do we keep pressing on in a ministry, and at what cost? When do we let go?

Elaine liked this quote from the 19th century missionary to China Hudson Taylor, no stranger to determining his own unique path of ministry. It goes a long way to revealing her faith: *"What God has given us is all we need; we require nothing more. It is not a question of large supplies—it is a question of the presence of the Lord."*[1] Her life reflected that yearning for His presence, from which she expected that every need of the Mission would be met. It takes a lifetime to acquire this quality—not just the hope of miracles in impossible situations, but an unconditional faith that no matter what we encounter, God will provide. All that we require is learning more fully, day by day, how to wait on Him.

SPADINA AVENUE

By Elaine Z. Markovic

I saw a man once,
withered arm held to his chest, protectively;
His heavy head drooped to one side
and one foot dragged.
People stared.
The lame foot faithfully followed
as he progressed down the street.
My heart was shouting after him,
"Tears to be wiped away, all things
Made New!"

Sometimes, even the elements
sympathize.
They rain down tears
from a mournful sky.
They too await the day of
Deliverance.

CHAPTER 1

Finding Laine

To say that Elaine was born into a missionary home means little today. There was a time when those words would have brought to mind exotic settings, foreign languages and intriguing new cultures. But she had her fill of that on the family mission field, Toronto's inner-city Jewish neighbourhoods.

She grew up near the bustling mayhem of Kensington Market, where Jews from around the world, especially after World War II, crowded into the teeming narrow streets to find a bargain or drive a deal. Colourful baskets of fresh produce were lined along the sidewalks where the air was punctuated by the noise of shouting merchants, car horns and live chickens still in their cages. Cobbled alleyways were vibrant with conversations over open barrels with pickles or herring. Families and couples were drawn by the aroma of European bakeries to get coffee and pastries and for *Shabbat* (the Sabbath) pick from at least five types of *challah*—sweet egg bread—sliced to order. Behind the large shop windows were piles of fish over ice, glass cases stacked with waxed rounds of cheese and heavy blocks of halvah in gold and silver foil.

It was an old-world marketplace in the heart of staid Toronto, a bland grey city where immigrants found a bank and a church on every corner and solid middle-class proprieties. As a teenager, Elaine might have been embarrassed by the shouting fruit peddlers and raucous conversation between tailors and seamstresses pouring out of sweatshops. Yet this is where she came to feel most familiar, surrounded by jarring accents on hectic street corners.

Even today, Kensington retains many of its original quaint narrow Victorian "gingerbread" houses. In summer, they boast vivid garden plots or small squares of grass. Similar houses had once lined the market streets before they acquired storefronts and then brazenly pushed their sales-goods to the sidewalk. A world away from the average Toronto church parish, it was a remarkable backdrop for life-size drama, and the market streets of Kensington were just steps away from the broad thoroughfares of Spadina Avenue and College Street.

By the 1930s, Spadina, running south of College, had become the arterial mainstay of Toronto's Jewish community. The avenue's wide sidewalks had room for everyone with an opinion and a voice to hold a crowd. There were missionary preachers, union organizers and street-wise politicians of every stripe. When there was outrage or a strike or the people opened their hearts to a new cause, there was a march up Spadina—as they did in 1933, 15,000 strong to protest the anti-Semitic laws in Nazi Germany.[1]

At its lower end, Spadina was growing into an industrial centre for the Canadian garment and fur trade—the *shmatte* business—with a lively cast of entrepreneurs. The avenue was lined with dusty storefronts, each one a standard bearer for immigrant expectations of making a living in hats or lace, buttons or business suits, retail or wholesale. Down the centre of the avenue rolled the familiar TTC red-and-cream streetcars (the original "Red Rockets"). When the front doors slid open, people squeezed their way through the stone-faced newcomers, gripping bags full of groceries or dry goods. There was always a baby crying while a mother comforted her in some unknown tongue. When you got off, you couldn't help noticing the chrome-gilded sedans filled with families who showed off the brash self-satisfaction of having arrived.

In November 1941, the Scott Mission was one of the newest ministries in the city but already one of the best known. Rev. Morris Zeidman and his wife, Annie, had been running the Scott Institute, a Presbyterian inner-city mission outreach to Jewish people, since 1927.

During the Depression years, the Zeidmans came to citywide prominence when they expanded their ministry, going to extraordinary lengths to assist those who were impoverished by the economic tsunami sweeping the country. But by the early 1940s, those hard times were past. A thriving economy driven by the war in Europe meant that most people—and most churches—were no longer worried about the poor. After years of effective ministry, Zeidman became subject to petty complaints from his denomination about minor expenses. In frustration, he resigned his position with the Presbyterian church, closing the Scott Institute at the end of October 1941.

Giving up the security of a salary, missionary housing on which he paid no rent and the guarantees of his position with the church, Morris secured a double storefront on Bay Street. The day after the Scott Institute closed its doors, newspaper ads announced, "The Scott Carries On." On November 1st the program of the institute would continue under a new banner: The Scott Mission. Even with a network of supporters and willing volunteers, they would face some very lean years.

The effect of all these changes on the Zeidman family happened well out of public view. The transition was hard on their four children, the oldest still only 13. They moved from the Mission quarters near Kensington at 307 Palmerston Ave. and College St. to a more conventional area in the east end of the city, north of the Danforth, between Woodbine and Main. The children considered themselves to be Jewish and had to cope with the culture shock of arriving in a typical Anglo-Canadian suburb. At the time, some 80 percent of Torontonians identified their origins as British. The open anti-Semitism among local children, even teachers, aggravated the family's sense of isolation. (Very few Jewish teachers during the 1930s and '40s were able to find work in Toronto schools.[2]) Nor did the neighbours bother hiding their prejudice. Some were particularly obnoxious, and one day the family came home to find the word "Jew" scrawled on the garage.[3]

Elaine, the younger daughter, had just turned seven. The family called her "Lainey"— spelled out as "Laine." She was surrounded by two older siblings and a younger brother, all of them born three years apart between 1928 and 1937. Her practical-minded older sister, Margaret, had arrived while the family still lived in the original old Mission building at 165 Elizabeth St. Margaret had inherited her mother's considerable musical skills in voice and piano. Alex, the older brother, was destined to carry himself with the bearing of a distinguished clergyman. He was a serious boy who enjoyed tinkering with mechanical projects, including a large crystal radio set, in the basement. The youngest, David, who would also play a leading role with the Mission, was a robust, happy child with great affection for his parents and siblings.

Laine was born in 1934 at the height of the Depression, a strikingly beautiful baby according to Margaret, but frequently ill. She was too young to remember her parents bringing her to Sick Children's Hospital with peritonitis, which in those days was fatal. The revered family physician Dr. Markowitz was able to secure penicillin, which had just become available. Her fate was uncertain until she rallied, taking months to recover. Laine would always have a sensitive stomach and remained prone to infections, never so vigorous as her siblings.

One of Laine's earliest memories was of her mother, thermometer in hand, deciding she was sick and hurrying them over to the family physician. Dr. Markowitz paid scant attention to the little girl, insisting that Annie immediately sit down and take a glass of wine.

At Christmas 1941, with the new Mission barely underway, Laine came down with scarlet fever. Public health officials treated the disease with extreme caution. Her parents couldn't afford the $12 a week required to put her into a special hospital isolation ward and paid off the bill in instalments. (This was decades before publicly funded health care.) Morris, using his clerical privileges, came to visit, and the little girl didn't recognize him under the full protective gown until she heard him say, "Laine, it's me."

By the time Laine returned home, her mother had the family schedule in order. Early each morning, Morris drove to the office, while she prepared the children for school. After they left, Annie took the streetcar and joined him downtown. It wasn't an era of working mothers. Annie discreetly employed a homemaker so that she could put in a full day at the Mission, usually coming home exhausted.

For the Zeidman children, the Mission schedule was closely linked to family life. They helped out as best they could through the year, joining in regular family programs through fall, winter and spring and then residing at the summer camp with the other kids. When needed, they were extra hands and feet for innumerable daily tasks. As they grew older, each one in turn would find a place in the work.

It was a lively house, full of music and its share of laughter. Occasional evenings were spent singing around the piano—Morris loved to sing, and Annie had trained in voice as well as piano at the Royal Conservatory of Music. Everyone kept up a sharp sense of humour. When Alex was a theology student at Knox, Laine knit him a tie in the purple and grey colours of the college. She'd made it a bit long, so one morning he showed up at breakfast wearing his usual college tie and Laine's knitted handiwork wrapped around his leg for decoration.

Despite their busy schedules, family members were expected to be home and gathered at the table for dinner, followed by a Bible reading with devotions. There were no more amusements once the Scriptures were opened. Morris and Annie were serious life-long Bible students. Only in time did Laine fully understand how much of the Word of God she'd absorbed from them, a lifetime's treasury of wisdom and comfort that came to mind when it was most needed out of the lessons from her earliest years.

The hours after supper were equally occupied. Annie used the time to teach her daughters how to play the piano, and later that was time for practice. To help make ends meet, she sewed a lot of the children's clothing. Morris, too, spent his evenings focused on studying and writing at the kitchen table. He relied on Annie to be his editor while he composed tracts and articles, plus his international correspondence. Always studying, Morris earned a PhD and was a Bible college teacher of Greek and Hebrew. Later, the children would recall vividly how Morris's bedroom was filled with books, newspapers and clippings from newspaper subscriptions that kept him abreast of international news—in English and Yiddish—from across Europe and America.

Afterwards, Annie would read to the younger children. Those moments became some of Laine's most precious memories. As a young child, she was encouraged to say prayers before bedtime. There was one she could easily recall and had taught to her own daughters:

Jesus, tender shepherd, hear me,
Bless thy little lamb tonight;
Through the darkness be thou near me,
Keep me safe 'til morning light.

During one of those prayer times, Annie wanted to know why her 11 year-old daughter was in an irritable mood. It eventually occurred to Laine that it was Miss Stacey's fault. During the Sunday school lesson, Miss Stacey had asked the children in her class, "Has anyone here given their heart to Jesus?" Laine was troubled because she couldn't say yes. So Annie began explaining how she could say yes, right then and there beside her bed. That was the moment when Laine prayed for Jesus to enter her heart.

As the family struggled to cope through numerous trials with the Mission over the next few years, Laine started to show a rebellious streak. During the first year of high school at Malvern Collegiate, her behaviour became a problem. She was seeing far too much of the detention room. Morris was embarrassed. He expected his children to the know the importance of education, but Laine didn't act interested anymore. She was falling in with the wrong crowd.

Annie had taken each child aside when they were eight or nine years old and taught them, "Remember who you are." They were responsible for being "a *Zeidman*." There were standards to maintain—the conduct suitable for children of clergy. Young as they were, the message was clear: "We're not like other families." By high school, Laine seemed to have had enough of that. Some of her attitudes might have come from her teachers. Neither of her older siblings had excelled at that school, and Margaret described the teachers as openly anti-Semitic.

Morris was determined that his daughter was not going to give up on her education. Despite the cost, he placed her at Moulton College, a Baptist all-girls high school associated with McMaster University, where families in ministry received financial considerations.

Soon Laine would find a supportive circle of friends, although that didn't seem so likely when she first arrived. The girls were fixing their place in the social order as each one answered the question, "Who's your father?" Of course, she knew that many of the girls had heard of her father or The Scott Mission, but Laine wasn't quite sure how to answer that question. Who was Rev. Morris Zeidman, and why was it so difficult being his daughter?

LUNCH

By Elaine Z. Markovic

As I make a lunch this morning
I wonder about the lad
Who offered his food to Christ.
Five small loaves and two fishes.

Did that one argue, "Loaves and fish again!
Mom, do I have to take it?"
Was she tired, too? And said,
"Don't give me lip. No lunch, no trip!"

But Jesus took the meal,
gave thanks, broke bread,
And fed
A crowd
Who soon would witness
The broken Bread of Life.

CHAPTER 2

An Interesting Wedding

In the glow of late summer, on September 2, 1926, Miss Annie Aitken Martin, draped in ivory taffeta and framed by the graceful high stone arches of the Knox College chapel, came down the centre aisle to meet her groom, in dark morning coat and white bow tie, the Rev. Morris Zeidman. Today, the chapel remains an inspired setting of hushed reverence near the centre of the University of Toronto campus. Sunlight pours down through tall latticed windows with a smoky yellow glaze. Dappled shadows from the trees lining King's College Circle dance over long dark rows of pews. On that day, before the college opened for classes, the pews would have been filled with many dear friends and ministry colleagues.

Newspaper accounts of the event, quite common at the time, give us colourful details: the bride's American beauty roses; the maid of honour and bridesmaid in pink and blue georgette with "old-fashioned nosegays." But the *Toronto Evening Star* hinted at something else when it called the event "interesting."[1]

The bride's mother had passed on a few years earlier, and her father, Mr. William Martin, was also absent. The papers said that he lived in Edinburgh, Scotland, but he'd been a long-time Toronto resident and moved back to Scotland only a few months before. In an era when cross-cultural marriages were frowned upon, it's hardly surprising that he had strong objections to his daughter's choice, described by the *Telegram* as a "Presbyterian missionary to Jews." Annie had come down the aisle on the arm of Rev. John McNicol, the distinguished principal of Toronto Bible College.[2]

Details of Mr. Zeidman's parents and family are also conspicuously missing from the newspaper copy. But a few inches of type could hardly explain how Morris, who had left an Orthodox Jewish home in Czarist Poland 14 years before, was now ordained and getting married in a Canadian Protestant seminary.

Another, less prominent, name in the newspapers draws our attention. The service was conducted by two clergy: Rev. Dr. J. G. Inkster of Knox Presbyterian Church, assisted by "the Rev. S.B. Rohold of Haifa, Palestine." Rohold had been Morris's mentor and predecessor at the Scott Institute, where the couple would begin ministry when they returned from their honeymoon. Rev. Rohold and his wife, Belle (later known as Bella), had literally travelled the world to be there. At the time, much of his work required him to traverse the length and breadth of Palestine (often by donkey) to assist the British in oversight of their new mandate in the region. The journey would have been a welcome respite for Belle (nee Petrie), whom he had met in Toronto. The event itself must have given them great satisfaction. After all, if anyone, apart from heaven, could lay claim to bringing the bride and groom together, it was Ben Rohold.

Only a decade before, Annie's family was a quiet model of Edwardian reserve, not likely to be identified with an interesting public ministry. Each Sunday morning Annie joined her parents in the great auditorium of Bloor Street Presbyterian Church, where she and her father sang in the choir. The large congregation had recently appointed one of Canada's finest preachers to its pulpit, the Rev. George Campbell Pidgeon.

Miss Martin was enjoying the busy life of a gifted pianist with her own students. She was also receiving the attentions of a certain young gentleman likely to be approved by her father. (He wasn't the one she married.) Then, sometime during the hard years of World War I,

Annie heard Rev. Rohold make an appeal for workers to help at the Jewish mission. Despite its location in a squalid district called "the Ward," she volunteered.[3]

Annie began supervising a program once a week that taught English to young girls from poor Jewish families whose first language at home was Yiddish. She loved the girls and enjoyed the work. Still, every week, she had a continuing irritation; his name was Morris Zeidman. Dark, short and energetic, he led the boys' club that met on the same night, perhaps in the same large room or an adjacent one. Morris would arrive early and round up all the equipment he needed, as if the boys had some priority. It seemed to Annie that he blatantly disregarded the needs of the girls. She'd arrive to find her class in need of chairs or teaching aids, thanks to Mr. Zeidman, whom she quickly decided was far too brash.

The offending young man's self-assurance was particularly irritating. He'd fled Poland only four or five years earlier from the city of Czestochowa. His mother, Hannah (Haindel), was the second wife of Alexander (Ziskind) Zeidman, a widower, and she oversaw a combined family of eight children—Morris had a younger brother and six sisters, although the oldest sister was by this time married and in her own home. A pious Orthodox Jew, Ziskind owned a prosperous fruit and vegetable store. Morris was born on *Shavuoth* (known to Christians as Pentecost) in 1894 and attended a neighbourhood Hebrew school. Haindel was a woman of sturdy common sense, frequently managing the business while her husband attended to daily prayers in the synagogue.[4] Charity—*tzedaka*—was very important. Whatever the family's situation, every week, well before the eve of the Sabbath (*Erev Shabbat*), Morris helped his father put together a parcel of groceries that he'd deliver to a needy family.

The region's painful history of Russian anti-Semitic persecution had bred resistance against Czarist rule. Some of Morris's contemporaries recalled his involvement in a small local socialist organization; then he was arrested for being in the street during a demonstration. The police station was in such a furor when Hannah arrived with two of his stepsisters that no one noticed when his mother left, ushering out *three* girls through the front door. No disguise, though, could help Morris after a second arrest and appearance before the local magistrate. While there's no specific explanation for Morris leaving Poland, the family memory was that he'd already been fortunate. One more arrest and he'd have been deported to Siberia. Life at home was increasingly uncomfortable; none of this had his father's approval.

Morris's passport, still a fond family keepsake, is stamped with the year of his arrival in the port of Montreal, 1912. After providing for the long journey and ocean passage, the family had little more to offer and only a few parting gifts. These included his grandfather's sacred phylacteries or *tefillin* (special bindings and boxes with Scriptures enclosed that are used in daily prayers) "so that he should not forget" the faith of Israel. With no English and few friends, Morris made his way to Toronto, where there was a growing community from his hometown in Poland. He was trying to find work as a manual labourer and often passed the time walking alone through the city.

Fellow Jewish immigrants would have warned him about the imposing three-storey brick building at the corner of Elm and Elizabeth Streets—the Jewish mission. Nothing was more contemptible for Jewish people than a *meshummad*, literally a "traitor," one who converted to the religion of the Gentiles. The local missionary may have been tolerated; getting too familiar with him would be suspicious.

But one Sunday afternoon, Morris, who'd been walking the deserted streets and brooding over a way to learn English for free, caught sight of the sign in a window. It said in Hebrew "The House of the Good News of Messiah for the Children of Israel." Morris, no stranger to controversy, discarded a lifetime of training to be wary of the *goyim* and found his way inside. Soon afterwards, he was enrolled in English classes and able to find employment in a machine shop, working 10 hours a day. He also received that forbidden book known in English as the New Testament. At first he may have tried to hide his copy from the Jewish family with whom he was boarding. When they found him reading it and talking like the missionary, they sent him packing.

Why did the Presbyterians have a mission to Jews in the centre of Edwardian Toronto? This proudly multicultural city has long since lost touch with the less tolerant society of the early 1900s. It was rife with anti-Semitism, and its growing number of Jewish immigrants was generally welcomed with disdain and mistrust. The newcomers often lived as peddlers, dealers in cast-off goods and second-hand clothes. Some found work in the needle trades or turned their homes into little storefronts in the city's poorest district.

In Toronto, that location was "the Ward" (properly called St. John's Ward), in the very heart of the city, bordered by College Street on the north, Yonge Street to the east and University Avenue to the west and extending south to Queen Street. Currently, it's a district that boasts major office towers and some of the city's leading hospitals. Back then it was a maze of narrow alleyways lined with dilapidated housing, some dating back to the 1840s. The drafty stucco frame homes were rented out by absentee landlords; many lacked indoor plumbing and had dirt floors. New immigrants kept the cheap housing in demand, and city officials ignored complaints from public health officials. Here, as in New York's Lower East Side and cities across North America, one of the poorest districts in Toronto became the hub of a thriving Jewish community.

According to the 1901 census, Toronto had 15,000 Jewish residents out of a total population of 208,000, but they quickly became one of the largest, most visible, immigrant groups. The vast majority of recent arrivals had fled Russia and its satellites: Poland, the Ukraine, Slavic and Baltic states. Their numbers grew even more dramatically from 1903 to 1906 when the Czarist government allowed indiscriminate attacks on the Jewish populace. Their homes and businesses were looted; families ran for their lives, while the Russian authorities did nothing. The Americans, also inundated by refugees, compelled the Czarist government to bring the worst excesses to a halt, though the immigrants kept coming.

A growing Jewish presence in the heart of Toronto was of special interest to local Presbyterian church leaders. All through the 19th century, Protestant Jewish missions were expanding. In England and North America, they would provide Jewish immigrants with English lessons, life skills education and family-friendly programs while their founders, a rising number of Jewish followers of Jesus, spread the gospel.

The rise of Jewish missionary efforts helped to spark a growing fascination in the fulfillment of Bible prophecies during the 19th century. Popular interpretations of prophetic Scriptures pointed to specific prophecies, both in the Jewish Bible and the New Testament, that "in the last days" Jewish people would experience a spiritual revival, be drawn to their Messiah and resettle in the Holy Land. With the impending close of the second millennium, visionary Christian leaders were preaching the Lord's soon return. Others recognized that centuries of Christian persecution had hardened Jewish people against the gospel. The emerging leadership among the Jewish believers in Jesus—Hebrew Christians of various denominations—began to form sizable missionary organizations and strongly influenced the Christian approach to Jewish people.

As early as 1838, the Church of Scotland was excited by this vision of Israel receiving the message of Jesus as Messiah and being restored to the Holy Land. During the 1840s, a fervent young Scot, Rev. Robert Murray McCheyne, travelled with a church commission to Palestine, seeking new avenues to bring the gospel to Jewish people. Returning to his parish in poor health, he passed away during a typhoid epidemic. McCheyne was only 29, but his diaries and sermons, published posthumously, became Christian bestsellers. His zeal for Jewish missions, combined with the rising interest in fulfillments of prophetic Scriptures, helped to sustain the popular wave of support to Presbyterians across the British Empire.

By the 1860s, Canadian Presbyterians were sponsoring their own Jewish missionary in the Middle East, the Rev. Dr. Ephraim Menachem Epstein.[5] When several Presbyterian denominations became a single national church in 1875—the Presbyterian Church in Canada—they looked for new Jewish ministries to support. While considering ministry opportunities in Canada, the Ward caught their attention. During the 1907 general assembly in

Montreal, a motion was carried "to commence a mission to the Hebrew people in Toronto, with the privilege of extending the work elsewhere in Canada as the circumstances may warrant."[6] A special committee was formed under Rev. John McPherson Scott of St. John's Church, Riverdale, in Toronto's east end. He was charged with setting up an outreach to the growing Jewish community in Toronto.

Scott was a tall, beloved great-hearted leader with a reputation for getting things done. (A local Jewish mission had already started with his help.) With typical efficiency, he took leadership of the committee in September 1907, and by the end of December he was able to recommend a promising missionary candidate: Mr. Sabati Benjamin (Ben) Rohold, then employed by a similar ministry in Glasgow.

Numerous photos of the period show Ben Rohold as a studious-looking figure with round wire-rimmed glasses.[7] His contemporaries respected his diligent, unpretentious and genuinely spiritual character and admired his intellectual gifts. (He grew up speaking Hebrew to his father, Spanish to his mother, Arabic to the children on his street, German to his tutor in secular studies, fluent English as a Christian minister and Yiddish for preaching and personal ministry.)[8] In April 1915, the first international conference to form an international alliance of Hebrew Christians in North America was held in Toronto, and out of all the dignitaries he was elected president.[9] He became the first editor of that organization's quarterly journal, was a writer and editor of books and wrote for numerous other leading missionary publications. Whenever Morris and Annie spoke of him to their children it was with sincere reverence.[10]

Born and raised in Jerusalem, the son and grandson of distinguished rabbis, Rohold had a thoroughly traditional Jewish education, including rabbinical training and extensive Talmudic studies. An encounter with a Christian missionary on the Mount of Olives (according to his personal account they began their discussion in the Garden of Gethsemane) led Rohold to the firm belief that Jesus of Nazareth is the Jewish Messiah. After weighing the costs of his decision over a period of years, he made an irreversible break from his parents and left for Great Britain; Rohold was only 21. A few years later, after graduating from Glasgow Bible College, he began to work in the local Jewish mission. Rohold had been there seven years when the Canadians offered him the position of mission superintendent, ordination, an annual salary of $1,200 and full provision for moving expenses (which largely meant shipping his books). By March 1908 he had arrived in Toronto.[11]

Rohold's storefront mission opened on Monday, April 6, 1908, in the centre of the Ward at 156 Teraulay Street (now Bay Street) at Elm. A number of the city's leading Presbyterians were there for encouragement, but there were other visitors more openly doubtful of the enterprise. In his book *Missions to the Jews* (1918), Rohold describes listening to their comments. "Some gave us a lease of life of three months, six months and the most generous 'one year.' But the good Lord was pleased to put the seal of Divine approval on the work."[12]

Scott and his committee were willing to be patient. Jewish ministries were expected to make slow progress. The Eastern European immigrants were isolated by the Yiddish language, a hybrid form of Hebrew and low German. They saw no difference between the Presbyterians and churches that had been persecuting them for the past millennia. A few of the young Jewish leaders had prepared their own welcome for the Mission; they set up a lookout to write down the names of anyone going in or out of the storefront. So when success came relatively quickly, it far exceeded the expectations of Rohold's superiors. Within five years there was not only a regular flow of traffic through the Mission doors but even a small, vibrant Hebrew Christian Presbyterian congregation.

Rohold envisioned a mission caring for a wide array of needs, reaching "the whole Jewish family." Comfortable reading rooms were stocked with newspapers in Yiddish from Europe and New York. Free services included night schools that taught English to separate classes of men and women, Sabbath schools, boys and girls clubs, recreation activities and a summer camp. A man of inexhaustible energy, Rohold visited widely in the community, distributing tracts and holding open-air services. On the Sabbath, he preached from the back of a wagon at Elizabeth and Agnes

(Dundas St.), where Jewish families strolled after synagogue. (The practice wasn't endearing to local Jewry or the press, although typical of missions at the time.)

The eventual key to success wasn't in Rohold's original plans. When he began visiting local residents, many were despairing and depressed by the shabby housing and unsanitary conditions. Frequently he heard "No one cares for us." While sharing the remarks with his volunteers, one of the women suggested he seek the aid of a retired druggist, Mr. T. C. Wilmott, who in turn enlisted the assistance of a physician, Dr. A. C. McClennan. Their services attracted an unusual level of attention, and after a free dispensary opened on May 1, 1908, and then a free medical clinic, the Mission never looked back.

Success didn't simply rely on the missionary's rigorous personal schedule. Here we see the authentic qualities that Rohold demanded of himself:

> In order to reach the Jewish people with the message of love, we must show them the reality of our message...The character, devotedness and spiritual power of the missionaries is really what a mission represents. The message that has entered their own life and soul is now entrusted to them, and this they must proclaim and exhibit in their life.[13]

These are the selfless values of faith that Morris and Annie chose to adopt and placed at the centre of their ministry.

From the beginning, the Mission gave meticulous reports to the presbytery. In Rohold's first year, the clinic treated 3,142 cases, 43 babies were vaccinated, 242 home visits were made to the sick, and 41 of those were maternity cases. Eventually a women's clinic was opened. By 1911, six doctors and a nurse were donating time to the Mission. Some practical assistance was offered, including rent subsidies and coal supplies.

In the fall of 1908, Rohold was ordained at Knox Church on Spadina Avenue. Meanwhile, demand for services on Teraulay Street was expanding far beyond the capacity of a storefront. An unfortunate incident in June 1911 would only briefly hamper Rohold's best efforts, although it would remain a memorable chapter for the Jewish community.[14] After another local missionary had made anti-Semitic comments that received wide circulation, Rohold's regular Sunday afternoon open-air service incited a violent riot. The front page of *The Toronto Daily Star's* late edition on Monday, June 19, featured a photo of the Presbyterian missionary in tabs and collar. The opening paragraph led with this statement:

> "I come from Jerusalem, the home of the prophets who were stoned, and I shall preach as long as breath is in me. Preach I must and preach I will."
>
> This was the declaration made to *The Star* this morning by the Rev. S. B. Rohold, the Presbyterian missionary who was preaching when the riot began in the Ward last night. Mr. Rohold looked perfectly fresh this morning…He is a gentleman under middle age with short dark hair and flashing eyes. He is full of fire and enthusiasm.[15]

He promised "to be on the same spot, Saturday and Sunday, preaching the word." Rohold denied that either his preaching or his work was an attack on the Jewish religion. "I simply preach Christianity," he said. He also spoke of the ministry plans to erect a new building that would allow the work to go on with "renewed vigor."

Scott's committee had secured land on the southeast corner of Elm and Elizabeth Streets and began construction on an impressive three-storey brick building to be called the Christian Synagogue at 165 Elizabeth Street. It's interesting that Rev. Rohold, in his interview, could already provide the final cost, which was $35,000 including the property.

The site boasted all the facilities needed to fulfill the missionary's vision: specialized rooms for the clinic and dispensary, activity space, reading rooms and a good-sized meeting hall for the Hebrew Christian congregation formed in 1913. It became one of the leading mission sites in North America. Doors were open from 8 a.m. to 9 p.m. every day but Monday (the workers' rest day). Rohold's 1918 book includes a series of excellent black and white prints of the building. A candid photo of congregants in their meeting room shows the words, "To the Jew first" (Romans 1:16) on the front wall.[16] Unfortunately, the impressive brick building is now gone, and the site has been absorbed into the campus of the Hospital for Sick Children, but this is where Annie and Morris first crossed paths—and swords.

JANUARY

By Elaine Z. Markovic

Look out that window
Through your sadness.
See those bare branches,
Not a hint of leaf
Or even bud;
And yet,
We know
That by the end of March
Small promises will appear
That foretell an abundant
New life.

CHAPTER 3

Holy Chutzpah—
The Challenge of a Call

Ben Rohold and Morris Zeidman had good reasons for a sympathetic rapport. Both were raised in Orthodox homes led by spiritually devoted fathers and dutiful mothers. Almost 20 years older than Morris, Ben respected the young man's keen mind and identified with the struggle of being immersed into a new culture. The free English lessons and a growing bond with Ben Rohold led Morris to a spiritual awareness that changed his life.

At 17, Morris became a follower of Jesus and was formally admitted into the Hebrew Christian congregation, according to the carefully handwritten 1914 records for the Christian Synagogue. It wasn't a decision made lightly. Spurned or silently ignored by former friends and neighbours, Morris was no longer welcome among the local fraternity of men from Czestochowa, his *landsleit*. Others, who recognized him in the street as a *meshummad*—traitor—would shout the word at him. Elaine recalled him saying that he had to return home one day to change his clothes because they were soaked with spittle.

As the young man dealt with the rejection, developing a genuine, maturing faith, Ben Rohold and John McPherson Scott began to appreciate his potential. Morris was working in the machine shop when Scott asked him to come by St. John's Church early one evening, prior to the mid-week meeting. A gathering of elders was waiting with Rev. Scott in the vestry. To the young man's surprise, the men circled around him. He received "the laying on of hands"—formal prayers setting him apart as one who might be called to ministry. Kneeling with them, he prayed for leading from the Holy Spirit, and eventually, he would sense a genuine call. It would mean an uphill battle for years to come, beginning with the task of completing high school at night in a new language and acquiring sufficient marks to attend college, then seminary.

Elaine, reflecting on that decision almost a century later, said, "I think it was holy chutzpah. Those were lonely years, because Messianic Jews are neither fish nor fowl. They are ostracized by their fellow Jews and oddities to fellow Christians."

Perhaps the feeling of isolation made the growing bonds between Morris and Rev. Scott all the more crucial. Scott remained a mentor until his untimely death in 1920. Five years later, the building that had been known as "The Christian Synagogue" was formally renamed: "The Scott Institute." Clients simplified that to "the Scott," and decades later it made sense for Morris and Annie to adopt the name for their independent mission. It's an enduring legacy to Scott's inspirational vision and commitment to bless the Jewish people.

The last page of Rohold's 1918 book, *Missions to the Jews*, has a photo of Morris in his full Boy Scout leader's uniform, surrounded by young men from the mission's Scout troop. Without referring to him directly, the closing paragraphs are written with a prescient faith:

> During the past ten years we have sought by every means possible to reconcile Israel with their Messiah, their only and brightest hope. We turn from the past to the unknown future in perfect confidence that He will continue to bless us.[1]

That picture would have meant a great deal to Morris; after all, he was probably leading this same group of boys when he first met the interesting Miss Martin.

There are numerous sepia-toned pictures of Morris and Annie from the early years of the 20th century showing their mutual affection. One of Elaine's favourite photos has the pair in matching "Ivy League" jackets and ties. It was, as she would confide, "a love match," despite a rather rocky start. Yes, they did maintain a certain Victorian decorum, but they always called each other "dear," and in front of the children Annie called him "Zeidy," a youthful nickname. (Another affectionate name—"Zeidle"—shows up in his correspondence.[2])

It's hard to know exactly how the ice melted, but Annie eventually severed the relationship with her original beau. (Family lore says that he didn't take the news very well.) The years immediately ahead brought a series of tests to help forge their persevering faith and mutual trust. Those qualities would shape the character of their relationship and form the bedrock of an effective ministry.

After graduating from night school, Morris entered the University of Toronto around 1919, the year when his name first appears on the Mission payroll. In a fragment of a report to Scott's committee dated that year,[3] Rohold affirmed his protégé's potential as a ministry leader:

> Mr. Zeidman has done wonderfully well since I am away. He is sound in his message and as a young man, is remarkably good in ability, earnestness and zeal, and we ought to encourage him in every way possible.[4]

Morris studied for three years at University College, earning a degree in Honours Orientals. (Hebrew and Arabic classes were less of a problem than English: final grade, 40 percent.) In the fall of 1921 he entered the Presbyterian seminary, Knox College, and academics were not his most daunting problem. He'd overcome challenges that would have discouraged anyone less convinced of God's call on his life.

Morris's father in Poland had passed away in the years following the war. With so many unresolved differences between them, the feelings of grief would have been deeply felt. The sudden death in 1920 of his fatherly mentor, Dr. Scott, was another tragic personal loss. None of this could be read in his demeanor. Student friends remembered Morris as a cheerful colleague, an unfailing optimist.

He needed that positive attitude to cope with a growing number of health issues. Not too long after his baptism, Morris's appendix was removed; then he was diagnosed with an intestinal problem, a so-called "tuberculosis of the bowel," the term used for a persisting colitis. The disease wasn't well understood for much of his life, and he endured regular painful flare-ups. When some old acquaintances said that he was under divine judgment, Morris ignored them.

Early in his second year at Knox there were new complications. During an operation to remove his adenoids, a blood vessel was accidentally severed. With his life hanging in the balance, friends and classmates rallied around him in prayer, anxious to do more. Fortunately, one had his rare blood type: Hugh Macmillan, future missionary to China and Formosa (Taiwan), who would become a lifelong friend. Years later, Morris would joke about being born Jewish but having "pure Scottish blood" flowing in his veins. Macmillan also made much of the story. While overseas, he described the transfusion to his Chinese audiences as a graphic illustration of receiving new life in Jesus by the grace of God. After returning to Canada, Rev. Macmillan had a distinguished pulpit career and served as moderator for the Presbyterian Church in Canada.

In the anxious days of waiting for news from the hospital, Miss Macdonald, a beloved elderly prayer warrior, spoke with assurance that Morris would indeed be healed, "but he would have to tread softly for the rest of his days." Her words proved true. Complications from colitis would reoccur for the rest of his life, though Morris rarely gave himself the luxury of slowing down. An extended recuperation took place north of Toronto in the town of Hillsburgh. Years later, he would return to the same area to relocate the new Mission's summer camp program.

While Morris was ill, his younger sister, Gitel—later known as Gertrude—arrived from Poland. Morris had sponsored her immigration and saved up to pay for her passage to Canada. She was only 14 years old, and she eventually settled in with the family of his New Testament professor, William Manson. Her affectionate relationship with the Mansons could have ended when Dr. Manson received a faculty appointment to Edinburgh University. Instead, she was officially adopted and moved with them to Scotland.[5]

Annie had her own share of complications. Her father didn't restrain his anger at her Jewish suitor, and there were unmerciful tirades. As the marriage plans were finalized, she took refuge in the home of a sympathetic local family. The painful rift between father and daughter never healed. William Martin's sudden death in Scotland a few years later was a shocking loss.

Just as Morris was entering his studies at Knox, Ben Rohold was invited to take on a new work in Palestine in an undeveloped area of the port city Haifa, at the foot of Mt. Carmel. He corresponded with numerous colleagues for many months before he finally accepted. Reluctant to leave one of the leading positions in North America, he had important reasons to consider the offer. The new British mandate was supposed to be laying groundwork for the Jewish state promised in the 1917 Balfour Declaration. His extraordinary managerial gifts and languages, combined with an extensive knowledge of both the British and Middle East cultures, made him uniquely capable of assisting in the restoration of a new Jewish homeland.

Rev. and Mrs. Rohold had been promised a functional mission property in Haifa on what was later to become HaGefen Street. Unfortunately, as Rohold explained in a long letter to Morris, they arrived to find horrendous living conditions. Months were spent working on the buildings while they lived out of two miserable cellar rooms. They endured as always and eventually planted a highly effective work with a medical clinic and reading room ministry, similar to the one developed in Toronto. Over the next decade, Rohold became highly esteemed in the region, often representing the interests of the Jewish community to the British authorities. He worked diligently to forge ties with the local Greek church authorities and even acted as a mediator for Moslem and Druse villagers. At the founding of Hebrew University in Jerusalem, Rohold was an invited guest.[6]

Their 1926 wedding was almost certainly Morris and Annie's last meeting with the mentor who'd been so important in their lives. In 1929, Rohold became quite ill, until his care required a move to a sanatorium in Egypt, where he died on February 14, 1931. He lies buried in the British Protestant cemetery in Old Cairo.[7] Belle—by then she was known as Bella—could have returned to Canada, but she proved to be as resilient in her calling as her husband. Mrs. Rohold led the HaGefen Street Medical Mission with admirable efficiency, especially during the critical post-war years, when Jewish refugees flooded in from Europe with extensive medical needs. Bella Rohold died in 1960 and lies buried in the city of Haifa, which honoured the mission in 1977 for its assistance and support of Holocaust survivors.[8]

Ben Rohold's departure from Toronto was received with a genuine outpouring of affection. He had not only done a remarkable work in Toronto, establishing a strong outreach with its own congregation; he also helped to establish a mission in Winnipeg. Both ministries would bear fruit for many years after his departure. The Toronto Presbytery noted his "faithful, earnest, successful and, we venture to think, unique service on behalf of Israel in Toronto, and other points in Canada...We therefore heartily record our appreciation of the remarkable success which has attended the ministry of Mr. Rohold."[9] Without him, the home mission board was uncertain about the future of the institute, and there were changes coming, marked by the growing divisions in the church.

As a budding "theolog" at Knox, Morris was keenly aware of the vision promoted by progressive Presbyterians, including his professors and the principal, Rev. Dr. Alfred Gandier. Decades earlier, as rural settlements across Western Canada followed the expanding railways, Canada's large Protestant denominations—Methodists, Congregationalists and Presbyterians—unified their plans of expansion. Rather than build three churches in every prairie hamlet, they pooled their efforts to allow each settlement to form a single assembly supported by all three denominations. By 1904, the model formed in the west led church leaders to explore a dynamic vision for Canada in the 20th century—a national denomination merged into a "United Church." After years of debate, a 1924 Act of Parliament allowed them to proceed, setting the date for union on June 10, 1925.

As the deadline loomed, each local Presbyterian congregation voted independently on whether or not to join the union. The process went on over several months, and sizable factions opposed the merger. Morris and Annie followed the fierce debates very closely under the critical eye of Dr. Pidgeon at Bloor Street Presbyterian, who became the first moderator of the United Church. The Methodist and Congregational denominations entered the alliance with almost no assemblies dissenting. In contrast, almost a third (30 percent) of Presbyterian churches voted no. They formed a continuing denomination despite the bitter prospect of court battles over property, even over the church name.

Morris's choice to remain Presbyterian "required a certain amount of firm determination and faith," according to the biography written by his son Alex. The resolve came "out of loyalty to the Church that had led him to Christ and to people who, like Dr. Scott had befriended him."[10] Nevertheless, the decision led to some painfully awkward situations. During his last year at Knox, the students and faculty on both sides—United Church and continuing Presbyterians—shared the college, until another seminary was built for the new denomination. Every day Morris endured the withering gaze of former teachers and classmates.

There had already been some frustrating shifts in the ministry of the Scott Institute. With Rohold gone, the presbytery tried to widen the scope of services with an "all nations" approach. The strategy stalled as few of the immigrant groups felt vested in the facility, while those who were actively using the building began to repel each other. Adding to the confusion was the pending question of which denomination would eventually own the site.

As graduation neared, Morris pondered his future. He'd been serving at the Institute for over a decade. It was an era when graduates were placed by the national church office after convocation. There was the possibility of receiving a call elsewhere, perhaps on a rustic charge in a frontier region. His future, though, was predetermined. He was appointed to lead the Scott Institute as superintendent of the Jewish Mission.

After the wedding, Morris and Annie headed east to New Brunswick. A leisurely two months were spent doing ministry in picturesque St. Andrews by the Sea on the Bay of Fundy. Six months later, the courts confirmed that the Presbyterian Church owned 165 Elizabeth St.

Together, Morris and Annie began taking the work in hand, refocusing attention on Jewish ministry, though Mission attendance had fallen to its lowest ebb. Years later, Annie told an interviewer that their first meeting at the Mission brought out "five Jewish people and a dog." Having overcome so many obstacles, they might well have thought that the worst was behind them. Indeed, they were briefly entering a period of stability and calm. Briefly.

DANIEL

By Elaine Z. Markovic

Soft light sifted through the iron grating above.
Glowing amber eyes watched me.
Padded feet paced nervously.
And then, the angel came.
As I stood trembling,
Those captive creatures stretched,
Lay down, relaxed and slept.

CHAPTER 4

The Soup Kitchen Years

L ong before most people in Toronto were aware of the Great
Depression, it came knocking on Morris and Annie's back
door. Their ministry magazine, *The Presbyterian Good News
and Good Will to the Jews*, described what was happening in the
February 1930 issue:

> Every day we were interrupted at breakfast, dinner and sup-
> per by men looking for work. It was impossible for us to
> refuse a bite to those hungry men when they approached us
> when we, ourselves, were eating.[1]

Before long, it was obvious that the growing number of homeless drifters lining up at the Mission door were harbingers of a
growing crisis.

The 1929 collapse of North American stock markets unleashed a
devastating economic disaster that lasted for the better part of a decade.
Not even the trials and triumphs of World War II could erase its impact
on a generation. At first, the federal government assured Canadians that
a healthy economy and stable banks would spare them from the worst
effects of a global downturn. That optimism faded quickly.

As the difficult years arrived, Canadian exports fell by a discour-
aging 50 percent from 1929 to 1933. During the boom of the 1920s
many Ontario factory owners had gone into debt to expand capacity.
With the American economy shrinking and foreign markets drying
up, businesses and industries all across Canada were forced to close

or restructure, laying off large numbers of workers. Banks and governments reacted with severe restrictions on credit, and commerce began grinding to a halt.

One in three Canadians lived on family farms. With limited credit, many farmers couldn't maintain their operations, harvest their crops or replace livestock. Those who failed to meet their debts were driven off the land. With no markets for their resources, the mining and logging industries began to shut down, with devastating effects on northern communities. "Main Street" in most small towns became a row of empty storefronts with yellowing newsprint in the windows. Larger cities were hardly doing better and were overrun by the unemployed seeking any opportunity for work.

Throughout the 1930s, hard-working individuals and families remained vulnerable, while Canadian governments seemed ineffective or even hostile to the growing ranks of those who were homeless and unemployed. Ontario tried to follow the lead modelled by President Roosevelt's "New Deal," mounting large-scale public works projects—many provincial major highways were first paved in this era—but there were still not enough jobs. The federal government offered no social assistance programs, no publically funded health care. Barely a decade before, many of the itinerant men riding the rails or hitching down the roads had been fighting in Europe, risking their lives for king and country; they were bitterly disappointed. Fearful of widespread social unrest, governments responded by setting up large work camps.

Toronto became a destination of hope for thousands seeking any kind of work or public aid. These were the waves of itinerant, displaced and homeless men and women who eventually came knocking at the door of the Scott Institute and every other downtown mission or charity. The Zeidmans could have kept them at arm's length or ignored the problem. They already had plans to move from the apartment in the old Elizabeth St. facility. Morris's official ministry responsibilities put no expectations on him, certainly not more than he and Annie were doing.

But after years of ministry in the heart of the city, they were determined to stem the tide of suffering. Their vision expanded to include everyone who came to them in need. A number of Morris's American ministry colleagues had opened up their own soup kitchens—feeding transients and the poor in major U.S. cities. The Institute also had a poor fund, but as Morris later wrote, "the meager sum at our disposal was less than a drop of water in the sea."[2]

By summer's end, the city's growing numbers of transients were a public concern, and winter threatened to make the situation worse. Early in October 1930, Morris dropped by the offices of the *Toronto Evening Telegram* (later the *Toronto Telegram*, until it closed in 1971). A chat with the editor-in-chief was interrupted by a phone call. The downtown Zeller's department store had 130 gallons of leftover turkey giblets after Thanksgiving. Did they know someone who would take it off their hands? That became Morris's first in-kind donation, large enough to launch a soup kitchen.[3]

A few weeks later, Morris sparked a lively debate at the local presbytery when he proposed the use of the Elizabeth St. facility to assist the growing numbers of hungry men. The next day (Tuesday, November 4, 1930), the *Toronto Star* carried a small headline on the front page: "Toronto Presbytery Allows Soup Kitchen." But there was one small caveat. The presbytery had no money for the program, and Morris couldn't expect any increase to his budget. Funds had to be raised separately, and he'd have to take that responsibility. This was the motion recorded in the notes of their regular meeting, November 3, 1930:

> That, at the request of Mr. Zeidman, we, as a Presbytery, authorize Mr. Zeidman to organize a soup kitchen in connection with the Scott Institute, for the relief of those suffering from hunger and poverty; and that he receive authority to collect money for that purpose.[4]

None of this delayed his plans. Morris launched the new ministry that Friday (November 7), giving his program a cheery moniker—the "Royal York Soup Kitchen"—and laying out 170 meals. Within three months of daily operations, the figure more than tripled; the Institute was providing food for 600 men daily. By that time, the ministry had already supplied 25,000 pieces of clothing to 8,000 men. On New Year's Day 1931, they hosted 955 guests, the meal supplemented with chicken provided by no less a personage than the lieutenant governor of Ontario. The ministry got lots of press exposure and attracted strong volunteer support. It continued until late spring.

A year later, Morris went back to his colleagues at the presbytery for permission to reopen the Institute for relief work. He generously credited "the Toronto Presbytery and the persistent urging of the general public" for encouraging him to resume. The next day, November 3, 1931, the *Telegram* reported that the work had received the necessary approval and that Morris had already been passing out restaurant tickets (1,137 of them) to those in need. He told reporters that he was willing to lay out his own money if he couldn't raise sufficient funds.[5]

As the Depression wore on, the first week of November annually marked the Mission's public opening for food and clothing distribution to homeless men, tirelessly feeding and assisting anyone who needed help until late April or early May. Men could come in off the street and be fed or clothed or find assistance. During the summer, the focus turned to the "Fresh Air" camping programs that brought inner city families—mostly mothers and children—out to the countryside. The mission's regular ministry services to Jewish people and Morris's ongoing personal ministry continued throughout the summer and into the fall.

The Zeidmans' vision and strength of character were nothing less than heroic. In addition to the exhausting daily schedule to sustain the ministry of serving meals and meeting individual needs, they also had to keep casting the widest possible net for financial support. Morris began regular Sunday afternoon radio broadcasts and an unending round of personal engagements at churches, clubs, fundraisers and community events.

Their determination needs to be seen against the backdrop of an era when government relief was minimal and average people felt overwhelmed. Morris and Annie had no great church at their disposal and no guaranteed funding. They were by no means the only charity doing this kind of work, but the public were impressed that the Zeidmans acted by faith, committing to feed and clothe hundreds of needy citizens when average people could hardly spare an extra dollar.

Their steadfast faith seemed capable of moving mountains and overcoming the impossible while others struggled to cope. Within a few years, the reputation of the Scott Institute and Morris Zeidman had spread across the city. Hundreds of touching letters (including amounts both small and large) came to Morris from across the country, entrusting funds to his personal care. People knew that their donation to "the Scott" would go directly to people in need. Every financial gift was carefully entered into the "Soup Kitchen Fund," which was fully separate from the Institute's regular budget. Morris regretted that the general board of missions, which received his reports with enthusiasm, never approved his requests for recognition as a home missionary program.

None of this changed his unique identity as an inner-city Jewish worker for the Messiah, a Hebrew Christian minister helping everyone in need. It was an unlikely profile for someone so widely known for community leadership. On occasion, his identity was a point of controversy, particularly with the rise of anti-Semitism during the 1930s. But no one succeeded in casting a shadow on his sterling character. Not even his severest critics could shake the public's well-earned trust in his integrity.

The *Evening Telegram* appointed a reporter, Rose Macdonald, to write a daily column on the work of the Institute. A typical newspaper article from the *Telegram* (November 1935) carried the headline "Mayor Praises Director as Scott Institute Opens."[6] The item describes Mayor Simpson's presence at the fall opening of the Mission's 1935 season of food and clothing distribution. Accompanied by the public welfare commissioner and the local superintendent of welfare, the mayor announced to the men who had assembled at the Mission, "The City of Toronto is particularly proud of him for doing this work...I hope you always will appreciate what Mr. Zeidman has been doing these past few years."

Occasionally the *Toronto Evening Star* also featured the charity. Their front page article on February 21, 1935, read "Get Behind Dance For Scott Institute" and promoted an upcoming dinner-dance for several hundred guests at the King Edward Hotel that had the "hearty support of Mayor Simpson and many of the city's most prominent citizens." At the end of each winter distribution season, both newspapers reported on the official statements of appreciation from the city, including the mayor and the board of control (city council).

The extent of the work followed the ebb and flow of the Depression years, but on average there were 500 to 700 meals served daily. During the toughest years (1935–37), that figure was closer to 900 daily meals. When the city of Toronto honoured the work of the Scott Institute with a special resolution of thanks on June 27, 1935, they received Morris into council chambers and read an address of appreciation, including this statement:

> The Scott Institute has recently completed another successful winter programme of work, during which…a total of 130,000 meals were served to the hungry in our midst…[by] the Reverend Morris Zeidman, assisted by his good wife and a corps of enthusiastic volunteers.

Not every year was a success. In 1938 the winter season of distribution closed in mid-April, weeks ahead of schedule, because of declining support. More than 60,000 meals had been served, but the accumulating deficit was close to $700. Morris told the *Telegram*, "we hope and trust that kind Providence will find the means for us." A year earlier, he reminded the reporter, they had finished with a $1,000 deficit, and a single donor wrote out a cheque for the full amount. "Another such miracle might happen!"[7]

As the services to homeless transients began to outgrow his expectations, Morris had one reason to hesitate. He feared that ministries to Jewish people would suffer. In particular, he feared that the women and children in weekly programs would be intimidated by the crowds of men. The response was quite the opposite, and he was able to write supporters that his Jewish ministry was expanding: "to our amazement it has increased and some services, like the mid-week prayer meeting, have trebled in number."

An increasing number of Jewish families would come to the Scott for groceries and financial help to pay overdue bills and rent. (Many would sit through the mid-week prayer service before approaching him about their needs.) Those who benefited were not placed under any obligation other than to accept that his assistance was a sign of his own genuine faith. Morris and Annie felt this was simply a reflection of the truth of the gospel.

Morris began experiencing a new level of respect from the Jewish community. In 1931 he noted with genuine surprise that "a prominent Jewish Zionist" had provided a generous bequest of 50 dollars "for the furtherance of our work." In time, he saw a quiet growing acceptance of the role as a charity for Jewish people in need. "The missionary," he wrote, "is looked upon as a welfare worker and carrier of the glad tidings of Christ."[8]

This story was told by one of Toronto's distinguished Messianic Jewish leaders, the late Rev. Dr. Edward D. Brotsky, who grew up in an Orthodox Jewish home during the Depression. Brotsky was a boy, about ten or eleven years old, when his parents ran out of food. Desperate, and with no idea where else to turn, they sent their son to get help from the Scott Institute. Young Brotsky approached the building but was too afraid to enter. He stood on the sidewalk until Morris, in his clerical collar, came outside and approached him. Hearing of the family's plight, he assured the boy that there was no need to come inside. Putting some money into his hand, Morris sent him home.

The role of friend and counsellor "in times of trouble" opened doors that would normally have been shut to a Jewish follower of Jesus. His relations with "leaders and rabbis" became more favourable, and this was reflected in donations he received, both in funds and in kind. A local Jewish newspaper even allowed him to place his advertisements in its pages. After all, Jewry holds charity (*tzedaka*) in high regard, and even today, there are many in Toronto's Jewish community who maintain a fond appreciation for the work of the Mission.

A few large scrapbooks in the Mission archives give us a closer look at day-to-day life for the Zeidmans during the Great Depression. The pages are covered with yellowing newsprint stories from *The Toronto Telegram*. Selections were usually grouped together by month and year; exact dates were not always recorded, and some aren't readable. While we know that the paper assigned Miss Rose Macdonald to cover the work of "the Scott," none of the stories included her byline. Nor are these regular news stories. The names of recipients are withheld to preserve their dignity and described with just enough details for readers to imagine themselves or a loved one needing similar help. Only portions of the stories are cited. Every column ended with a list of recent donors: individuals, often with donations of $1 to $5, and businesses that provided food or gifts in-kind.

November 1935
NEEDY MOTHER GETS CARRIAGE FROM "ANON."
Clock Also Sent to Home to Regulate Feeding Time Necessary for New Baby

Appeal was made in *The Telegram* the other day on behalf of one of the Scott Institute's protégées, a young mother who had just brought her baby home from the hospital—a delicate baby. The infant's feeding timetable needs to be followed meticulously—but there was no clock in the home, nor was there money to buy one. Response to the appeal was prompt. An anonymous giver sent a brand new clock, and a much needed baby carriage was supplied by someone else. The mother, the Scott Institute folk and *The Telegram* join in saying "thank you" to those who helped so spontaneously.

January 21, 1936
MEALS SERVED DAILY AT SCOTT EXCEED 600
Task Is Heavy, But Gratitude Gives Encouragement to Institute Workers

They are serving over 600 meals a day at the Scott Institute, a big piece of work in terms of meat and vegetables to be prepared and cooked and served—and paid for. But the gratitude and independent spirit of many of the men who sit at the Scott tables is to Rev. Morris Zeidman and his helpers a heartening encouragement to go on with the work.

There were two young men, for instance, who came from out of town on their way to take jobs. They had no money to tide them over here. At the Scott Mr. Zeidman saw that they had food to eat and a place to stay. The young men were most insistent that they pay their way by serving the Institute on Elizabeth Street at their own trades. There was, however, at the moment no need for such services...The offer, nevertheless, was appreciated.

January 23, 1936
CRUTCHES, LONG STORED, AT LAST FIND THEIR JOB
Scott Institute Able to Answer Call—Sleigh Helps Family Get Fuel—Many Pleas For Aid

"You never know when it will come in useful." Everybody has said it sometime or other. The Scott Institute has proved the truth of the observation.

Since last spring they have had a pair of good crutches about the place. But nobody seemed to need them. What to do with them has often been the suggestion.

They have been given to a woman, bereaved last month of her husband, who had been an invalid, confined to bed for two years. Scarce had her husband died than further misfortune befell her. She broke her foot and has since had it in a plaster cast. She and her sister prayed for crutches. They didn't get the crutches just then, but they did get the idea of putting in a request at the Scott Institute. The pair on hand proved just the thing.

A young lad came with a note from his mother. There were four children at home, all down with chicken pox. Could they have a sleigh so that the older boy could draw wood or coke? They needed fuel. And could they have bedding or warm clothes?

There really was a sleigh for them. Bedding too.

December 26, 1936
BOUNTEOUS HOLIDAY FEAST GIVEN BY SCOTT INSTITUTE
Children and Parents and 150 Men Have Bang-Up Dinner

"The children had the loveliest time yesterday," Rev. Morris Zeidman, superintendent of the Scott Institute, said today. "There were about 20 of them, and the families sat down to a real turkey dinner, with all the fixings, including plum pudding. And Santa Claus had presents for everybody, besides candies and fruit." The dining room with its fine tree was gay, too, with Chinese lanterns.

About 150 men had their dinner in the big dining room, with chicken, plum pudding, candy and fruit and so forth.

Numbers of contributions came in for the Scott right up to Christmas Eve.

51

March 1937
EVICTED FOUR COME TO SCOTT JUST IN TIME
Deserted Mother and Three Children Make Pitiful Picture—
Feet Blistered by Trudging

If the city pavements could speak they could tell sad tales. Sometimes these tales do find a sympathetic and helpful audience, and this is one of them. It comes from Rev. Morris Zeidman, superintendent of the Scott Institute.

"We had a family consisting of a deserted mother and her three children come in," Rev. Zeidman told. "They had been evicted from their home and all day long had been tramping the streets looking in vain for a new one (they had only the assurance of a night's lodging).

"We had just locked the doors and were preparing to leave when they came, and we just couldn't send them away hungry. We opened the kitchen, prepared soft boiled eggs for the children, got ready meat and fried potatoes for the mother, and there was plenty of bread and butter and fresh fruit for them all.

"The poor children were very tired—the youngest was only two and the eldest five. The mother washed them all and then took off her shoes to rest her own tired feet, all blistered. Her stockings, we noticed, were in holes. Well, we were able to fix the family up comfortably, give the mother some milk to take to the night's lodging and some food.

"We see many men in need here but occasionally one comes whose case especially touches us. For instance, we had one man, a respectable, neatly dressed fellow, an elderly bachelor, who has worked all his life and says he can still do a good day's work at his trade…He had nothing to eat for two days. Then he came here and asked for a meal, for which he wanted to work.

"The poor fellow cried. It just broke our hearts," Mr. Zeidman finished. "There was timely help for him, of course."

March 26, 1938

MUST SCOTT INSTITUTE SHUT? NEED $50 DAILY TO RUN IT

Contributions Now Average Only $15 to $20 a Day—
Pitiful Cases Come for Aid

Will the Scott Institute have to close its doors against the needy because of lack of adequate support? Rev. Morris Zeidman hopes not. But it takes something like $50 a day to maintain the work of emergent relief...Mr. Zeidman would continue to provide meals for the hungry until the end of April, but he feels he cannot incur the responsibility of debt piled up...

Mr. Zeidman pointed out to *The Telegram* reporter that he was receiving no civic assistance...He finds, however, that large numbers of young men of the best type are coming without tickets, such as are issued to hostel residents. These young men have been able to find lodging for themselves, though for some of them this must be a precarious matter, but they do need food—their pale lips show that.

Then, there are the men who for infringements of rules lose their welfare department tickets temporarily—for instance, they haven't done their exercises for the day, as they are required...Mr. Zeidman feels, that even so, they can't be left to starve when they come for a meal.

"It's awful hard to turn them away," he said.

December 31, 1938
SCOTT INSTITUTE FIGURES UPSET CLAIM OF CRITICS
Good Food Is Provided All, Including Those Who Lack Meal Ticket—
Needy Cared For

Rev. Morris Zeidman, superintendent of the Scott Institute, comes back with a neat riposte in reference to a recent criticism of the Institute's relief measures, and specifically to the statement "that a man must have a ticket from the relief office before eating there."

Mr. Zeidman has provided figures from his books showing meal-by-meal, for a week, the number of ticket holders cared for, the number of non-ticket holders. Adding these two figures it is found that during the week of December 21–28, there were 1,399 meals provided for ticket holders and 786 meals to non-ticket holders...

Having disposed of these matters, Mr. Zeidman went on to tell of some of the more pathetic instances of need...[on] this holiday week. A woman came in with her baby, perhaps two months old and very sick with intestinal flu. The little family is not on relief for the husband earns a meagre wage, not sufficient to keep their cold house adequately warm for the baby.

"We have taken them in hand," said the Scott superintendent.

April 22, 1939

SCOTT INSTITUTE SHUT DOWN AFTER HEAVY WINTER'S WORK

Rev. Morris Zeidman Completes Voluntary Job for Season—
No Meals After Monday

The Scott Institute will close on Monday, *The Telegram* was told today. Thus will be concluded a great winter's work, voluntarily undertaken by the Institute's superintendent, Rev. Morris Zeidman, at the request of welfare authorities. It has been carried on often with difficulty, for emergent relief dispensed on the scale required involves serious financial responsibility. Friends have come splendidly to the support of the work, it is true; but it has taken the most careful management some times to bring ends anywhere near to meeting.

"While we will stop giving meals on Monday, we will for some time have people coming to us for help," Miss Dixon, of the Institute, said today. "We will still give out as we get in. We are especially in need of men's shoes and suits."

April 26, 1939

REV. M. ZEIDMAN LAUDED FOR WORK

Board of Control Commends Scott Institute for Assistance to Needy Persons

On motion of Mayor Day, Board of Control endorsed a resolution commending the work of Rev. Morris Zeidman, of the Scott Institute, in aiding those who find themselves in need of assistance.

The Mayor explained the institute had served about 680,000 meals since it started operation.

"They are doing a very fine work," Con. Fred Conboy agreed.

Welfare Commissioner Laver informed the board that the institute had supplied 33,000 meals to single unemployed this year, and since 1930 had supplied 676,146 meals to needy persons, without cost to the city.

WHAT IS THE MEASURE? (1953)[9]

By Annie A. Zeidman

What is the measure of Thy love to me,
O God, my King?
An ocean without bounds, a shoreless sea.
What is the measure of my love to Thee,
My Lord, my King?
A cup of water to a thirsty soul.
But this my goal:
To stand with my poor cup beside Thy sea.
And dip for all a measure of Thy love to me.

*For whosoever shall give you a cup of water to
drink in my name...he shall not lose his reward.*
(Mark 9:41)

CHAPTER 5

That Jewish Gentleman

In his public ministry, Morris had emerged as a singular figure of extraordinary faith. His denomination appeared to be supportive, and he quoted Presbyterian church leaders in his pamphlets. At the annual general assembly meetings each June he was well received and widely admired for his reports. Privately though, Morris and the family coped with numerous aggravations—and many were caused by the church.

Daily, the family had to manage their awkward living quarters above the Mission facilities at 307 Palmerston. These were shared with a deaconess, Miss Caroline McArthur, appointed as Morris's assistant by the presbytery. The home's single washroom was barely adequate for a family of six plus one. The unfinished children's bedrooms were another frustration, especially during the freezing cold of winter. Regular requests for funds to have the rooms completed went unanswered.

No matter how successful Morris was at promoting the ministry, his financial allotment remained fixed, and he wasn't paid for any extra work. For most of the 1930s, that budget was about $3,250 a year, including all salaries and ministry expenses. In his reports, he occasionally noted that his work had expanded much further than ever—but not his budget. In pre-Depression years he'd received as much as $15,000. It's no surprise that his complaints fell on deaf ears—almost everyone in the church felt overstretched, underpaid and grateful for their salary.

Since the fracture of the denomination in 1925, Morris had been a steadfast Presbyterian. Loyalty was a trait he valued and tried to foster in others. In 1928, a mission in St. Louis had offered him an attractive leading position. Aware that he couldn't be replaced, the denomination raised his salary and confirmed their intention to move the Institute's headquarters to a more appropriate location.

A few years later, his loyalty was quietly tested again. The mission archives include a yellowed piece of correspondence, dated June 21, 1934. It's a letter to Morris from Sir Leon Levison, president of The International Hebrew Christian Alliance (IHCA). In his day, Levison was something of a living legend; in later years he remained a visionary who admired Morris's abilities. From the IHCA offices in Edinburgh, Toronto may not have seemed such an important assignment as Levison had in mind. The typed letter mentions a vacancy in the Church of Scotland "station" (mission) in Jaffa, "practically centred at Tel Aviv, the 100 percent new Jewish city in the Holy Land." Levison wrote,

> I feel that in view of the important position which Palestine is going to hold in Jewry throughout the world, and also with the Jews aiming to make Palestine not only their national home, but the centre of Jewish culture, it is imperative to have a Hebrew Christian of education and character as well as of experience to be at the head of the Jewish station.

Levison also reminded Morris about the IHCA's plans to start a Hebrew Christian colony on a site near Gaza. Urging him to apply immediately—"by return of post"—Levison assured Morris that he would "endeavour to use my very best influence to help you." He also requested confidentiality, as he knew most of the committee who would make the appointment.

Morris couldn't respond as Sir Leon requested. Neither his well-hidden colitis nor his family situation (Elaine had been born May 1) made it reasonable. There were more immediate demands on his time and energy. He'd recently returned from the annual general assembly meetings and was busy starting up the summer Fresh Air camp programs. These would bring more responsibilities than usual because Annie— who oversaw much of the program—was looking after a newborn.

Levison had added a postscript in a few handwritten lines: "Would you consider the question of your being appointed General Secretary of the IHCA and work with me in Great Britain? L.L." We have no record of Morris's reply. He occasionally travelled to London, but he went on to serve the IHCA as general secretary from 1934 to 1944. That role would take him far afield in attempts to expand the work of the alliance, whose numbers were growing, particularly in Europe. He travelled to Europe, across the United States and Mexico and, on the very eve of the Second World War, to South America. He was returning by ship when war was declared.

Closer to home, Morris's networking for public support led him in some unexpected directions. In the 1930s he became a member of the Orange Lodge, a Protestant fraternal institution with strong Presbyterian links. The lodge exerted a strong influence on Toronto politics, promoting the interests of conservative politicians and businessmen. Morris became a member of the local John Knox lodge and was elected chaplain and a senior member.

The religious prejudices of the Orange Order against Catholics were by no means hidden. Every year, city lodges celebrated the Battle of the Boyne with a grand parade. The battle (neither important nor decisive) is supposed to mark the defeat of James II, Great Britain's last Catholic king, and his replacement by the House of Orange. (Similar parades are still held in parts of the former British Commonwealth.) In the mid-1930s, Toronto's parade was a major event involving many of the city's leading politicians. As chaplain, Morris was a noticeable dignitary. After the war, the influence of the Orange Order declined, and its religious prejudices were no longer socially acceptable, a change that Morris also welcomed.[1]

In recent decades, since Vatican Council II in the 1960s, Torontonians have become used to an increasingly ecumenical spirit between Catholics and most Protestant denominations. The atmosphere of the 1930s was a stark contrast. The differences in theology and practices between Christian denominations were fiercely debated. Some of the earliest religious radio programs featured strongly partisan Catholic and Protestant preachers.

In the biography of his father, Alex Zeidman explains that Morris had a continuing interest in Roman Catholicism, the dominant religion of his native Poland. That curiosity was almost certainly fanned by the anti-Semitism so prevalent in Catholic circles, with its emphasis on blaming the Jewish people for the death of Jesus—that is, all Jews, of every generation. In the aftermath of the Holocaust, these teachings were critically re-examined and rejected by Vatican Council II in 1965. Pope Paul VI declared the views inconsistent with the Scriptures, and they are no longer openly tolerated. (His statement is called *Nostra Aetate*—"Our Times." Further progress in relations with the Jewish people has continued since then.)

Commercial radio was still relatively new in Canada in the mid-'30s. *The Catholic Hour* was broadcast as a Sunday news program for Toronto audiences by an organization called the Catholic Radio League. Programs featured the strong opinions of Father Charles B. Lanphier and were broadcast from St. Michael's, the cathedral church of the Roman Catholic Archdiocese of Toronto. Father Lanphier's views were increasingly controversial with the onset of the Spanish Civil War (1936–39). In keeping with the official views of the church, Lanphier was a staunch supporter of General Franco, who received military support from Hitler and Mussolini. Meanwhile, in April 1937, Canadians were reading the first press reports of the Luftwaffe bombings of civilians in Guernica—a glimpse of the terror to be unleashed on England in the Nazi *blitzkrieg*.

The medium of radio appealed to Morris's entrepreneurial personality. While he kept up his busy schedule of public appearances across Southern Ontario, including church pulpits and social clubs, the radio broadcasts reached thousands more and gave voice to his wide-ranging views on theological and topical issues.

Morris launched his own Protestant radio league in 1934 with a series of radio messages, some of them quite controversial. While the league had an advisory council, Morris was responsible for the scripts and presentation. His "subscribers" were only required to indicate their support of the programs, without other obligations. *The Protestant Hour* caught the attention of Protestants and Catholics alike, and the Mission scrapbooks contain many newspaper columns on the ensuing controversies.

The Telegram, well known for its conservative politics and support of Morris's ministry, was attacked for promoting anti-Catholic views. In fact, the paper printed numerous letters and articles on both sides of the radio controversies. One particularly lengthy response to the paper's managing editor suggested that Morris was only one in a series of individuals used by "the Tely" to "attack the Catholics." The writer noted that his predecessors were at least "of Anglo-Saxon origin…but to bring to the microphone a foreigner is just a bit raw. Don't you agree? Last Sunday, when I sat listening to your friend, the Jewish gentleman, I felt that Hitler knew what he was doing when he showed the Jews the gate."[2] Similar protests reappeared regularly in the paper for the next few months.

Not only was commercial radio in its early stages, so was the Canadian regulatory body that was supposed to maintain order over the airwaves. Government censorship became a problem for Morris, though it often seemed arbitrary. At one point, the issue reached the floor of the House of Commons. J. Earl Lawson, member of Parliament for South York, questioned the minister of transport, C. D. Howe, as to why a message on "the exclusive mediatorship of Jesus Christ between man and God" was not allowed on the air. The minister was pressed to explain "what possible justification there could be for censorship on a sermon of that nature."[3] Another message that Morris prepared on birth control was censored only hours before he was to go on air. Government regulations put limits on Fr. Lanphier as well, and at one point both broadcasters were banned by the federal government.

A few local churches actively supported Morris's radio ministry, but the local presbytery was noticeably uncomfortable. The raucous tone of the presbytery meeting on February 1st, 1937, was evident in the report of the *Toronto Telegram*, which opened, "'God knows we have enough strife in Canada as it is without adding religious squabbles,' declared Rev. Stuart C. Parker, D.D. of St. Andrew's Church, yesterday afternoon as he moved to have the question of censorship by the Canadian Radio Commission of radio broadcasts by Rev. Morris Zeidman referred to a special committee of Toronto Presbytery…His motion carried unanimously."[4]

A month later, Rev. Parker, as head of the investigating committee, presented its report. The committee refused to censure Morris, and some of the comments were positive. They noted that "Mr. Zeidman alone was responsible for the broadcasts and that no newspaper or organization was behind them." The committee did not correct or criticize the text of his messages. "Those of doctrinal character set forth aspects of the Reformed faith and were orthodox in respect to their substance. Those dealing with current affairs expressed views which might legitimately be held by anyone. Both types, however, were controversial and had in view, first and foremost, the repudiation of Romanist doctrines and attitudes. In style and language, the Committee found Mr. Zeidman 'did not overstep the bounds regarded as legitimate in such controversy.'" It was neither an endorsement nor a vindication. After all his bluster of the previous meeting, Rev. Parker could give no reasons for a reprimand: "your committee is unable to see any ground for disciplinary action in respect to Mr. Zeidman."[5] Although the broadcasts continued, Morris's regular travel to radio stations around southern Ontario—including Hamilton and St. Catharines—were simply too great a strain on his health to sustain for many more years.

While the Depression lingered on, Morris made a pointed and very public stand against Canadians' refusal to respond to Europe's growing number of Jewish refugees. The government's deliberate inaction, so fully evident in the debacle of the *St. Louis* (a boatload of more than 900 Jewish refugees from Germany who were refused entry to Cuba, numerous South American countries, the U.S. and Canada), was abetted by the silence of Canadian churches and their apathetic response to the spread of anti-Semitism.[6]

"During the last few years," wrote Morris, "we have had to engage, not only in preaching the Gospel to the Jews, but also in combatting anti-Semitism among Christians."[7] As one of the few mainstream Canadian voices boldly supporting the cause of Jewry, he was pointedly confrontational in his writings and speeches, insisting that

Christians must show moral leadership and genuine biblical values in their attitudes toward the Jewish people.[8]

The rise of anti-Semitism in a period of international economic turmoil was no coincidence. Extensive propaganda, a lot of it originating with the Nazis, blamed the world's financial crisis on "an international cabal of Jewish bankers." Emboldened by the laws against Jews in Germany, groups of Nazi sympathizers became a common sight in some Toronto neighbourhoods.

Mounting tension on the streets led to one of the city's worst riots, during the summer of 1933. A mid-August series of softball games at the city's Christie Pits parklands included a team with a large contingent of Jewish players. At one of their games, a blanket with a swastika was openly displayed in the stands. Nothing happened, though the police were warned that any more provocations could be dangerous. The caution was ignored, and the next day, August 16, the offending swastika was unfurled a second time. The team on the field and their supporters rushed the stands. Hours of brutal combat went on late into the evening, described by the *Globe and Mail* as a "Christian-Jewish pitched battle" along Bloor Street.[9] The next day's *Toronto Star* described the incident:

> While groups of Jewish and Gentile youths wielded fists and clubs in a series of violent scraps for possession of a white flag bearing a swastika symbol at Willowvale Park last night, a crowd of more than 10,000 citizens, excited by cries of "Heil Hitler," became suddenly a disorderly mob and surged wildly about the park and surrounding streets, trying to gain a view of the actual combatants, which soon developed in violence and intensity of racial feeling into one of the worst free-for-alls ever seen in the city. Scores were injured, many requiring medical and hospital attention.[10]

Morris's repeated public statements were confronting the anti-Semitism entrenched in Canada's leading institutions. Well-known social clubs and hotels were "restricted"—Jews were not allowed. Ottawa's elite institutions, including the Rideau Club, a renowned haven for its leading politicians and highest ranking civil servants, had a "Christians Only" policy.[11] Universities had well-known quotas for the number of Jewish students allowed entry to law and medical schools. Canadians could legally refuse to sell real estate to Jewish people, based on the premise that their property values would be reduced. Those statutes were not struck down by the Supreme Court until 1955, a full decade after thousands of Canadians had died to defeat Nazi Germany.

One of North America's best-known promoters of anti-Semitism was Rev. Gerald B. Winrod of Wichita, Kansas. When he was invited to speak at a missionary conference at People's Church in Toronto held in April 1935, Morris organized a peaceful picket line and protest in which many Jews also took part. Morris vocally urged ministry colleagues to see the full consequences of Rev. Winrod's "Gospel of Hate."

> The time for keeping quiet has passed. They are not only slandering the modern Jew but are besmirching the names of the patriarchs. They are sapping the life of the Church like a canker. If we do not cut that canker out of our Church in America it will be Nazified, like the Church in Germany. No, we cannot remain quiet. If we should, the very stones would cry out.[12]

Despite the widely known terrors of Germany's persecution of Jews, Canadian church leaders vacillated on taking in Jewish refugees, even when they openly condemned the Nazis. Many Canadians had little understanding or sympathy for Jewry— Europeans or local—while anti-Semites vocally warned that a flood of Jewish immigrants would come and take their jobs. An official rejection of Hitler's treatment of Jews and other minorities only came with the onset of World War II. By then, the worst years of the Depression were fading into memory. Decades would pass before Canadians recognized their culpability for closing their borders to all but a very few Jewish refugees prior to the Holocaust.[13]

After more than a year of war, the Canadian economy had stabilized. By 1941, there was no lack of jobs or opportunity. Despite uncertainty over the future of Europe, the difficult years of privation had passed. The Zeidmans could look back over a decade of exceptional, if controversial, ministry. Morris was confident that his superiors at the home missions board would finally recognize his achievements. At last, he'd be compensated for his remarkable success, both with the "soup kitchen" ministry and the outreach to Toronto's Jewish community. Unfortunately, the board did not see things that way.

SEEKING THEE AT CHRISTMAS, LORD (1937)

By Annie A. Zeidman

Seeking Thee at Christmas, Lord,
We cannot cross the sea,
The deserts or the mountains
To bring our gifts to Thee.
We cannot see the angels
Or the star in Judah's skies,
Or all the wonder dawning
In Mary's gentle eyes.

So we see Thee nearer, Lord,
Where poverty's dark tide
Flows ever past the door
Where grief and misery abide;
Raiment and bread for myrrh and gold,
And love for incense sweet,
In attic bare for stable rude
We lay them at Thy feet.

*For I was an hungered, and ye gave me meat: I was
thirsty, and ye gave me drink.* (Matthew 25:35)

CHAPTER 6

The Scott—and the Zeidmans—
Carry On

A series of letters—most of them written between February and September 1941—reveal the frustration and disappointment that finally led Morris and Annie to leave the Presbyterian Church and strike out on their own. Most of these passed between Morris and his superiors, the local and national leaders of the home missions board.

The first one, dated February 19, 1941, was sent from Morris to George Beare, convenor of the home missions sub-committee on Jewish Work. Like most church correspondence of that period, it's typed and has a very formal tone. The letter was also quite lengthy. Beare had been a strong supporter of Morris's work, but the many irritations among his superiors had left Beare and his colleagues with tough questions to answer about the ministry.

No one accused Morris and Annie of enriching themselves. Everyone had struggled through the Depression years, yet Morris had developed a national profile and had won a rare level of public trust. While his peers in the church couldn't fault his tenacity or vision, the reaction to his broadcasting ministry had shown their growing disaffection toward his work. Meanwhile, they were all too aware of his excoriating comments on those who lacked his moral resolve concerning the fascist powers and Nazi anti-Semitism. All this had won Morris many admirers and the grudging respect of colleagues, but few friends.

Morris wrote to Beare at the urging of the "Committee on Jewish Evangelization," his own ministry support group, and mentioned familiar problems: The "Evangelistic Centre" residence with its "bare attic rooms" had been affecting his children's health. He also urged an end to the awkward living arrangements with Miss McArthur and suggested that she "move out."

His arguments were a bit more emphatic as he looked back over 21 years of service to the church. The strenuous pace of the past decade had forced him to neglect his family, though he wasn't complaining: "We have been very happy in the work, and it is that very happiness and blessedness which...has made us ignore any discomfort." He did have other suggestions. Annie ("Mrs. Zeidman") should "be recognized at least as a part-time worker" considering that she began her duties daily at 9 a.m. and was doing Mission work well into the evenings.

Reminding the committee of his "loyalty to our Church," Morris discreetly referred to his accomplishments: "I am merely trying to point out that our success...and the blessings we have received as a result, are the only things we have sought for." He requested, prayerfully, for the committee to "do what is best for the work." Given the country's improving economy, he hoped that his family's needs might get some attention or at least be acknowledged. Nothing in the Mission archives suggests that he received any assurance of that kind.

A few months later, the trail of correspondence picks up again with a letter dated June 9, 1941. It's a letter of response from Morris to Rev. Ross Cameron, the convenor of the presbytery's home missions committee. The accounts submitted for payment of the institute's expenses for January to April 1941 had been delayed. A number of items were being questioned.

The tenor of Morris's reply is extremely defensive. The committee had focused on minor incidentals including: "Car Tickets...$20...Gas $8.00...Parties, Sunday School $4.00...Car Tickets, Sunday School $15.00..." Morris explained these in order: The first represented the five dollars per month that he was allowed to charge for transportation (the rate had been set by his predecessors); $2 was the amount allowed monthly for gas used in cooking (the gas bill was actually higher); third, a charge for the annual Christmas party, which had been severely cut back during the Depression but, again, cost more. The last item included the $3.50 per month used to help invalids and poor children who attended the Sunday school program. Tickets were also given to volunteer teachers "who cannot afford to pay their own carfare."

The ministry had always been managed with careful attention to detail, especially after its allowance was cut by 10 percent in 1932. The missions board had set many of these rates before Morris became superintendent. Now he was being scrutinized for trifles. To bring home his point, Morris listed 20 additional items for which "we never charge," the last two being "14 pairs of curtains/14 pairs of curtains must be washed periodically and many other expenses which our workers pay out of their own meagre stipends."

On the morning of Wednesday, July 9, Morris was interviewed by Rev. W. A. Cameron, secretary of the general board of missions, and Rev. Ross Cameron (there's no evidence that they were related). The Presbyterian church archives include a copy of a letter on file for that date from W. A. Cameron to Ross Cameron.

> In regard to our interview with Rev. Morris Zeidman this morning I have thought that, in view of the fact that these expenses which we questioned have already been paid by the workers to those who had the parties and were given car tickets, we ought to pay the accounts in full...However, I think that from the 1st of July these items of parties, milk and car tickets for the Sunday School should not be paid.

The letter goes on to address what Rev. W. A. Cameron calls "the situation in connection with the Jewish work."

> What I mean is...that there is no Communion Roll, nor is the Sacrament of the Lord's Supper observed and that those who become Christian become members of some of other Church and give financial support to that Church. It ought to be indicated too that no offering is taken at any of the services... it is our judgment that with a view of placing responsibility on the Jewish people we should recommend that an offering be taken at every regular service of worship.

The writer's attitude speaks for itself. The religious meetings described were largely evangelistic, so Rev. Cameron was insisting that Jewish people start paying to hear the gospel. He's also unaware that Jewish people don't usually take offerings during religious services, a point on which Morris was always sensitive. In regard to placing new Jewish believers into churches, Morris had already publicly commented on his experience. In one of the city's leading evangelical Presbyterian churches, the congregants had openly objected to taking communion with Jewish believers.[1]

While the summer Fresh Air ministry went on as usual, Morris weighed his alternatives. His resignation letter to W. A. Cameron is dated August 11 from the camp at Grimsby Beach.

> I herewith tender my resignation as Superintendent of the Jewish work in the Presbytery of Toronto...I wish to be released from my duties by the end of October, as I hope to have all Camp bills and accounts paid, and an audited report ready.

On August 22, he formally tendered his resignation to the clerk of the Toronto presbytery. A week later, August 29, George Beare wrote to Rev. Ross Cameron with some minor complaints about the summer camp. (Mr. Beare's letter has numerous typos.)

> Whether or not Mr. Zeigman's [sic] resignation is accepted „ [sic] or whether he continues in charge of the work, this and other matter ought to be goine [sic] into, and his resignation would seem to me to afford a good opportunity to get some of these things adjusted as they ought to be.

Rev. W. A. Cameron's response to Morris, dated September 25, was more respectful.

> After taking into account as carefully as we could all the circumstances, it was decided to accede to your request, and to accept your resignation at the end of October...
> The members were not unmindful of your long association with us in the work, and recognize that your going will be greatly felt...We wish you the highest success in your future endeavours.

Alex Zeidman's biography of his father notes how the presbytery tried to hold its October session "in camera," that is, behind closed doors. Morris prudently refused to take part in a meeting that might imply that there was an issue of moral misconduct under discussion. The proceedings went on as usual, and his resignation was accepted. Morris remained a minister on the appendix to the roll of the Toronto presbytery without any income from the church.

Only much later, in a letter to the *Toronto Star* in December 1942, did Morris shed more light on that earlier meeting with the Reverends Cameron. At the time, he was responding to a letter that W. A. Cameron had sent to Toronto city council following a request for funds from the Scott Mission. Morris's reply explains that, while the board of home missions had paid his salary as a Jewish missionary, they took no part in his relief work, and it adds choice words for the Toronto presbytery committee:

> Not one cent was contributed by the board for the general relief work of the Scott Institute...Far from co-operating, presbytery's committee hindered and discouraged relief work. Any relief work I have done, has been done in spite of them, and not because of them...
>
> I have never given the reason for my resignation and Mr. Cameron has, on numerous occasions, given reasons for my resignation which are not true. I now wish to say that my only reason for resigning was that he objected to my giving car tickets to a poor destitute child coming to Sunday school in the winter time. And he called it bribery! This the Rev. W. A. Cameron said in the presence of the Rev. Ross K. Cameron...His other objection was to my providing tea and cake for special meetings of underprivileged groups.[2]

Morris had been running his ministry to the poor from the Scott Institute building on Elizabeth Street since 1931. That name—still so precious to him—had become indelibly linked to his own. Looking around the neighbourhood, Morris located an empty double storefront at 724–726 Bay Street. To secure the rent, he cashed in his life insurance policies, and Annie gave up her few precious pieces of jewellery along with her wedding ring. Later, Morris confessed that he'd never been so scared. As he signed the $100 a month lease, his hand was trembling.

When they opened the doors on their new Mission, a box advertisement appeared in the local dailies under the headline "The Scott Carries On":

> Today, November 1st, the Rev. Morris Zeidman, B.D., resumes the 16th Annual season of service to the poor of downtown Toronto…Our Special Ministry—Visiting the Sick, Feeding the Hungry, Clothing the Naked, Proclaiming the Gospel of Hope to all…
>
> A new policy has been adopted to give all citizens the opportunity to share in this great task. Our Mission is now non-denominational in character, as our services are extended, and relief is distributed to all needy, irrespective of race, colour or creed.

Below the announcement, a new name appears in bold letters: "The Scott Mission."

If there was any reason for Morris to believe that he could survive on his own without a church salary, a home or an expenses budget, it was written into the 1941 report given at the general assembly in June. He included an impressive summary of his relief work during the Depression: "over a million meals" were served and "several hundreds of thousands of articles of clothing" were distributed, along with "many thousands of beds, stoves, pieces of furniture, bedding, layettes, medical appliances, medicine, and all sorts of necessities of life."

Perhaps the most impressive statement is the "Total Cash Receipts" (all financial donations) received from November 1930 to June 1940: $94,943.72. That amount is more than double the stipend Morris received from the church during the same period and doesn't include the material goods received in-kind. He also mentions an amount for legacies: $12,032.32. This was a bit complicated. No one could be sure if funds from a gift in a will designated for the Scott Institute could become the property of the Scott Mission. The courts had to settle the question.

That issue brought the estate of Jane M. Houston before the Supreme Court of Ontario in 1943, and it wasn't settled for a year. The Presbyterian Archives has a copy of the deposition given by Morris "in the Supreme Court of Ontario." He outlines the history of the institute and his work for the poor. A separate document includes part of the lawyer's report for the Presbyterian Church in Canada. The lawyers quote his reports to the general board of missions and the general assembly, describing his relief work as a ministry of the church. Despite those statements, his superiors had frequently announced in print and in public that the work of the Scott Institute was "without cost to the church." And, of course, this had been the original stipulation for the "Soup Kitchen Fund." From the start, Morris had to raise those funds with no promise of aid from the church.

The final ruling was decisive. The court was "not able to find that the Church took any part in the work of charity being carried on by Mr. Zeidman under the name of the 'Scott Institute.'" The Scott Mission became the sole recipient of legacies for the institute.[3] There's no record of any significant challenge to that decision, which eventually helped lay the financial foundations of the ministry.

Elaine was barely ten years old when the decision came down, but she remembered it as an important victory—moral and financial—for her father. Unfortunately, he had little time to savour it. Everything that Morris and Annie knew about the life of faith was about to be tested.

THE BOMBER
("The B-29 Near Ontario Place")

By Elaine Z. Markovic

There was a time
The whine of dropping bombs
Pierced the sky around you.
And you, yourself, were prey for
"the other side."
Today, your stilled propellers
Are choir-stalls for cheerful sparrows
Rejoicing with a new song.

CHAPTER 7

The Lord Will Provide

T he phone was ringing early on a Sunday morning, and Morris took the call. It was May 24, 1942, another disheartening year of the war. Grim reports from Nazi-occupied Europe filled the papers. Radio broadcasts from London were defiant, but the British had barely survived the Battle of Britain, and Allied forces hadn't yet won a victory. On the continent, Germany had created "Fortress Europe," and Hitler was poised to attack the Soviet Union. In the Far East, Imperial Japanese armies had overrun most of mainland China and South East Asia, while its immense fleets controlled the Pacific. Closer to home, after less than eight months, the meagre finances of the Scott Mission had scarcely held out through the winter.

As Morris put down the receiver, matters appeared considerably worse. During the night, a fire had started on Mission property north of the city. The site had been acquired a few months earlier for a summer camp. Tragically, an elderly woman had died; she was the mother of a faithful supporter.

Annie stayed with the younger children while Morris and Margaret began the long drive north of the city. Decades later, Margaret had vivid memories of the day. The route, about 90 kilometres, led through rolling green hills and black newly-tilled farm fields to the small town of Hillsburgh, south of Orangeville. Morris had spent time there recuperating from surgery when he was still a student at Knox. The camp property was next to the highway, but Morris didn't stop until he reached the home of Miss Catherine Carmichael. Her mother had died that morning.

In spite of exhaustion, Miss Carmichael insisted on coming with them into the old house, where the fire had raged only hours before. Margaret recoiled from the acrid odor as they walked through water-stained walls—some still smoking. Miss Carmichael led them to the room, under scorched timbers, where the firefighters had found her mother. Sometime early that morning a kerosene lamp had overturned, starting the blaze. At its height, flames had penetrated the ceiling, and through a jagged breach in the roof came a startling shaft of sunlight. (Both Margaret and Elaine were visibly moved as they recalled the memory, decades later, of the open rafters and the column of light in the gloomy darkness.)

Only a few months before, in March, Morris and Annie had left Miss Carmichael's home feeling energized, their faith revived. All winter long, they'd been trusting that the Lord would help to relocate the Fresh Air summer camp programs. Since 1929 they'd enjoyed their own lakefront grounds at Grimsby Beach, near the orchards of Niagara—a welcoming summer haven for busloads of inner-city kids and mothers, far from the cloying heat and drab concrete of downtown Toronto. Over the decades, they had renovated two old cottages on the bluffs where they could catch the breeze coming in off Lake Ontario. Dormitories were added later. A trail led down to the beach for swimming. Laine and her siblings would lie in their cots at night and fall asleep to the lapping of waves. Because of the Mission's new independence, the Grimsby site was no longer available.[1]

An appeal to supporters had led to the offer from Miss Carmichael, a long-time donor. Despite opposition from neighbours, family and even her lawyers, she invited Morris and Annie to see her inherited property—three acres next to the main road through Hillsburgh. It wasn't much by any standard: an open field, a little barn and a small old house off the highway. Yet there'd be many poor campers glad to come and enjoy the country air in Hillsburgh for a week. Annie and the children would stay all summer.

As she finished the original tour for Morris and Annie, Miss Carmichael mentioned one last condition of passing on the deed. Her elderly mother occupied the house and shouldn't have to leave. Morris, thinking of his own mother half a world away in Nazi-occupied Poland, went in to speak with her. Taking her hands, he promised, "We will never move you from your home."[2]

Leaving the charred house, all his plans were now cast in doubt. The shock of the tragic death and the added financial challenges of preparing the grounds made him hesitate. School was ending in a matter of weeks, and he would face some tough decisions. The Mission was promoting the new campgrounds to summer clients, and he had already appealed for support of the campers. His vision and the reputation of the new Mission were in jeopardy.

Soon afterwards, Morris drove Annie and the rest of the family to Hillsburgh while they considered what to do next. The setting left an unforgettable impression on eight-year-old Laine. As they walked through the old house, the family entered a small room that might have been a parlour and found an old Victorian sampler that had survived the fire, smoke and water damage. The delicate handiwork was still easily read: "The Lord Will Provide." Abraham had given that name to the mountain where God had called him to sacrifice his son Isaac. As he was about to take the boy's life, an angel interceded and another sacrifice was provided—a ram with its horns caught in the nearby bushes. Afterwards, God confirmed His original covenant promises to Abraham (Genesis 22).

"Once they saw those words," Elaine said, "Morris and Annie took hold of that promise as if it had been spoken aloud from heaven." Since the early morning phone call, they had been carrying a tremendous burden. Here, at last, was a sign of divine provision. From that moment on, they were determined to stand in faith, believing that all their needs would be met. The summer program would go on as scheduled.

The property had its share of problems. In time, the camp ministry would thrive, even if the setbacks seemed intimidating. Morris set the immediate priorities: bring in electricity and mow the overgrown fields. The electrician and the mower arrived on the same day, and the first set of electric lines was shredded into spaghetti-size lengths. But the well water proved to be the finest for miles around. The summer camp ministry opened up with Alex and David still nailing chicken wire to bed frames as the first campers arrived at the gates.

As for the site at Grimsby Beach, the family returned there a few years later. Sadly, the bluffs in front of the houses had caved in, and the grounds were no longer safe for camping. Elaine would later reflect that this must have been God's hand at work, moving them on at just the right time.

So, too, the Hillsburgh facility was eventually replaced by a larger, more suitable facility in Caledon where today the framed lacework hangs at the back of the campground chapel. A small plaque under the words "The Lord Will Provide" tells the remarkable story of the fire and the sampler—words of faith in the midst of tragedy and the promise of miracles yet to come.[3]

A lengthy typed letter, buried in the archives of the Scott Mission, reveals how desperate the situation had become when Miss Carmichael called. Dated June 6, 1942, it's addressed to Dr. Fred J. Conboy, mayor of Toronto, and follows an appeal made months earlier. Dr. Conboy, a dentist by profession, was a politician with a strong public Christian commitment and a history of supporting the Scott Institute's work through the Depression. Morris clearly expected the mayor to give his appeal a sympathetic hearing. He wrote,

> The Scott Mission is going through a very critical financial period...On March 21, I addressed a letter to you, explaining my request, but so far nothing tangible or definite has resulted...
>
> I wish to point out that my request is based not so much on the work that we do now among the poor, worthy as that work may be, but on the 10 years of service during the most critical economic period of the City of Toronto...If the City of Toronto had paid me as they have paid other institutions at the rate of 10 cents per meal, I would have received $70,000. [He describes several instances of taking in families and individuals sent by the city welfare department and helping police to maintain public order.]

Strictly speaking, I am not asking for any favours... merely asking the Board of Control to recognize their financial obligation to my Mission in a financial way as they have done to others.

...Even now I am not asking for the full reimbursement, but merely a fraction of the money...to see me through the crisis in my Mission's finances.

Hoping that you will consider my request favourably...

Years later, Annie described how Morris was left distraught when it was obvious that the request to the city would go unanswered. Afterwards, Morris declared himself fully aware—more than ever— that the work must go on "by faith." The memory of this event remained with every one of the Zeidman children. Annie spoke of it as a personal "turning point." Underneath the text of the second page, Alex added a short handwritten note:

Letter of request which was not granted. M. Zeidman said this was when he learned to trust God completely & not look to man for provision for the Mission.

Living by faith meant accepting that tomorrow was in the Lord's hands, and it was best to face it with a good sense of humour. One of Elaine's favourite stories involved a client who was coming weekly for groceries. Finally, the man declared that he'd found employment, the words spoken with confidence that this would be his last week at the Mission. A week later, Morris was surprised to see him in the grocery line again.

What happened? The man pointed down to a pair of brand new patent leather shoes. "I've always wanted a pair like these," he said, "and they cost $100."

There was a heart-sinking pause, and Elaine heard Morris say, "All right, one more week of groceries."

WINTER

By Elaine Z. Markovic

It snowed last night.
A child without boots,
A child without coat,
A child without love,
Came here today.
And that other Child without a bed,
No place to lay His head,
Provided.

CHAPTER 8

Confronting the Holocaust

T hreats of war hung over Europe in August 1939 as Morris was making plans to bring Jewish refugees to safety. His annual vacation would be spent in South America, as he told a reporter for the *Telegram*. The International Hebrew Christian Alliance had hopes of "establishing an agricultural colony for Hebrew Christians from Germany and Central Europe." There were already similar colonies in Argentina and Chile.[1]

A memento of the trip is a large photo of Morris in Buenos Aires, standing with members of the local Hebrew Christian congregation outside their worship hall. That picture in the Scott Mission archives confirms that he was there to discuss the proposal with local Hebrew Christian leaders. When Germany invaded Poland early in September, he was onboard a ship in the mid-Atlantic, travelling home.

During the first frantic weeks of the conflict, as Poland was overrun by German forces, Morris and Annie anxiously worried about the fate of his aging mother and married sisters, Rachel, Libby, Leah, Reizel and Yochet, with their husbands and children. There was also a younger brother, Joseph, with a wife and child. They received one last letter from his mother, stamped with a swastika and lines blacked-out by the censors. She asked him to send her a little bit of oil. Morris sent a pleading note to a missionary colleague in Holland, Leon Rosenberg, asking him to send funds to his mother, promising to reimburse any expenses. A few months later, the letter was returned by the RCMP. There was nothing more to be done.

Only gradually did Morris come to accept the full scale of terrors that the Nazis were unleashing on Europe's captive Jewish populace:

> All during the war, the family and I were praying for those unfortunate ones in Poland who were under the Nazi occu-pation and oppression. We had heard, and read in the newspapers of the wholesale murders and tortures, the beatings, the crematoriums; but we had hoped against hope that these were only war atrocity rumours and that surely such bestial, inhuman treatment and such deliberate destruction of non-combatant Jewish men, women and chil-dren was inconceivable.[2]

Determined to do more, he and Annie began a campaign to inspire the hearts of Canadians. They placed on city streetcars and buses hundreds of 4" x 5" printed cards decorated with two crossed flags—the Canadian Red Ensign and the Union Jack—and uplifting words from Scripture. Readers were encouraged to trust that God was with them. The program eventually expanded to Ontario mili-tary buses to Camp Borden (a major training facility for Southern Ontario), then to Hamilton and the northern railway.[3]

Elaine recalled that Psalm 91 was a Scripture that Morris and Annie often recited during the war years, especially the promises of its opening verses:

> *He that dwelleth in the secret place of the most High shall abide under the shadow of the Almighty. I will say of the LORD, He is my refuge and my fortress: my God; in him will I trust. Surely he shall deliver thee.* (Psalm 91:1–3)

Another ministry evident in the Mission archives is found in copies of the brief encouraging letters that Morris sent to leaders of the Allied cause—including Winston Churchill, General Eisenhower and Canadian prime minister William Lyon Mackenzie King and oth-ers—assuring them that they were in his prayers and in the prayers of the Scott Mission staff. Alex's biography notes that Eisenhower, alone, sent a personal reply of thanks.[4]

The work of the Mission, caring for the poor and destitute, continued uninterrupted during the war. There was, however, one group's welfare that was of special interest to Morris: German prisoners of war. Morris began a series of appeals to the Canadian government, offering to bring spiritual comfort to POWs. During the war years these letters went unanswered. Finally, as the war ended, the government responded, allowing Morris and Annie access to German prisoners in a camp near Drummondville, Quebec. According to Elaine, Morris and Annie brought chocolate, cigarettes, Bibles and the gospel. After several trips to the camp, they won the hearts of many, some of whom stayed in touch after they returned home. One showed his gratitude with a beautiful large wood carving for Annie fashioned from the top of a barrel.

Despite the sufferings of his family and the Jewish community in Poland and throughout Europe, Morris refused to allow himself any thought of revenge against the German people. Elaine remembered how he used to say that he had to forgive. She always thought of that quality as one of the most touching signs of his spiritual discipline.

All through the war years, a spiritual impulse had assured Morris that he would return to Europe and deliver practical and financial aid to the ravaged communities of his homeland. As he learned the terrible news of the devastation among the Jewish communities of Poland, he was anxious to seek out any survivors of his family. The prompting remained on his heart as clear and strong as any call in his life. Despite occasional physical weakness and continuing trials from colitis, Morris hoped to set out as soon as possible, yearning to comfort those he loved.

His plans were not only dangerous but highly improbable while Europe lay in ruins. Morris gave over the entire project to the Lord, resigning himself to months of quiet prayer. He wrote that he wanted "a sign that it was His will that I go, and that my desire was directed, not by selfish impulses but by His Holy Spirit."[5] Besides, as he explained, "Passports to leave the country were difficult to obtain; a visa to travel behind the 'Iron Curtain' was next to impossible to get. Passage on board ship or transatlantic planes was not available, and our own Foreign Exchange has very strict rules in regard to taking money out of the country."[6]

The extensive reports that he produced after his return make it apparent that by faith he'd been preparing for years, laying aside clothing and funds, "so that when the war would be over, I could immediately proceed with the much needed help."[7] The breakthrough that allowed him to go is somewhat obliquely described by Morris and later by Alex, who says that he went "on behalf of Canadians with relatives in Poland."[8] Morris is much more florid in his comments: "The Lord in His mercy took me at my word, and He miraculously, without any effort on my part, secured for me passport, visa, passage and the permission to take out of the country the necessary sum to be distributed among the poor and the needy in Poland."[9] Clearly, some form of government permission had been given, though we have no knowledge of any specific conditions.

Unfortunately, as Morris made his final plans to leave for Europe, he received news of brutal attacks on Jewish Holocaust survivors. In many reports, Jews returning to their homes in Poland had been murdered. Once again, Morris put his trust in the prayers of faithful believers. These continued throughout his travels, and he credited the petitions of God's people for keeping him safe until his return. Morris admitted that he left Canada with great apprehension. Saying farewell to his family, he saw his wife and children choke back their tears—all except for twelve-year-old Laine, who "broke down and cried bitterly."[10]

In August 1946, almost exactly seven years after he had left on a journey to bring European Jewry to South America, Morris was steaming across the Atlantic on the Swedish ship S.S. *Drottningholm*, to reach out to survivors. He was surprised that the ship had no program of Sunday worship and received permission to conduct services. Preaching on "The Love of God for Sinful Man," with his "heart full of tears," Morris saw many in his audience who were touched. He made several important contacts, including other clergymen aboard and a Polish official from the Ministry of Health who later guided him through Warsaw.

As the ship approached the Polish port of Gdynia, Morris stared out at the gaping steel wreckage of two massive German battleships. The spectacle foreshadowed many scenes to come. The devastation and heartbreak to which Morris would become a witness was perhaps more than he could bear. His family later said that he never truly recovered from the effects of this journey. Although he'd spent years assisting the neediest people from the streets of Toronto, the work of the next eight weeks would be the most draining, arduous task of his life.

The full extent of Nazi crimes against the Jewish people weren't yet fully tallied, but in his 1946 report he could claim, "Here in Poland, a destruction has befallen the Jewish people, the like of which, for its cruelty, bestiality and monstrosity, it is difficult to find in the long annals of the history of God's ancient people, the Jews." A tour of the shocking ruins of Warsaw, where most of the homes and public buildings were destroyed, convinced him that there was no way to fully comprehend the distress of those who had lived through it: "The suffering they endured, the ghastly fear of being blown to bits any minute, the hunger, the cold, the despair, and the frantic attempts to save themselves...beggars description."[11]

Repeated tours of ghettoes in Lodz, Krakow, Czestochowa, Soanowietz and many others revealed the horrors that Nazis brought upon the Jewish populace. Many Jewish families perished as they hid in cellars or homemade bunkers that couldn't withstand the Nazi onslaught of bombs and shells. Each day he spent most of his time listening to survivors with an insatiable need to speak about what they'd seen and experienced. The stories poured out "from early morning until late at night, of the valour, the tragedy, the heroism, the martyrdom of the men, women and children of the ghetto."[12]

It was an exhausting process. "Every hour and every minute of the day," he wrote, "I had to hold on to the hand of God and feel His presence, and claim His grace, without which it would have been humanly impossible to hear in detail the works of the devil and the deeds of men who had forsaken the living God."[13] Absorbing and recording these accounts might well have been the greatest burden of all, yet he did more.

Morris conducted detailed studies of the conditions in his native city, which he recorded as "Czenstechowa." [Other Jewish sources also use this form. The common Polish spelling is Czestochowa.] He was able to contact the family back in Canada from here, and the original Canadian Pacific cable, dated "1946 SEP 16 PM 11 16," is in the Mission archives. It reads,

> INTERVIEWING SCORES JEWS OFFICE PLACED MY DISPOSAL TRYING ORDEAL HEARING CONCETRATION [sic] CAMP WOMEN BEYOND ENDURANCE TO LISTEN HOW FRIENDS RELATIONS LIQUIDATED HEALTD [sic] FINE HOTEL COMFORTABLE FOOD PLENTY LOVE
>
> ZEIDLE

This was the city where the extended Zeidman family had lived: his mother, five married sisters with husbands and children, and a younger brother with a wife and two-year-old child. The Jewish population of 30,000 had been reduced to 500. Here, as elsewhere, the Nazis had used every possible method of terror for one end: "death, under the most humiliating and most excruciating torture."[14]

In each town, Morris heard similar tales of the ordeals that allowed only a few to survive, and most of these were destined for the gas chambers. He wrote, "My own dear ones and loved ones were among the first to be dispatched into eternity by this bestial and devil-inspired method."[15] From what he had gathered, his mother and his sisters' families had perished by 1942. His brother, Joseph, was hiding in nearby caves with his wife and son until they were also seized in the Nazis' relentless pursuit.

Morris documented the living hell of the concentration camps, where death was meted out by every possible means of cruelty. Inmates were tortured for any infraction and otherwise worked to death. Many who did not perish from sheer exhaustion died of various diseases, including typhoid and tuberculosis. Finally, in the winter of 1945, as the Germans lost their foothold on Europe, the guards led their prisoners on forced marches that killed many more. "The human mind is not capable," he wrote, "of enduring the strain of comprehending the wickedness and depth of its own baseness and depravity."[16]

In the aftershock of such tragic devastation came the violence against survivors who attempted to return home. The Poles remained adamantly hostile to their former neighbours; Jews found that they were "shunned, boycotted, and threatened daily." And the memories were too vivid. It was, they told Morris, "like living 'beside an open grave.'" He began to see that the future for European Jewry was bound up with the hope of a Jewish state in the Holy Land: "thousands of Jewish young men want to enter Palestine or die—for it is their only choice—there is no other."[17]

He also found a very different group of Jewish survivors: those who had gone "underground" and effectively assimilated, often by intermarriage. Many of these, with the assent of the Polish authorities, were maintaining their assumed Gentile identity and had become Roman Catholic. What would be the legacy of this generation, Morris wondered, when a growing spiritual hunger made them question the rituals and doctrine of Roman Catholicism? In so many conversations, he had found a yearning for truth and meaning among Jewish survivors. He wrote, "Man's extremity is God's opportunity."[18]

The welcome he received as he distributed financial assistance and hundreds of pounds of clothing brought from Toronto was full of heartfelt thanks and even reverence because he had come not merely to write reports but to provide relief for body and soul.[19] He was particularly moved when he was able to bless fellow Jewish believers in Jesus—including those who had passed through the horrors of the Holocaust and found the Messiah. "I shall never forget," he wrote, "how in sheer delight and with tears of joy I was told in the City of Lodz by these brethren: 'You are the first Hebrew Christian that has come to us with help from America.' And they blessed me with many blessings."[20]

His efforts, he conceded, were "only a beginning;" so much more help was needed, and yet this would cost him dearly. Alex tells us that over some two months of travel, Morris lost 15 pounds and had very little sleep. He wrote constantly, recording as much as possible. In addition to all that he had heard, there was the personal anguish of discovering that virtually nothing was left of his family; even his father's gravestone—like so many others in the Jewish cemetery—had been obliterated. He would eventually learn of a few cousins who had escaped through the sewers of the Warsaw ghetto and settled in Israel. He would also receive a precious keepsake: a sister's Hebrew prayer book found in a Polish bookstall. Through it all, he was conscious of God's leading, writing in his diary for October 16, 1946, "It is nothing short of miraculous how the Lord has been going before me."[21]

Travelling back through Great Britain (including meeting with the leaders of the IHCA, who eagerly took up the work of assisting Europe's Jewish refugees), he spent time in Edinburgh with his sister Gertrude before returning home. Despite weariness and the worsening effects of colitis, Morris immediately began speaking and writing about what he had seen. In the coming decades, he and Annie were committed to assisting Holocaust survivors by every means possible, especially if they could bring them to Canada. The Mission provided assistance and advice that allowed them to settle into a new life— whatever their background or beliefs. In fact, Morris himself was about to make a move, and it would put him right back in the centre of the Jewish community.

IF COMES THE DAY

By Annie A. Zeidman

If comes the day when Tyranny roars down our carols
Stamps out our candles, stifles all our joy,
Still Thou remainest, Lord, unchanged, unchanging
Still shine Thy stars;
In faithful hearts the heavenly host still praises and
adores thee,
Thy love our Glory, Thou Thyself our joy.

CHAPTER 9

The Good Samaritan of "Czenstochova"

In the 1940s and 50s, one of Toronto's foremost Jewish figures was J. B. Salsberg. J.B., as he was known, had gone from being a union organizer to city alderman and then won a seat in the Ontario legislature. His riding was St. Andrew, which included Spadina Avenue and a large percentage of Jewish voters. Though Salsberg was recognized by his peers and the premier as a capable, well-spoken member of the provincial Parliament, his term in office was controversial: he sat as a member of the Communist Party, holding his provincial seat from 1943 to '55.

Within a few years of leaving public office, Salsberg severed and disavowed all connections to Communism and the party, becoming a successful businessman. In time—with many of those old associations buried in the past—he re-emerged as an elder statesman in the Jewish community and a leading columnist for the *Canadian Jewish News (CJN)*. In two consecutive *CJN* columns written in December 1982, he shared several stories about his encounters with Morris Zeidman. These provided some intriguing insights on the Mission from the viewpoint of its Jewish neighbours.

Those exchanges wouldn't have happened if Morris hadn't been forced to relocate the Mission in 1948. There'd been no intention to move from Bay St. until the restaurant owner next door decided to expand his operations into a cocktail lounge.[1] When the landlord wouldn't renew the lease, Morris made alternate plans and started promoting a building fund.

The site at 502–504 Spadina Avenue, where the Mission relocated—and later built a major facility—is a few doors above the northwest corner where Spadina meets College Street. Originally, it had been two separate houses. These were joined together by an addition in the front, and the combined buildings had operated as a fur factory. A disagreement between the two factory owners had reduced the price. Taking another step of faith, the Mission purchased the property at a cost of $32,000. Building fund donations allowed them to give a down payment of $10,000, although Morris admitted to a few sleepless nights about the other $22,000. Calling on friends and volunteers to help, the Zeidmans began renovations. A major task was transforming the factory floor into a hall that would serve as a chapel, Sunday school and dining area with room for 100 at one sitting: ten tables with ten spaces at each table.

In the mornings, transient and homeless men would line up for breakfast, and for many years not all of them could be served at once. Thus began the familiar sight on Spadina of men lining up outside the Mission door. At holiday times, when a large meal was available, the lines would stretch quite long, but only 100 could sit down at a time.

The location was attractive for a few reasons. Not least of these for Morris was its setting under the distinctive arched windows of No. 1 Spadina Crescent. That gothic structure and its tower can be seen down the length of the avenue. In the late 1940s, it was the site of Connaught Laboratories and garnered fame when Dr. Jonas Salk used their expertise to make the first large batches of polio vaccine. But for any graduate of Knox College, it was affectionately remembered as "the old building." Built in 1875, this had been the original site of the college prior to its move onto the University of Toronto campus in 1915.

More important than nostalgia was its immediate prominence on Spadina among his Jewish neighbours. The Mission instantly became a visible landmark at a major intersection of the Jewish community near many local institutions—synagogues, restaurants, union halls, the B'nai B'rith offices and other landmarks. The local M.P.P., Mr. Salsberg, kept his riding offices there and would inevitably cross paths with the Rev. Morris Zeidman.

Salsberg recalled the original "Scott Mission" from its days on Elizabeth St., but he knew few details about Morris. Joseph Baruch Salsberg (1902–1998) had also been born in Poland and immigrated to Toronto in his early teens. His first *CJN* column on Morris begins by broaching the "hard to define relationship" between the Jewish community and the Mission, a relationship that Salsberg described as "neither peace nor war." The little that he knew about Morris was not always accurate, including the suggestion that Morris "was ordained in an English missionary school." (The details might have been confused with those of Rev. Rohold.)

He did appreciate the difference between Morris and the open-air missionary preachers from an earlier era. Salsberg recalled their public ministries for "bombastic proselytizing speeches" that led to confrontations on street corners and outside synagogues. Above all, he affirmed Morris's Jewish identity, referring to him as "Rev. Morris Zeidman, a Polish Jew of the city of Czenstochova." (Note the similar spelling of his home city that Morris had used.) While the column avoided presenting Morris in too positive a light, Salsberg didn't minimize the Mission's practical help for the needy. Nor did he deny his awkwardness at being seen with a missionary in the street. He wrote,

> Since this odd Christian Mission in the midst of Jews didn't carry on any overt proselytizing activities there developed an uneasy truce between Zeidman and the many Jews who knew him and with whom he was eager to retain some contact...
>
> But I, too, had moments of embarrassment with the said Rev. Morris Zeidman...
>
> There was Zeidman, north of College St. on Spadina Ave. and there was I, whose constituency office was on College St....and our path did cross from time to time.
>
> What was I to do on such occasions—reject his friendly approaches? And then again, what might people say when they found me speaking with Zeidman in a zaftik Yiddish in public?[2]

In those post-war years, both the politician and the clergyman had a shared concern about the distressing plight of Jewish Holocaust survivors from their native Poland. Soon after his return from Europe, Morris began making impassioned pleas to Canadian evangelical Christians, describing the plight of 100,000 displaced, homeless Holocaust refugees. Many were clamoring to enter Palestine, while the British were blockading the ports. Morris's appeal compared the treatment of Jews to the settlements offered Germany and Italy:

> What fair dealing is there in the fact that the United States and Great Britain are offering a billion dollars to Germany to re-establish herself; an Italian statesman has been offered one hundred million dollars...but millions are spent to maintain a navy, air-force, and army, to keep Jews away from their God-promised and man-promised national home, and keep them shut up in concentration camps in Belsen, in Cyprus, and in many other places...in the terrible nightmare of old camp surroundings?
>
> The 100,000 Jews in concentration camps and in Poland...would go anywhere, to any hospitable shore that would allow them to start life anew.
>
> The writer of these lines receives, daily, letters from would-be immigrants in Poland...pleading for us to help them get out.[3]

In the midst of this tragedy, Morris's journey to Poland didn't escape the notice of Salsberg or the fraternal organization of Polish Jewry from Morris's home city: the "Chenstochover Aid Society." They were led by Moyshe Tarnovsky, who Salsberg described as "the highly respected and universally recognized leader of all Chenstochover landsleit in Toronto." (The term *landsleit* refers both to individuals and the associated members of the original Polish community. This type of association was familiar to Salsberg's Jewish readers and didn't simply aid the needy. They extended mutual aid, co-operating to provide personal and spiritual support—often acting as family for each other—while they transitioned into North American society. Over time, these groups helped to establish synagogues, retirement homes, cemeteries and other Jewish community organizations.)

Sadly, even Polish survivors with Canadian families found the way "barred and almost unpassable," wrote Salsberg, noting that Rev. Zeidman offered more than just news from home.

On his return to Toronto Zeidman approached Tarnovksy and a few other leaders of the Chenstochover Aid Society with the following proposition.

Through his influence he was able to secure from Ottawa permission to bring a number of Chenstochover Jewish families who survived the Holocaust. What he needed to realize the plan was individual sponsorships from Chenstochover landsleit for each of the families still located in their native city. Further Zeidman assured his landsleit that he would privately raise all the funds necessary to cover the cost of the entire project.

Moyshe Tarnovsky came to see me about his painful problem. Of course, he assured me, the Chenstochover in Toronto would eagerly participate in any rescue plan. But they were afraid of a partnership with Zeidman. They feared that he would utilize his involvement to gain religious influence over the newcomers and ultimately draw them into his Christian missionary plans.

"How," he asked, "can we assume such a moral responsibility?"[4]

The end result was that the society declined the offer but allowed local families to participate according to their consciences. They had to accept, as Salsberg wrote, "Zeidman's assurances that his interest was not conversion to Christianity but to bring the surviving Chenstochover Jewish families to Canada." Salsberg records that he personally knew "a number of those families did arrive, but I do not know whether Zeidman kept his promise not to proselytize."

Salsberg adds that Morris's efforts weren't limited to those he could bring to Canada. He recalled a passing encounter in their neighbourhood pharmacy when Morris "insisted that I hear from the druggist as to the frequency and volume of his drug purchases for his Chenstochover landsleit which had to be shipped by the druggist. They were many and frequent, the druggist assured me."

One more curious tale rounded out Salsberg's second column. It involved Morris's sister Gertrude, who had been living in Edinburgh, where she had moved with Professor Manson's family. The news that she was arriving in Toronto made its way to Tarnovsky, who was unfamiliar with her situation and would have assumed that she was a Holocaust survivor.

He convened a meeting of senior members from the aid society. They decided that "since Zeidman's young sister may not be aware of her brother's apostasy, they, her landsleit, were morally obligated to inform her of this fact immediately on her arrival." Salsberg describes what followed:

> Thus it happened that on the morning when Zeidman's sister was due to arrive at the Union Station Moyshe Tarnovsky and a group of landsleit were at the station awaiting the train. The train did, indeed, arrive but, alas, there was no sign of Zeidman or his sister. As was later discovered Zeidman outwitted his landsleit. He had travelled to Montreal the day before and received his sister at the Montreal railway station where no one knew of the critical meeting between the head of the Scott Mission in Toronto and his surviving young Jewish sister of Chenstochov.[5]

Morris and Annie continued aiding survivors over the next decade. Alex refers to second- and third-floor apartments at 502 Spadina that were refitted to accommodate "four or five immigrant families" from Poland. As additional properties were acquired to the south of the Mission building, these were also used for immigrant housing. Less visible were the many letters that Morris wrote, advising survivors about the best ways to leave war-torn Europe, or the numerous metal drums that Annie would faithfully line with clothing to be shipped overseas over the next two decades.[6]

Although Morris publicly appeared to have returned to his Mission duties with vigor, the long-term effects of the overseas trip were telling. He persisted in making trips to speak in other parts of Canada and the occasional trip abroad, but his strength was failing. Morris responded by giving more attention to preaching, writing and teaching ministries and became active in some unexpected circles.

The separation from his Presbyterian roots had left a vacuum. Morris became isolated from long-standing ministry colleagues and was open to new avenues of fellowship. For some years, he'd been warmly received in Pentecostal circles where pastors and congregants alike had a strong interest in the Jewish resettlement of Palestine and Jewish evangelism. He began to cherish their support of his ministry. Alex later reflected that his father's involvement in these circles appeared to coincide with a desire for a deeper experience of the person and work of the Holy Spirit.[7]

An increasing number of invitations came from local Pentecostal pulpits and eventually their conferences and camp meetings. A favourite congregation for Morris was Evangel Temple, a leading church in downtown Toronto. The liberty of Pentecostal services meant that he'd be recognized from the pulpit and invited to lead the congregation in prayer. When the Eastern Pentecostal Bible School was located in Evangel Temple, Morris became a lecturer in Greek and Hebrew, influencing the next generation of denominational leaders. As a teacher he was both loved and respected. Some of those students eventually came to work at the Mission, either at the camp or as staff members for various lengths of time. During the 1940s Morris became a regular contributor to *The Pentecostal Testimony*, a denominational magazine where his articles included "The New Order of New Birth" and "The Jewish View of the Holy Spirit." (Some articles were later reprinted as pamphlets by the Mission.)

In "The Jewish View of The Holy Spirit" (1946), Morris begins by expounding from rabbinic sources, including the Zohar and the targum of R. Jonathan ben Uzziel. He employs extensive scholarship to support one emphatic point: the supernatural experiences of the first-century followers of Jesus described in the book of Acts are available for believers today. The blessings are not only accessible—they are "to be desired and coveted...by Christians in every place and in every age, until He come." Rather than conform to their denominations, he suggests that sincere followers seek the Lord on this question and decide for themselves.

As Morris expanded his writing ministry, he decided to give Christian readers a greater understanding of Jewish topics and religious practices. He launched an advertising feature called "IQ on Jews and Judaism." Beginning in 1945 until 1960, *The Gideon Magazine, Sunday School Times, The Sword of the Lord* and *The*

Evangelical Christian ran these informative short pieces, which drew a wide audience. The format usually followed a question, such as, Is Judaism adequate as a world religion? What is the Passover Haggadah? What is the number of Jews in the world today?

For secular newspapers, the Mission created "The Good Samaritan Corner" in a very different style. Starting in 1945, both Morris and Annie authored weekly summaries of their ministry for the Toronto Saturday "church pages." Each weekend, readers of the *Globe and Mail*, *Toronto Star* and *Evening Telegram* found heart-warming illustrations about the challenges and blessings of caring for their poor and vulnerable neighbours. While the Mission's Depression-era reputation was receding into memory, the columns drew support and appreciation from a new generation of readers.

Early examples of "The Good Samaritan Corner" show that the style and content owed only a slight debt to the daily sketches that Miss Rose Macdonald had prepared for the *Telegram* in the 1930s. Morris and Annie added Bible references and spiritual encouragement and often closed with a few verses from a hymn or Scripture. And, like J.B., Morris and Annie knew that one of the keys to holding people's interest was sharing a good story.

FEBRUARY 14, 1948

Two women are waiting for relief groceries, and as we come along the passage to talk to them, we cannot help overhearing part of their conversation. The young one nearest the door is saying "Yes, they bin good to me here. Two weeks ago my kids were near starved. I'd never bin to the Scott before, but I couldn't stand their crying no longer, so I came over here and told them I needed food, and my man wasn't working again (I never mentioned the kids) and they never asked me nothing. They gimme potatoes, and porkanbeans, and they gimme some swell soup. I tell you, my kids had a swell time that day." We tiptoe away so that we can get over the picture of those poor babies and their "swell time" on potatoes and beans and soup. (You may read about hungry children in Canada…we see them right here in Toronto, and thank God, we can do something about it.) This young mother went home with food more suitable to provide a "swell time" for her little tots.

So they come and go, our friends, and very often we feel that we ourselves are missing something precious because we must hurry them along to make room for others. We are cramped and crowded, and we are working under adverse and uncomfortable conditions with inadequate equipment, but we are working together with God, and looking to Him to grant the larger place for the larger service. Please stand with us in prayer and fellowship, and remember the "Building Fund."

DECEMBER 4, 1948

"In my distress I...cried unto my God," said the Psalmist (Psalm 18:6), and he was not the first one to do so, nor the last. Only yesterday a man came in and cried in distress out of the depths of sin in the gutter. He was dirty and filthy, but he cried to God. He wanted a chance to get out of the depths where he lay helpless. Between him and decency there was a gulf, but it could be bridged by the forgiveness of sin...and clean clothing. Jesus cleansed him from sin...now to get rid of the dirty clothes and put on the new and clean. These the Scott Mission provided. Two thousand years ago in Bethlehem a baby boy, His mother and His foster father could find no lodging—there was no room for them in the inn. This week a young man with his two boys, one six and the other four years old, could find no lodging. The mother had left her two children and her husband, who came to the city to find work. It was about 11:30 in the morning when they arrived in the Mission, and the boys and the father had had nothing to eat that day. The children were pale, hungry, weary and haggard. Could we pay for their room over the weekend and feed them, the worried father pleaded with tears in his eyes, as the tragedy of the family was unfolded. We surely fed and provided lodging for the father and his two little fellows. The money? "Seek ye first the Kingdom of God" is the motto of the Scott Mission. Tuesday was the end of the month, when the Mission pays its bills. Our bank account is overdrawn, but tomorrow, Sunday, at 10 a.m., 150 hungry men will be waiting at our door to be fed—and maybe some children and women, too. Would you, dear Reader of this column, turn them away? Of course you wouldn't, were you to see the cold, hungry, haggard faces. You can help us feed them by your prayerful support and freewill offering. Please write to us now, while you think of us.

But to do good and to [share what you have with others] forget not: for with such sacrifices God is well pleased. (Hebrews 13:16)

FEBRUARY 21, 1949

This week we have had a record number of men, women and children seeking aid, material and spiritual. In all, over eighteen hundred souls were ministered to. Many of the destitute old men say with tears in their eyes, "We'd starve to death if it wasn't for the Scott Mission." The following letter with $2 in it shows the appreciation of those who are being helped by us. "Dear Sir: Just a small token of appreciation of a few lunches I needed and received at your Mission last winter. Thanks for the lift. Two dollars is not much, but a lot when you have nothing in your pocket. Yours truly, R." Here is a request from a frantic lady: "Dear Mr. Zeidman. I wonder if you could help me out. Could you give me some clothes for this boy? His mother deserted him three years ago, and my husband and I have been looking after him ever since. I am beginning to find it awful hard as I have five children of my own, and my husband makes only a small wage. I can't get enough clothes for my own children." Scores of such requests come to us daily. We are in need of men's, women's and children's underwear, men's trousers and ladies' winter coats; also men's and women's shoes. The work at the Scott Mission is a challenge to every Christian citizen in the city and province. A Christian ministry is maintained on a large scale. Funds are needed to carry on the work and necessary expansion. Your prayerful support will help in this indispensable Christlike ministry. Pray for our Building Fund Campaign, which opens officially March the 1st (D.V.). If you have a building or residence available, please write to us about it.

MAY 14, 1949

Very often strangers visiting the Scott Mission watch the people come, each with a burden of need or sorrow, and then they turn to us and say, "How do you stand it?" Well, we can tell you that we could not stand it very long if we had not learned to cast all our cares on Him, the Great Burden Bearer, because He cares for us, or in other words, because He does our "caring" for us. Sin and sorrow and sickness, bitterness and despair, poverty and loneliness...these are our portion every day. Often we are faced with problems and needs that seem too big for us, and if we could not take them to Him, our hearts would break. Just yesterday we were asked for nightclothes for a three-year-old boy who weighs 18 pounds. One distress has complicated another throughout his little life, and the diseases he has suffered have seemed to overlap. A bad case of "red tape" has not helped matters any, either. We did our best to provide what was needed, but it seemed so inadequate when his poor, wasted, wee body was in misery, when his short past was one of unhappiness, and his uncertain future far from promising. And yet, we do know that the Good Shepherd loves this little lamb, and will surely carry him in his bosom.

Our office is a haven these days to many bewildered folk from over the seas, strangers in a strange land, understanding neither its speech nor its ways. The Mission is also an oasis where they can refresh their soul in almost any one of the European languages...and we use the word "refresh" advisedly...you would know what we mean if you could see their faces when they hear friendly greetings in their own mother tongue. And all the time, the Lord Himself stands by to counsel and strengthen and help us. He it is who does the work— we are only His instruments.

The Scott Mission Review was one of a series of pamphlet quarterlies that Morris and Annie published over the years for their donors. The September 1952 edition (it was only eight pages) includes an article with touching descriptions of Holocaust survivors among the camp participants, including some who have come to North America via Israel, and a letter from Israel. Another letter (not reproduced here) is from a doctor in Wiesbaden, Germany, thanking Morris "for all the good you are doing now and have done for us in the past."

SCOTT MISSION FRESH AIR HOME—1952
By Annie A. Zeidman

So often we have thought how wonderful it would be if you who uphold our work and our people before the Mercy Seat might just have the opportunity of meeting all the precious mothers and children, yes, and fathers, too, who have been your guests—and God's—at the Scott Mission Fresh Air Home this summer. Since, however, for most of you this is not possible, we should like to bring a few of them to you in this short article.

A special and blessed feature of the work which the Lord has given us to do this year is the number of new arrivals from Israel. These dear souls, having survived the torture camps, the D.P. camps—having escaped, or wandered, or travelled to Israel—having found there hunger, fear, and disillusionment, are now trying to build again a new life for themselves and their children in Canada. Small wonder that they are fearful and nervous; small wonder that their children are a constant source of anxiety to them—as one mother said in apology to us, when she was unable to stop worrying because her little one had a slight cold, "Excuse me for worrying. She is my only one. And children die so easily."

In imagination let us sit on the step outside the kitchen door, and from this vantage point watch the mothers and children as they come and go about the camp grounds. See that little girl coming toward us for a "love"? She is six years old, and each of her birthdays has been spent in a different land, always one step ahead of terror and tyranny. Her parents are both doctors, and are also Jewish followers of the Lord Jesus…

Please notice this sad-eyed young woman walking past us, holding a little child by the hand. Notice the string of numbers tattooed on her arm. Numbers like these are tattooed on the arms of practically every man and woman in our company— the dread symbol brought with them from the extermination camps. This little child is not her firstborn. Ah no! He lies in a common grave with his father, aunts, uncles, and all their families, shot down in the market square of a little town in Poland. After the war, the young widow married again, and now, with another sweet child, is trying to rise above the past.

These are only such a few out of the many who share your hospitality.

LETTER FROM ISRAEL

To our dear and precious friend, Mr. Zeidman:

Shalom!

First we wish to tell you that we are all well here and pray that you too are enjoying good health. I regret to inform you that I was laid up in bed for four weeks with a broken leg—the result of heavy work, undernourishment and difficult conditions under which we live.

Your food parcel was a Godsend to us as it arrived while I was sick and was unable to earn a living for my family. My wife gave birth to a little girl two months ago, we were therefore so glad to receive the rice in the parcel and also the meat, for which we are most grateful.

My wife and three children are praying for you that our kind Heavenly Father may bless and prosper you. Please do not forget our needs. Words cannot express our gratitude to you for your kindness to us.

The Wasserman family

BETHLEHEM IS FAR AWAY (1955)

By Annie A. Zeidman

Bethlehem is far away, far, and long ago,
Oh, could we but travel there tonight, and bend low,
Enter through the stable door,
Offer up our treasure store
To Him, the Lord of Life, God's Gift of Love
To you and me.

But just down the street, perhaps around the corner,
Is Bethlehem in poverty, Gethsemane in tears,
Nazareth misunderstood, Calvary unpitied
May we dare to seek Him there?
Friend, let us go!

For God so loved the world, that he gave his only begotten Son. (John 3:16)

CHAPTER 10

Growing Pains

The first time that Marilyn Nelson saw Elaine was the opening day of grade 10 at Moulton College. Neither one had arrived at school—they were both on their way, dressed in the school uniforms. At least, that's how Elaine thought she was dressed.

"I was on the streetcar," said Marilyn, "and saw her getting on the Bloor car with black silk stockings instead of the required black lisle [cotton] stockings. She had just turned 15 and never wore them again. I think of her with those legs with the silk stockings. Everyone just looked at her because her legs were thin."

That image—a slight, vulnerable young woman who didn't want to be noticed—reflected many of Elaine's anxieties as a young teen. Grade 9 at Malvern hadn't gone well. A classmate of the young Glenn Gould, Elaine was also gifted at the piano, according to her older sister, Margaret. Unfortunately, she lacked the determination, or as Margaret said, "It wasn't an obsession." Her choice of friends became another problem, and Elaine had spent too much time in the detention room.

"I wasn't a very serious student," Elaine said. "It may have been rebellion." She recalled how Morris refused to accept her lax attitude. Over his daughter's objections, he enrolled her at Moulton College. The school was an excellent setting to learn Christian values, which did nothing to make it appealing. "I knew that my father was a Christian minister," she said. "I didn't like that during my teenage years. I would have liked to have been 'Joe Cool' rather than Elaine Zeidman."

Moulton College occupied the old mansion of Canadian senator William McMaster at No. 34 Bloor Street East, on the north side near Park Road, less than a block from Yonge Street. The vine-covered three-storey Victorian mansion radiated a comfortable, gracious atmosphere. The site is now marked by an Ontario Heritage Trust plaque inside 2 Bloor Street East, a large retail and office complex covering the old site. The plaque states,

> Senator William McMaster's former residence, Moulton Ladies' College was opened in 1888…His widow, Susan Moulton McMaster, then conveyed the residence to the university for use as a preparatory school for girls. The Ladies' Department of Woodstock College, an older Baptist institution, was transferred to the Toronto college, named Moulton in honour of Mrs. McMaster. For 66 years Moulton College served with distinction both day and resident students from junior grades to university entrance. The buildings were sold in 1954 and demolished in 1958.

With its long association with McMaster University and strong Baptist roots, Moulton had become a high quality Christian school with women in every faculty post. Opening day was always the second Tuesday in September. Chapel was held daily at 9 a.m., and this is where Elaine memorized many of her favourite hymns. The principal in those years (1949–53) was Miss J. Marjorie Trotter, who held the religion classes in her sitting room. She was remembered by her students as "a tall, imposing woman" with a love of nature, especially camping. A brief history of the college wrote of her, "Every girl cherishes memories of Miss Trotter's faith in her and of her urging to higher things."[1]

Apart from graduation, the highlight of the year was "Class Tea," usually held in November. Students and their parents were received in the wood-panelled drawing room. The principal and teachers in evening gowns welcomed the visitors and a special guest of distinction invited for the occasion. Both Elaine and Marilyn recalled the girls' frantic preparations to look poised. For many, this meant walking around the college balancing a book on their heads. Special events aside, the school made appearance a priority. "I tried to keep my uniform in pristine condition and shined my shoes every night," Elaine said.

Fortunately, she wasn't long in finding friends, including Marilyn Nelson, who was so small in grade 9 that she got the nickname "Pee Wee." There were four of them in her circle, young women who saw in each other a committed faith. "Our lifestyle was different from the others," said Marilyn, "and we were always more interested in spiritual things, even at age 15." In addition to Marilyn and Elaine, there was Lorna—a Baptist minister's daughter—and Ethel Mae, whose parents were Pentecostal missionaries in Africa. The Zeidmans by that time had moved to a house on Bayfield Crescent, not far from Broadview and Danforth. Every morning over the next four years Marilyn and Elaine would do their best to meet at that intersection.

Marilyn didn't see Elaine as needing discipline, only that she liked having fun. "We did impish things," said Marilyn. "And Elaine was always in on these. She had a way of arching one eyebrow and closing the other, like a great big wink." They enjoyed harmless hijinks, like the time three of them quietly opened a window and threw wet paper towels at Elaine during a late afternoon Latin class.

Elaine's skill at the piano—she never needed sheet music—gave her lots of positive attention. She played for the chapel and often when her friends got together. There was a piano at the Zeidmans', where Morris loved to sing, and one in Lorna's home, where her father often enjoyed hearing Elaine. The girls formed a quartet, and Margaret prepared their four-part arrangements for hymns. Marilyn recalled them singing at a ladies' meeting in the church where Lorna's father was the minister. During one of the songs, the girls broke into some untimely laughter. Elaine just kept on playing.

Her grades began to improve markedly. Marilyn recalled Elaine as a very capable scholar who didn't enjoy the limelight. In grade 12, Elaine became a sub-prefect and then, in grade 13, a prefect. The position recognized her standing as a model student. She was widely nominated to run for head girl in her last year but declined. "It meant going to a lot of dances," Marilyn said, "and we had our friends from church." There was lots of fun to be had with the various young people's groups at People's Church (next door to the college) and Evangel Temple. If there wasn't a party, they would go skating at the Riverdale Terrace.

Marilyn saw how Elaine was always helping out at the Mission, often doing "whatever work had to be done." In particular, that meant working all though Christmas Day, an unimaginable sacrifice for a teenage girl, and one she saw Elaine make year after year.

There was also a vulnerable side to Elaine. Marilyn felt that she was sometimes too concerned with what other people thought of her. After she had been working full-time at the Mission, she saved up for a fur jacket. At a young people's meeting, she heard someone say, "Work at the Scott Mission and buy yourself a fur coat." It was a callous remark, but Marilyn noticed that Elaine never wore the jacket again.

By the time that Elaine had graduated from high school, her older sister, Margaret, had become tall and confident and was utterly focused on a career in music. Margaret's high school teachers agreed that she was talented, and then Annie had noticed that there was a new course at the University of Toronto specifically for high school music teachers. Margaret was able to enter the program and found herself surrounded by veterans back from the war. One of her teachers was the distinguished professor Leslie Bell. He had a choir, and she was admitted to The Bell Singers, though, in her opinion, "I wasn't a very good singer."

The experience helped Margaret decide that she wasn't interested in teaching. Her goal was to become a professional musician. She picked up the syllabus from the Royal Conservatory to become a piano accompanist and looked around for a teacher who specialized in that skill. He wasn't just any teacher—Weldon Kilburn coached, accompanied and eventually married Lois Marshall, Canada's leading soprano at the time.

After Margaret auditioned, he told her, "You'll have to learn to play the piano first." She began piano studies all over again with formal exercises, until one of her fingers was caught in a car door. It was crushed, unusable, and she didn't want to lose time while she had an injury. Margaret also felt that to be a good accompanist one had to be able to understand singing, so she began singing lessons and appeared to do quite well. Her piano teacher finally confronted her. She had to make up her mind: voice studies or the piano.

Secretly, she had always wanted to be a singer, but this meant an unstinting commitment to conservatory studies. For some years she'd been paid to function as the Mission's bookkeeper, managing the accounts and overseeing the banking. She approached her father and asked, "Is it all right if I keep studying singing and I will work here as much as I can?" With his approval, Margaret kept loose hours while going to school. Morris encouraged her talent, taking his daughter with him to sing at his speaking engagements. She eventually graduated with her bachelor of music degree, specializing in opera.

When she was ready for the conservatory final exams (the ARCT or Associate of The Royal Conservatory diploma for performers, which is the highest academic standing awarded by the conservatory), Margaret won the highest marks in Canada, the gold medal. "That made me understand that I could sing," she said.

While her studies continued, she built up her repertoire and began getting engagements. One of her most satisfying career experiences was to become the soloist for Sunday services at Bloor Street United Church. It was a joy to be in the great sanctuary where her parents—and grandparents—had worshiped decades before, and a number of congregants remembered Morris and Annie affectionately, including those who recalled Annie's excellent voice. And Morris was equally pleased with her appearances there.

"He knew," she said, "that meant that I was among the best." She was a soloist at the church for 14 years, and her daughter, Jae, well remembered attending services with her mother. She, too, at the age of 12, sang a solo at Bloor St. United. "By the time I did my solo," said Jae, "it was four generations who'd sung there." (Later, Jae won a stained glass art commission at the church, and her work is on permanent display.)

Margaret's success was interrupted by a brief and unhappy first marriage, which ended with her husband's departure. Their daughter, Jae, was raised as one of Morris and Annie's family. Unfortunately, the father chose not to be a part of his daughter's life. (Jae shares more of her story in a later chapter.) Being a single parent was much less common for an accomplished career woman in Toronto during the 1950s and 60s. Margaret had the caring support of her parents and siblings, who helped Jae experience a loving family home.

True to her artistic goals, Margaret developed her skills as a singer, earning an international reputation, and eventually as a coach at the opera school. In the 1960s, she was a rehearsal accompanist at the Stratford Festival for about three years and copyist for the performance music. In one of the plays, she was a singer. During that time, she received a Tyrone Guthrie Award—an honour shared by a number of staff and cast members each year, which includes a financial gift for training and personal development.

"We weren't brought up to make much of ourselves," she said, but because her career had focused on genuine excellence in her field, she knew that Morris was proud of her success.

PHARAOH'S PHOLLY

By Elaine Z. Markovic

There were frogs on the table,
There were frogs on the wall,
Frogs in the pantry,
And frogs in the hall.

Incantations from the wizards,
Exclamations from the king
Only multiplied the numbers
And the frogs began to sing.

In unison on the verses,
With harmony the refrain
Such amphibian modulation
Has never been heard again.

CHAPTER 11

Elaine Begins Her Mission Career

I just fell into working at the Scott Mission. I just wanted to do it," Elaine said, reflecting on her choice. Of course, she had also spent years promising herself that she'd never work there as a career. So the process leading up to her decision was a bit more complex.

After leaving Moulton College in 1953, she might have explored numerous opportunities. As graduation approached, she talked over her options with Morris and Annie. They wanted her to consider Bible college. They encouraged all their children to seek further education, and they could recommend excellent schools locally or in other provinces where she might prepare for ministry.

"That didn't really appeal to me," Elaine said, recalling how young women going to Bible college were often teased about seeking a husband. Certainly, she had no intention of being diverted away from her parents' ministry. Margaret and Alex had become focused elsewhere; Elaine was determined to make it her priority.

Her friend Marilyn Nelson was a graduate in lab technology from the Toronto General Hospital. She recalled that Elaine certainly would have had her pick of schools. "She could have gone to university," said Marilyn. As a young teen, Elaine had viewed the Scott with disdain and told herself, "I will never work at the Mission. Who needs it?" All that changed by grade 12.

"She never talked about doing anything else but the Mission," said Marilyn. "When she took a secretarial course at Moulton, she was preparing to work in the office." She had even decided on her new position, expecting to become Morris's secretary.

"I thought I would help my father with typing and stenography. I wasn't bad at it, but I wasn't good," said Elaine. Instead of assigning his daughter to do paperwork, Morris placed her at the reception desk. Initially it seemed like a demotion, until she realized that the role fit her perfectly.

"I was more of a people person," Elaine said. "It surprised me. I don't know if it surprised him. But I had been around the Mission long enough to hear how people were treated and what could be done. And that's what I wanted to do." There were only about a dozen people on the staff, and Elaine was on the front line. She understood what happened at the Mission. She had worked in the clothing department from about 1948, after the move from the Bay Street location. There were few jobs at the Mission that she didn't know or hadn't done.

The Mission in the 1950s was inside the converted premises of the old fur factory at 502 Spadina, where the new building would later be erected. Elaine worked at a desk in the reception area with a glass partition. Clients came in and took a number, most of them waiting in a long hallway on chairs for groceries or access to the rooms where men's, women's and children's clothing were kept. Someone always had to be at the front desk, so they developed a system where the groceries department was right underneath the reception area. A hole was cut in the floor, and bags could literally come straight up or an order be placed for pickup.

Elaine soon realized that her job meant handling every possible need or situation. She remembered how one man had been drinking all night and sold his pants for a bottle of wine. He came in wearing the pants of his 12-year-old son. It was awkward and ridiculous—but where else could he go? Others would occasionally handle the reception desk, but that became her area. Morris and Annie were there to guide her at first, but over time, Elaine was considered fully capable of making decisions.

Marilyn was impressed by Elaine's dedication. She watched her best friend give up much of her social life. Elaine was exhausted after very full days, spent weeks away at summer camp and supervised after-school children's programs. She wasn't just sacrificing her time. At a Billy Graham ministry rally, Marilyn saw Elaine donate her entire savings for the cause.

She'd followed the call, but now Elaine felt insecure about proprieties and keeping up the image of a Mission worker. "I was struggling with issues that shouldn't have been a struggle," said Elaine. "Makeup and dancing, things you should do and things you shouldn't do." She was surprised to find that her parents weren't all that restrictive.

"They never said, 'You mustn't,'" she said. Instead, they led her to seek guidance from the Holy Spirit. "It was a wise answer. I was counselled toward praying and to ask God about it. Talk things over with them, but pray. They were people of prayer," she said.

Having a position at reception didn't limit her to a desk job. It meant pitching in to do whatever was needed, whenever it had to be done. She was mentored to do what she saw her parents do: everything.

For example, each Saturday evening at 7 p.m., Elaine had an appointment at a supermarket in the east end of the city (the Dominion on the Golden Mile). She'd drive the Mission station wagon to the store's rear entrance and have it loaded up with bread. The entire back compartment would be filled and block the view from her rear view mirror. More loaves were piled on the seat next to her. During winter evenings that meant driving in darkness and arriving alone at the back door of the Mission. She'd rouse the janitor and help him unload the contents. Afterwards, she'd try to make it over to People's Church in time to join friends at the regular Youth for Christ meeting. (The church was then located at 100 Bloor St. East.)

During those years the Mission struggled to accommodate each new wave of immigrants transforming the Kensington area and the city. Elaine began to sense the hand of God preparing them before they were inundated. "Someone would come in and ask for work [at the Mission] and they would speak Portuguese," said Elaine. "After that, many Portuguese immigrants would arrive and we'd find that we were prepared. Then there was the Hungarian wave after the

[1956] revolution. Again, we had a staff member who was Hungarian. If you couldn't communicate with someone you couldn't help them."

From 1951 to 1953, Elaine recalled the Mission setting out a regular meal at 4:30 in the afternoon for 50 to 60 immigrant men. They went out looking for work in the mornings and couldn't come in for breakfast. Many were post-war survivors from Europe: Germans, Austrians, Hungarians and others. A lay pastor was among the group, and Morris often asked him to say grace.

Some afternoons, Elaine saw men who were desperately hungry. "We had to feed them," she said. "At one point the Yugoslavian water polo team defected, and they came to the Mission to eat. I don't know how they heard about us." There was a sense of God's provision, because along with the extra men, the necessary food was also there. "It came in from restaurants and bakeries, and I went to pick up what was offered," she said.

That brought a deeper awareness of her parents' faith. She learned to admire that they had always been consistent. "What they were at home," she said, "was what they were at the Scott Mission."

There was a new appreciation of Morris as they worked together, and she saw how he was always thankful, always prayerful. A number of times, she'd walked into his office in the morning after the mail had arrived. "He would have his hand on the mail, thanking God and praying over it," she said.

"He would always be giving credit to God," Elaine said, for upholding the work. "It was natural for him to do that. And he believed that God gave him ideas and he followed them up. One time, we had to go downtown to Eaton's, and by chance we met a gentleman who promised he was going to send a large donation of goods." Morris later turned to her and said, "Isn't it wonderful how the Lord had me run into this man?" At times like these she saw that quality of gratitude so essential to his faith. "He had a thankful heart," she said.

In time, she came to fully identify with Morris's faith. "I couldn't help but see that what he said was true," said Elaine. "It wasn't something we had to learn," she said. "We grew up seeing it, and you couldn't deny it."

MISSION CHARACTERS

There is no better way to get a feel for the work of the Mission in that period than to read Elaine's personal recollections about some of the clients and her co-workers. We can see how Morris tried to help immigrants and those who needed a second chance. The concluding anecdote about Annie and the chocolate pudding is something of a legend around the Mission.

Doctor Goodchild

"Doc," as everyone called him, was a sad man. He was severely alcoholic when I knew him. I have memories of him being around the Mission for 30 years at least. He was always polite. When I was in a car accident and wore a brace on my neck, he asked kindly how I was feeling. He had a wife and two sons. He wore an engraved watch that had been presented to him by the University of Toronto for some accomplishment.

His downfall came when he assisted in an illegal procedure and was caught. His license to practice was cancelled, and he began drinking heavily. I remember that he was badly beaten up one night and lost the sight of one eye. Doc was quite fragile physically.

We tried to set up an appointment with one of his sons. The son told me that he hated his father and would only see him out of respect for his mother. "She must have loved him at some point to have married him," he said. "I'll see him for her sake and memory. You can tell him he has two grandchildren."

The appointment was made for them to meet at the Mission, but the son did not show up. Doc did not seem surprised. He had put the family through sheer hell, according to the son.

We do not see the fear, economic hardship, verbal and physical abuse, unreliability and humiliation of so many families who have had to cope with alcoholism. We only see one side of the coin here at the Mission. I do not remember any of the details of Doc's passing; we heard about it some time after the funeral.

Miss Bishop

I never knew Miss Bishop by any other name. I never heard her first name used or her called anything other than her surname. All the men who ate at the Mission knew her. They would call out, "Hi, Bishop," when she walked up the street to go into the Mission. In those days the men had to line up outside on the street, as we could only accommodate 100 inside at a time. We often had 600 to 700 in a morning. She would respond to them with a small condescending smile and a nod of recognition.

When I was just a kid, I asked my mother how come so many of the men knew Miss Bishop. I don't recall what she answered, but I was satisfied that my question had been adequately addressed. It was some years before I realized why everyone, particularly the men, knew Miss Bishop.

Miss Bishop always wore a dress, never slacks. She seemed to choose dresses that draped across the waist. I remember one in particular, a dark faded forest-green crepe. Summer or winter, she always wore a large silk fuchsia-coloured flower on her shoulder. ("Delta Dawn, what's that flower you have on? Could it be a faded rose from days gone by?" Whenever I heard that song I immediately thought of Miss Bishop.) Her pumps had a heel about three inches high. She took short quick steps, carried a purse and kept perfect posture. And she had no teeth.

In her younger days, Miss Bishop must have been very pretty, with high cheekbones and an oval face. She wore a little rouge, lipstick and eyebrow pencil (black) and face powder. Her hair was quite grey, and she always had it permed, wearing it swept up on top of her head. She was always a lady, very polite, gracious, but I am certain she could have held her own with anyone. I was never sure of her age.

Her health was poor. Under the powder, her face was not a good colour, and I think there were problems with her vision. She never wore glasses and probably never would. For all her poverty, she was a little vain.

She seemed a bit embarrassed when the men would call out, "Hi, Bishop." She would not ignore them but smile and answer a quiet "Hello." Sometimes she would stop and have conversations with a particular man; they seemed to be genuine conversations. I never saw her walking with anyone. She certainly did not come to any of our meetings or appear to have any special friends.

She was from another generation, and it may well have been hard for her to come to the Mission for food. Miss Bishop died in hospital. We did not know she was ill and so were unable to visit her. It was good to have known her.

Luba

Born in Poland, Luba came to work at the Mission after the war to cook for the staff. She spoke very little English, never smiled and always complained. She had a perpetual frown, a mouth that was always turned downward and a tremendous sadness, which was very tiresome. She did her work as though it was a complete bore but also took every ounce of her energy. She apparently felt completely unappreciated for her mediocre efforts. One day she sliced up a cantaloupe and served it alongside ravioli on the same plate. Different. Another time she made chicken a la king and called it "chicken mit de king," which became a byword around the Mission. If things did not work out well, she would raise her hands above her head and say, "Well, what can I do?"

I eventually learned from Annie that when the Nazis invaded, they took Luba's first husband. He died in a concentration camp. Luba and her pregnant daughter were also rounded up. Because she was not "work material" the daughter was immediately shot and went into premature labour. Mother and infant died in front of Luba. Because of our privileged life, we could never really understand. It's a wonder that she was not completely mad, having witnessed such evil.

Luba remarried someone she had helped during the war. He'd also been in a concentration camp and was a barber. Short, with shiny black hair, he was a dapper dresser and a womanizer. A story went around about his exiting a house of ill repute during a fire. He was seen climbing down the ladder holding onto his trousers, in his hands.

One day, Alex had played a trick on Maureen and me. To get back at him, we prepared him some coffee with snail shells in the bottom of the cup. He took a sip, and the shells knocked up against his teeth. All he did was set down the cup and say, "Oh, snails." Luba was watching and doubled over with laughter until she had to hold on to the kitchen sink. She said later that she hadn't laughed like this since before the war. So, it was worth it.

119

Franz Kurilla

Franz was a Finnish evangelical pastor. He spoke absolutely no English at all and could hardly say "Hello." We hired him as a janitor's helper. Slightly over six feet tall, he weighed about 350 pounds. He was a large cheerful Christian with a wonderful voice. When we had morning devotions, we always asked him to pray in his own language.

He sang hymns in Finnish to himself when he would swing the mop, washing the floors. It probably made the job easier because he mopped in time to whatever song he sang. His favourite seemed to be, "I am Thine, O Lord, I have heard Thy voice, And it told Thy love to me; But I long to rise on the arms of faith And be closer drawn to Thee." He had the most beautiful bass voice, and when he sang the chorus, we all would listen as he gently sang in his own way, "Draw me nearer, nearer, blessed Lord, To the cross where Thou hast died; Draw me nearer, nearer, nearer, blessed Lord, To Thy precious bleeding side."

Franz must have been in his 50s and just did not seem to get the hang of this language. When our truck pulled into the driveway to be unloaded, he would call out, "Trucky come, trucky come." His heart's desire was to be with his dad, who lived in Wisconsin, and lead him to Christ. The father was a staunch Communist. Franz was called as a pastor to a Finnish congregation in the States, and his father did receive Christ before his death.

Other Custodians

Mr. White was our custodian when I was quite small. He would go to Grimsby Beach with us. He enlisted in the army, even though he had flat feet. He looked great in his uniform. He would almost stand on his head trying to distract me so that I would eat. He would make me laugh, and when I opened my mouth the spoon would be popped in and, hopefully, I would swallow. One day, a large dog came into the kitchen at the camp, and I scrambled up on top of the icebox and would not come down until Mr. White got rid of the dog.

Percy was small, about 4'10." He had been a jockey until alcohol took over his life. He was from England and a nice little man. Then there was another Percy who called my mother

120

"Mrs. Snyman." Percy III was a singer, at least when he was drunk. We always knew when Percy had been drinking, because he would never appear upstairs from his basement quarters where he lived. He was supposed to be on duty when the staff arrived in the morning. When the front door was still locked when we arrived, we knew what awaited us. We could hear him singing "The Holy City" at the top of his lungs. Morris knew that Percy would not be of any help that day.

The problem of a custodian was always with us, and finally my father telephoned a local pastor to see if anyone in his congregation was looking for employment. The pastor sent us a little man who was a Christian, and he was most eager for the position of custodian at the Scott Mission, so he was hired. He did not smoke and he did not drink. He also did not work. He would just hurry around the place with a duster in his hand as if he was about to do some dusting but never got around to it. Then there was the morning that my father opened his desk drawer to find that there was no bottom in the drawer where the petty cash was kept. The custodian had helped himself. When we checked the clothing area, we found that he'd also taken a couple of good outfits, leaving his clothes behind, so we immediately recognized the thief.

Tom, who worked for us at 726 Bay Street, was a Scot. His accent was so thick that he could hardly be understood. He said "eh" before every comment, such as, "Eh, Mr. Zeidman, shall I shovel the snow?" One day, a donor sent in a small paper bag with four sets of false teeth inside. Tom got excited and tried all four sets before deciding that the ones he owned fit best.

The kitchen was on the second floor, and the stairs were very long. My mother had made some chocolate pudding in an enamel baby bathtub for dessert one day and asked Tom to carry it downstairs to the dining room. At the top of the stairs Tom stumbled and dropped the tub, which slid to the bottom, and he slipped all the way down after it, landing right in the chocolate pudding. Tom was angry, but he looked pretty funny. Unfortunately, money and food were in short supply, and the dessert was ruined. My mother didn't know whether to laugh or cry.

◈

FROM ELAINE'S CORRESPONDENCE

In her early days at the Mission, Elaine knew how to have fun during times that were often rather mundane. This letter to Annie was typed on Mission letterhead and shows Laine's great sense of humour (although it includes some sad community news, which has been left out in consideration of those who are named) and happens to mention her brother Alex.

June 23, 1954

Hello Dear Momma:

I have just come back from lunch.

1. I was ironing and all of a sudden the iron is gone broke. Is flying sparks, blue ones, so I am dropping quick the iron. She went cold and I was not from finishing the ironing. I was azoi mad. I say to myself buy another one. So, I [bout—crossed out with slash marks] got a iron at a sale. I had no money so I pinned Daddy down to giving me the dough [H—crossed out] he [oughed—crossed out] owed me from so long time. I was walking along College to get some sunglasses and I saw a feather-weight iron in the window. I asked the guy viffel costis and he says $10.95, regular $14.95. So I have it. Do you want me to bring it to camp? Or maybe the old one. There aint nuttin wrong with the iron itself you know, just the bloomin cord.
2. Oi vey, that chicken. I said to Daddy, "Daddy, how's the chicken?" So help me it was falling off the bones. He says "tough." I says, "Tough!! It's falling off the bones." He says, "Well not exactly tough, stringy!" He managed to choke down a whole leg and thigh.
3. The bus leaves Toronto 1:15 p.m. so I'll be in Hillsburgh when I get their [crossed out] there.
4. [includes mention of a leading in prayer]
5. [difficult news]
6. Peewee [Marilyn Nelson] and I are going to Li Chee Gardens to celebrate the end of her exams tonight. I don't know where Daddy is going to eat but I think he won't let

himself starve. I just showed him the new iron and he looked over his glasses and said "Hm Hm." If he would have to press his own pants he would have been a little more impressed...

Powie [the family housekeeper] said she saw Alex hitch-hiking on the highway three weeks ago; he was with Ron.

I must goø. I am gumming this whole letter up anyway.

See you on Saturday if everything goes o.k.

Your ever loving dotter,
Laine.

MRS. ZACCHAEUS'S TEA

By Elaine Z. Markovic

Oh, poor Mrs. Zacchaeus!
Tea's to be served in an hour
To a total stranger.
"His strangers have been here before,"
She grumbles.
"And they leave with half the silver."

She hurries to the freezer and sets out
The tarts to thaw, deftly mixes the batter for scones,
And while they bake, spoons strawberry preserves
Into a cut-glass jam-jar, puts out Crown Derby cups
On the tea wagon. Tarts in the silver basket.

They're at the door!
She is introduced to company
And finds she is serving
With great Joy.

Peace permeates the home
And she understands now,
The Prince Himself
Has been the Guest.

CHAPTER 12

Public Choices—Private Struggles, Part 1

W ithin a year after she had started working at the Mission, Elaine felt that she needed a larger Christian perspective—"a wider outlook"—than the one she saw daily. She began attending Sunday church services and the young people's meetings at Knox Presbyterian Church on Spadina, several blocks north of the Mission. Morris and Annie had been on the church roll since 1925, but this was the first time that Elaine attended regularly. Knox was renowned for its preaching and popular with young adults. Happily, Elaine struck up an acquaintance.

Maureen Sherwood, a tall attractive young woman, was about her own age, 19 or 20. Like Elaine, she was already employed, doing secretarial work at an engineering firm. They began a friendship, and Elaine's stories about the Mission drew Maureen's interest. Over many months, as the two slowly developed a rapport, Maureen felt secure enough to share her hopes for the future.

"I had been seeking God's direction for my life," Maureen said. "Then one day while I was at the office, I told her that I was looking for something more meaningful." Elaine responded by saying that her father needed a secretary.

"Come to our house for supper tonight," Elaine said, "and meet my dad."

That evening, Morris offered Maureen a position. "I had been praying," she said. "It felt like this was God's answer to what I was looking for." She remembered taking the job right around the time of her 21st birthday.

The Mission was a rough contrast to the offices she'd left. She described the work as "functioning in makeshift fashion." Maureen began doing stenographic work for Morris, preparing his letters and accompanying him to the bank. She didn't find the work difficult. Morris was very focused and rarely spent time chatting. He would call her up to his office on the second floor whenever he needed assistance, and, as Elaine may have warned her, "He did not have a very orderly desk." Her own desk was next to Elaine's in reception.

She'd also heard from Elaine about Alex, who had graduated from Knox in 1956 and received an assignment that year at Val d'Or in northern Quebec. Soon after Maureen came on staff, Alex came home for a visit. She immediately felt drawn to him. With Morris's health so obviously in decline, she quickly grasped the situation. Both parents, especially Annie, wanted their son to come home and help his father at the Mission. The visit was brief, and Alex left without giving any commitment. There wasn't even a hint of a decision, and he was gone for several months.

Maureen had barely spoken to Alex, yet her reaction was unmistakable. "It was love at first sight," she said, "but I didn't reveal this to anyone. I tucked away some very special feelings." There were occasional visits, but Alex gave little hope that he would change his mind and work at the Mission.

These were the final years of Morris's oversight of the ministry, and, as Maureen remembered, he didn't speak to her at length about the work or the people they served. At first, Maureen found the clients intimidating. Elaine became her guide to understanding the ministry: "I got my education watching her," Maureen said.

Elaine knew how to cope with the variety of needs and expectations that came in off the street every day. "She was young, but very gracious and patient," said Maureen, "even with the most broken and wounded people." Elaine could also keep things light, bantering with good humour. Maureen was touched by the way that she managed situations when clients' problems seemed overwhelming. Others would call in and she'd pray over the phone.

"I can see now that she had wonderful gifts working with people," Maureen said. "I fell into the role of organizing things that she was doing. Elaine was not a delegator. She would get swamped doing it all herself. I would suggest how to organize projects, like the Christmas hampers.

"At times it got difficult," Maureen said. "We were on the front line of ministry, and when Morris was absent, Elaine and I held the fort." Though her title was secretary to the director, it hardly described her full range of duties. She learned that you had to help out wherever help was needed. In the midst of it all, she and Elaine often had fun, enjoying each other's company. The clients now seemed colourful. Sadly, Morris's health was declining, and he was finding it harder to come into the office. He was seriously ill in 1958 and would, for the first time, spend the entire summer recuperating, at a new campsite.

More than 700 kilometres north in Val d'Or, well away from the influence of the family, Alex was wrestling with the decision to return to Toronto. The city had no appeal for him. A true introvert, he was most content in the solitude of nature; that was his ideal setting for spiritual peace. During his university summers he had found work in a logging camp in British Columbia. According to family lore, after his lengthy refusal to write, Elaine sent him a letter with multiple-choice answers. He only filled in the checkmarks and sent it back.

While at Knox, he relished any opportunity to take his summer placements in rural charges. After graduating with his bachelor of divinity, Alex was assigned to a "three-point" pastoral charge (three churches) in the small northern mining community of Val d'Or, Quebec. By all accounts he was thriving and prepared to start a long-term career in the pastorate.

Alex conferred with his university friends about the decision to return to the Mission. There'd been a particularly serious conversation with Morris, but he remained uncertain. Later, as the director of the Scott Mission, he gave a lecture at Knox College titled "What Is Ministry?" It was an issue he knew well, after spending so many months agonizing over that question: if he took on the Mission he would, in certain ways, be leaving the ministry as it had been defined by his education for the pastorate. He also knew intuitively, as Elaine would later reflect, "The Mission can become a giant in one's life."

His older sister, Margaret, was fully aware of the struggle. She was travelling in western Canada and happened to meet someone from Val d'Or, and they, too, gave her an exceptional report of Alex's ministry. As much as she admired Alex, Margaret felt that he might be coerced into setting aside everything that made him happy. All that he'd done since entering seminary pointed to a pastoral vocation.

Alex's choice to serve with the Mission entailed a measure of personal self-sacrifice that he kept very private. When he wrote his father's biography, *Good and Faithful Servant*, all those reflections were dismissed in a single line: "Alex had resigned his position as minister at Val d'Or, Quebec, to become assistant director at the Mission in 1959."[1]

Determined to fully commit to the Mission, Alex never spoke of it again. As Maureen said, "If he'd had his druthers, he would have been off to some mission field in Africa; he had that spirit. Downtown Toronto wasn't appealing, but it was a call, and he was a reluctant recruit."

Years later, long after Alex and Maureen were married, their children grown and the Mission operations were well established, they remained open to new possibilities, even a new calling. "We prayed and sought God's guidance," said Maureen. "He never felt released."

&

No son could have planned to be more faithful or supportive of the family ministry than the youngest, David. Like each one of the children, he responded to Morris and Annie's expectations that he had a future in his parents' ministry. "I had a sense that this is what my parents wanted," he said. "My mother was emphatic that I would work at the Mission."

He was genuinely respectful of Morris and enjoyed their times together weekly as he'd accompany his father on regular chores around the city. Some of his fondest early memories were of leaving school a few weeks early every June to help Annie and Alex prepare for the summer camp program. After high school, David took an undergraduate degree at Waterloo Lutheran University (now Wilfred Laurier) with courses in both theology and business. During the difficult years while Morris was beginning to decline physically, David was away at school. He returned to help Annie find a new camp facility just as Alex arrived to take up a leadership role with the Mission.

Alex's new role made perfect sense to David and eased his way forward. "My whole background came to the fore," he said, "taking economics at Waterloo and learning the business stuff I had picked up from my father," he said. "Alex would lead the ministry, and I'd work on the business side."

David became responsible for handling the hidden but indispensable duties around the Mission: working on accounting issues and maintaining the various mechanical, electrical and heating systems. He had some contact with the clients but rarely served as a front-line worker. During a typical day David might start out managing the finances and then be asked to check on problems related to the building or to oversee the work of a contractor at another Mission site. Many cold, snowy mornings found him busy clearing the road onto Mission properties.

Under Alex's leadership, David said that he felt fulfilled "doing whatever needed to be done," but these weren't minor duties. Reports of the board show that he was frequently charged with handling important financial matters, including the management of long-term investments. Later, when Alex proposed that the Mission develop a ministry to First Nations in Northern Ontario, David did extensive legwork for the board, leading to the creation of a facility for Native young people that became known as Homestake House in Kenora (near the Manitoba border, over 1850 kilometres from Toronto).

"The leadership in spirituality came from Alex; he was a people person," David said modestly. "I was concentrating on other things."

David met his wife, Elizabeth, at Knox Church, and they were married in the early spring of 1961. She was a devoted staff member for many years. They had three children: Madeleine, who also worked at the Mission, Kate and Jonathan.

HOPE (1978)

By Annie A. Zeidman

By the side of the train as it snuffled its way
Through the yards to the city
Ran a gully, foul, stagnant;
But out of the mud and the muck sprang a tree
Young, slim, a paper-white birch,
(nourished by what hidden source)
Its frail branches reaching in hope to the smoke-laden sky.

I met a girl like that once, young, gentle, pure,
Rising from squalor and evil
(nourished by what Source)
Stretching the wings of her soul toward Heaven.

Where is she now, I wonder.

CHAPTER 13

Public Choices—Private Struggles, Part 2

E laine was becoming more involved at Knox, playing piano for the junior church on Sunday mornings and singing in the choir Sunday evenings. Then a Mission co-worker invited her to join a special dinner party. Elaine almost didn't go. Earlier that evening she was with her parents, who were hosting their old friend Dr. Nelles Silverthorne[1] and a member of the mission board. Elaine found Dr. Silverthorne's company fascinating and privately asked her mother if she could get out of the other engagement. Annie felt it was a bit late for that, so Elaine made her apologies and left.

The party was a traditional Serbian celebration called a *slava*. Among the guests was a young man, Miodrag "Mica" Markovic, who knew their host from his hometown district in Serbia. (His first name is pronounced "Mee' cha," and the final "c" in the surname is also pronounced as "ch.")

Mica had been born into a well-to-do farm family, and during World War II he was a young child when an advancing Nazi army marched through their property. German officers commandeered the house while his father, a soldier, was away. The occupying troops didn't leave empty-handed. They took a horse and the cow and would have stolen all the beans to seed next year's crop if little Mica, painfully straining his back and knees, hadn't hidden some of the sacks.

After surviving the horrors of war, the young man watched the Iron Curtain descend on Yugoslavia. The rise of the Communist Party offered few prospects for rural landowners. Because of the family's resistance to the new political order, Mica's father was sentenced to hard labour in Belgrade.

A beloved grandfather, Nikodije ("Ni-ko´-dee-ye"), was forced to surrender family property to the party. After refusing to sign over everything, he was also imprisoned. As a well-respected county overseer and pillar of the local Eastern Orthodox Church, Nikodije had the wrong sorts of connections. Mica was expelled from the local high school. Doggedly persistent, he tried to get into a school in the next town, appealing to the nation's minister of education. At a last meeting with his grandfather in prison, he was advised to leave: "Your future in this country is finished."

Travelling in soccer uniforms, because it was the season when people were used to soccer teams moving openly around the country, Mica and a friend made their way toward the Italian border. Any attempted escape would be risky—they could be shot on sight—but it was the only hope for a better life. Finally, they were hiking through fields and fell asleep in the afternoon. They woke up before sunset and continued walking while it was still light. They could see lookout towers but no guards to stop them. Pressing on, they crossed the border to Trieste, where American troops took them in. Later, after nightfall, they could hear rifle fire and snarling dogs tracking down others making the same journey. Mica was told, "No one thought you'd do this in broad daylight."

It was around 1951, and Mica was only 18. He considered going to Australia, until someone told him about Canada. He landed in Halifax on Pier 21 and eventually got to Ottawa. He recalled becoming a "DP"—a displaced person without a country, only a number—as one of the most humiliating experiences in his life. Hired onto a family farm near Smith Falls, he spent a year paying off his passage and then left for Toronto.

Entering Ryerson as a chemical engineering student, Mica was unable to keep up his grades while he worked at night. By the time he met Elaine in 1958, he'd found a good job working for the Canadian subsidiary of Pathé Deluxe, a film company, where he was splicing sound to film images.

Elaine and Mica found each other's company intriguing. Elaine absorbed Mica's tales of survival. Decades later she could recite his war and post-war adventures in elaborate detail. Mica was fascinated by what he called Elaine's "intellectual beauty." The feeling of acceptance that he got from Morris also touched him deeply.

"There are similarities, that he came as a very young man to this country as I did," Mica said of Morris. "His life was threatened, as was mine. We had quite a bit in common. We got along very well; as a matter of fact, he was the one who persuaded me to work for the Mission."

According to Elaine, when Morris found out that Mica was an excellent cook and offered Mica a position on his kitchen staff, the young man thought that the prospect seemed "exciting." Mica's reflections were a bit different.

"It was a difficult situation for me," he said. "They couldn't afford to pay me the same as I was making. By that time, I was going with Elaine and I was volunteering—subconsciously to be close to Elaine. But the more time that I spent there and got involved with the clients, my attitude and my perspective on what the Mission was doing dramatically changed."

There was also a growing connection with Morris. "My grandfather was deeply involved in the church when I grew up back home. There was a spiritual similarity to my grandfather and Elaine's father. His personality and his beliefs persuaded me to work for the Mission for one-third of what I was earning." Mica not only provided effective oversight of the kitchen, but in time he also ran the distribution centre in the basement and was responsible for purchasing. Eventually, as the operations grew, purchasing for the Mission became his main responsibility.

Elaine's continuing involvement at Knox encouraged Margaret and David to begin attending there as well. Meanwhile, her social life was becoming much more focused. Elaine and Mica were married on May 5, 1962. They had two daughters, Lois and Sera.

❧

By the time that Alex returned to Toronto, Maureen was already part of the extended Zeidman family. As Elaine's closest friend and

133

co-worker at the Mission, Maureen naturally began to spend time with Alex at family get-togethers and in the course of Mission duties. With Elaine paired off with Mica, Alex and Maureen were now being paired together by the family. For Maureen, who had been silently disposed to the idea for a while, it was more than a happy coincidence. Alex was less comfortable in a situation with romantic overtones.

"He didn't talk a lot about his feelings," said Maureen, "nor did Elaine." Most of the family's conventions about not revealing their emotions were from an earlier era. For Maureen, an emotionally attached young woman, the result was endless frustration.

"They were Victorian," said Margaret, a stage performer who didn't like hiding her feelings and saw this as one of the more irritating Zeidman family qualities.

"I knew how I felt," Maureen said, but it took her some time to understand Alex's nature as an introvert, who was six years older. "It wasn't his personality to talk about himself, express emotions or feelings. He was a man of few words. He kept it all in until he was certain. He did take me out, but I wasn't getting anything specific from him." She wanted to confide in Elaine, but it felt awkward. Meanwhile, Elaine was discreetly trying to be supportive.

"There was a part of him that wouldn't be pushed," Maureen said. "Alex had to be his own person. I was thinking that I should quit the Mission. It was very hard."

The last straw for Maureen came at Elaine's wedding. She and Alex had been dating, and, as she said, "Everybody kind of knew we were a sort of a couple." A couple where one had strong feelings and the other was uncertain. Then she heard Morris saying, "We hope we'll have another wedding soon."

Maureen decided that she had to do something. "I surrendered the whole thing to God. I said to Him, 'I accept whatever Your will is.' And I don't know if Alex went through that. I knew that approaching him wouldn't work. So I waited."

Alex finally made a decision. Once it was made, he had no hesitation, second thoughts or dawdling. Maureen and Alex's engagement lasted only a few months. Despite the Christmas rush at the Mission, the couple was married on December 1, 1962, and would have two children, Anne and Andrew.

❧

During the 1960s, Margaret refused to lose sight of her goal to be an accomplished musician in her own right. "I was slowly building a repertoire and getting more exciting engagements," she said, and she began to coach at the opera school in Toronto. She gained a reputation while singing with the smaller local symphonies around southern Ontario. As a coach in the School of Music at the University of Toronto, she was invited by the distinguished Canadian bass singer and actor Jan Rubeš to join him on tour across Canada. Together they did over 400 concerts in schools around the country, alternately accompanying each other's performances on the piano. (Margaret used the term "accompany" a bit lightly, since she was a much better pianist.)

Margaret was still testing the limits of her ability when she turned down an offer to teach at Banff and arrived in Italy to pursue further opera training. During an event where she was invited to perform, she caught the interest of Giulio Kukurugya, an American based in Italy who was an accomplished singer and had a rising career as a director of operas (his surname is of Hungarian origin). Giulio was very impressed—and intrigued—by Margaret's work ethic and absolute refusal to pay any attention to him until after her performance.

They married in 1970, and Margaret, together with her daughter, Jae, moved to Europe. Later, the family settled in South Africa for some years, although Margaret and Giulio continued travelling for performances. They also moved to follow Giulio's opportunities as an opera director and later work as a screen actor in film and television. At 18, Jae was recognized as a gifted artist and returned to Toronto to enter the Ontario College of Art and Design.

In spite of Margaret's extensive travel schedule over the next few decades, she continued to be a board member of the Scott Mission. Giulio, too, had tremendous respect for the work of the Mission and her family legacy, but the couple now moved in very separate worlds from the one in which Margaret was raised.

THE COUPLE

By Elaine Z. Markovic

It is the close of the Sabbath.
The last rays of the sun
Cast patterns of lace curtains
On the white-washed walls of the room.
He is in pain.
Rocking in the chair comforts him.
He watches her peel potatoes at the table,
Her lower lip in its perpetual pout.
He thinks about the two wee graves by the kirk wall,
The strong young man lost at sea.
He closes his eyes, gently rocking,
"Glory to Thee, My God, this night."
He murmurs to the Lord, in evening devotion.
As he continues, she suddenly cries out,
"And do ye not see the fire dwindling?"
She rushes to the hearth,
Grabs the iron tongs,
Angrily rearranges the logs.
The sparks fly into the room.
A fitting accompaniment to her temper.
"What she could do with cymbals!" he muses, and then,
"Ah, Lord, Ye've afflicted me,
But a'ways in love,
A'ways in love."

CHAPTER 14

"The Miracle on Spadina Avenue"

Less than a week before Christmas 1958, an article on the Mission appeared in the first section of the *Toronto Star* Saturday edition under the headline "The Miracle On Spadina Avenue." It began with a description of Morris talking with Sam Campbell, a *Star* reporter. Morris was describing preparations for Christmas morning. That year the Mission expected to host about 600 men over the course of Christmas Day. Each one would be expecting to sit down for "a mouth-watering turkey dinner with all the trimmings."[1]

Since many readers knew the cost of feeding an average family, Campbell began by asking, "Where does such a tremendous amount of food come from?" Then he described Morris "facing this annual Christmas chore with only six turkeys and not a worry in the world." As Campbell noted, "that's where the miraculous element of this story begins to appear."

"You'll see," said Dr. Zeidman, "enough people in Toronto will be moved before Christmas to send us the necessary number of turkeys as well as the vegetables, fruit, pie, candy and everything else we need…They have never failed in more than 25 years. People who win extra turkeys in raffles send them to us, and people who have two birds given to them forward one to us. It is truly miraculous the way we have been sustained."

The article continued, "Just yesterday, to prove the director's point, several cases of canned gravy—more than enough for 600 plates—came to the Mission 'out of the blue.'"

Campbell also mentioned the recently arrived gift of "300 pairs of heavy woollen socks," which Morris planned to make part of "a little Christmas package" for his guests, although he still needed to get another 300 before the big day and to add sufficient quantities per person of candy, an orange or apple and a chocolate bar—which had not yet come in. Men would be lining up for the length of two city blocks, waiting until 10 a.m. Morris would then open the doors with a hearty "Merry Christmas" for the first hundred to be admitted to the first of the six sittings.

"Christmas with the Zeidmans is not like Christmas in your house," Campbell explained. The family, including Morris and "his wife, Annie, his two daughters, Mrs. Margaret Rowan and Elaine, and his son, David, will be up well before 6 a.m. and downtown in the Mission by 7 a.m....they'll all pitch in to peel potatoes and carrots and start carving up the turkeys."

Morris's reward is "the extra little squeeze of a stranger's hand-shake...the tears of gratitude glistening in the eyes of a transient." The reporter concluded, "Christmas for the Zeidmans means giving—their time, their energy and their hearts to a cause dear to them. There is no fanfare, no ballyhoo. They give in the same quiet reverent spirit as the Wise Men of old gave their gold, frankincense and myrrh."

The article covered the top half of page nine and featured a large photo with Morris, Annie, Margaret and Elaine. The closing para-graphs invited readers to "take part in this 'miracle'" and call or send funds. "Since the Mission station wagon is running almost around the clock...if you can possibly deliver your contribution it would help."

A few weeks later, on January 2, 1959, the *Star* did a follow-up article with the headline "Second Miracle as 600 Again Get Mission Treat." The opening lines read, "Miracles—like lightning—are not supposed to happen in the same place twice. Yet New Year's Day at the Scott Mission on Spadina Ave. was a repeat of Christmas Day. Again, almost 600 homeless men sat down to their first meal of 1959—a turkey dinner with all the trimmings."

In the follow-up piece, Morris was asked to describe the impact of the first article. "The response to that story was fantastic," said Dr. Zeidman. "People from all walks of life were touched in various ways." One inspired donor dropped by to see the children's program and sent 300 hula hoops.

A special New Year's Eve dinner was also laid out for 30 homeless Hungarian refugees. These men had been of great concern to local Hungarian clergy. Describing their meal, the story closed on an upbeat note: "Few in the group understand any English. Most have had a rough time finding jobs because of the language barrier. And all might have been lonely and unhappy exiles on New Year's Eve. Instead, they smiled and sang in their own tongue for the first time since the Hungarian revolution days."

Campbell, a well-known court reporter, was admired by some of Toronto's leading lawyers, judges and police officers. He enjoyed assignments on the charities supported by the paper's "Santa Claus" and "Fresh Air" fundraising drives. In subsequent years he wrote more stories on the Scott Mission; none had the impact of "The Miracle on Spadina Avenue." He retired after 38 years with the *Star* and died, age 90, in 2010. The obituary headline next to his name said "Helped raise millions for children."[2]

Afterwards, the Mission adopted the title "The Miracle on Spadina." The name has stayed relevant to this day. It thoroughly describes the faith and experience of the Mission staff, and, as Morris once wrote, "Miracles happen daily at the Miracle on Spadina."

"I never get tired of the miracles," said Elaine. "There are miracles happening all around us, I know that, in the lives of the people that come. You may not see them visibly change, but you don't know the miracle of the switch inside the head of the people who come here day after day. It may be the smallest response from us that makes the change. But when you see the miracle of a changed life *at just the right moment*, it knocks you off your feet," she said.

And then there are real-life inexplicable events. "We got a donation of strawberries, whipping cream and Mary Jane cakes," Elaine said, remembering how they had put everything together—cakes with strawberries covered with whipped cream—just so nicely for a women's meeting. Considering that the donations to the Mission were always "whatever came through the door," they were delighted. It was a bit nerve-racking when more women showed up than expected. As the meeting went on, Elaine and Laura Dupuis, who ran the program, were feeling frantic, wondering what to do. They needed another 15 desserts. There were cookies to be had, but nothing else on hand. Then a knock came on the back door. It was a man carrying a tray—he looked like he'd been just sent out to bring them the very same desserts that they were serving. And he had exactly 15.

One of the first miracles that Elaine recalled included a similar crisis around meat pies. They had prepared a lunch of meat pies for the men and were running out. They had no idea what they were going to serve, and then a truck pulled up with a load of meat pies—just as if it had been dispatched to refill the order.

That memory brought to mind a very similar situation that had happened 50 years later, when they were serving beef sausages for the men's lunch. The kitchen ran out, and a delivery came in the back door with the exact same brand that they were serving, once again as if it had been sent to the Mission to meet a specific order. And all of these goods were donated from different sources at random.

Many staff workers have shared similar stories. David Cross, a member of the board, and his wife, Marti, were in awe of God's faithfulness through the years. They had particularly special memories of Christmas: "You could see God directing the Mission," said Marti Cross, "the cheques, the food, Ed Mirvish coming with a limousine full of turkeys and tickets for the *Nutcracker*."

When a reporter wrote about Rev. Alex Zeidman describing his experiences after more than 20 Christmases of sending out appeals, he recalled how Alex had said, "It is truly amazing to watch, and it's also humbling. It reminds us more of the miracle of the feeding of the multitude rather than the nativity story."[3]

"You know that it's God," said Elaine, "because there's no other way that these things could happen."

Lois Markovic as a toddler in the front office of the Mission;
Elaine working in back

Elaine Markovic

At the Hillsburg Camp property

Zeidman children dressed up for Purim

Annie Zeidman

Annie Zeidman at work in the front office of the Mission

Zeidman family at Caledon Camp in the late 1960s

Maureen and Bob Topp; Elaine and Mica Markovic

Elaine Markovic

Elaine and Mica

Elaine and Mica

*Morris Zeidman (far left) is pictured as a member of the
University of Toronto Debating Team circa 1920.*

Sabati (Ben) and Belle Rohold, whom he met and married in Toronto.
In Israel, she was known as Bella.

*Annie Zeidman packing relief barrels that were sent to Poland
and other locations overseas after WWII*

Zeidman children in the early 1940s: Margaret, Alex, Elaine and David

Alex Zeidman at camp

Breaking ground ceremony for 502 Spadina. David Zeidman, Rev. Alex Zeidman,
Frederick G. Gardner, Philip Jackson (construction), Rev. Morris Zeidman,
Basil Ludlow (architect), Robert Jackson (construction) – May 1960

Morris Zeidman with the plans for new 502 Spadina Avenue building

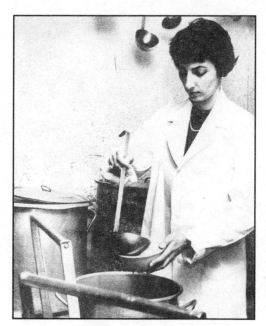

Elaine serving soup at the Mission

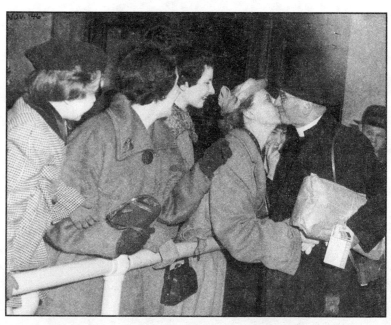

Elaine (second from left), Margaret and Annie Zeidman welcome Morris home after trip to Poland shortly after WWII (November 1946) at Union Station, Toronto

In February 1961, Morris received the Canadian "Citizen of the Year" award by The Progress Club of Canada, as voted by readers of the Telegram *during a dinner in his honour at the Royal York Hotel.*

Annie Zeidman cleaning washrooms at camp

Elaine and Mica's wedding on May 5, 1962.
The flower girl is Margaret's daughter, Jae.

The Zeidmans look at the plan for The Scott Mission's new building

*Rev. Morris Zeidman with Mission staff and volunteers
in front of the Bay St. storefront, where The Scott Mission first located after
Morris's break from the Presbyterian Church.*

Morris out for a hay ride with Fresh Air campers circa 1920s.

Men line up in front of 502 Spadina

Before the new facilities opened in 1961, there was space for only 100 to be seated in the dining room, which led to the familiar sight of long line-ups for a meal each morning outside the Mission.

SEE, LORD, THE HANDS (1949)

By Annie A. Zeidman

See, Lord, the hands that we raise to Thee, open;
See, Lord, our hearts open too;
Fill them, we pray, with the oil of Thy comfort,
Let them o'erflow with the wine of Thy love...
Here in the dust of the road near Jericho,
Here by the wounded, the naked, the poor,
Help us to bind up their hurts and their heartaches,
Lord! fill our hearts and our hands.

And to know the love of Christ, which passeth knowledge. (Ephesians 3:19)

CHAPTER 15

One More Vision

L ooking back over 30 years of ministry, Morris could well remember the state of the Scott Institute when he and Annie inherited the Mission work in 1926. By then, most of his Jewish neighbours had moved west toward the Kensington Market neighbourhood, and the missionary enterprise was barely viable—despite the fine building that Dr. Scott had built at 165 Elizabeth and Rev. Rohold had turned into a landmark ministry. After the home missions board had been convinced to move the outreach headquarters to the corner of Palmerston and College, Morris's use of the building on Elizabeth Street for the Depression needy had made it one of the city's most recognizable inner-city ministries.

When his denomination no longer had a heart for the work, he had the vision of a widely supported outreach that was non-denominational and strongly evangelical. Despite little encouragement and constant financial challenges, he had accumulated the resources and a donor base to outlast his naysayers and prove the doubters wrong. By extraordinary determination, energy, dedication and faith, he and Annie had transformed the potential of the Scott Institute into the Scott Mission.

Yet as Morris's health continued to decline, his legacy remained uncertain. As the leader of a family-run operation, his best years were behind him. Meanwhile, he was now watching the Jewish population move away from the Kensington Market neighbourhood. This time they were relocating north to attractive new middle-class suburbs. His

Jewish neighbours were inevitably replaced by new waves of needy immigrants, who would come seeking his help. Of course, some of his clients didn't seem to change, and the lineup of transient men outside the Mission every morning was filling the dining room above capacity.

Financially, the Mission remained conservative and cautious. Morris never received more than a modest clergyman's salary, and the salaries of those who served with him were equally moderate. In 1951, after having led the work for some 25 years, he received $5,000 annually. No one would consider it overly generous. Alex's starting salary in 1964 as the new director was $8,000. In time, an independent board committee set the compensation standards for all staff.

As funds became available, there was a focus on buying the properties around 502 Spadina, which were slowly and carefully acquired. The bequests of long-term supporters and those who had been helped in the Depression years would eventually provide the foundation to expand Mission services. Wisely, Morris and the board had segregated those funds as long-term investments unless they were put to use for the capital costs of expanding facilities.

While he continued to widen the Mission's base of supporters, travelled across Canada to inspire church audiences about the work and purchased nearby properties to expand the operations, Morris began to cast one more vision—the Scott Mission of the future. His mentor, Dr. Scott, had pointed the way forward a half-century before: he had built a sizable well-equipped facility for those who were committed to the work. That could be done again.

Better facilities were already needed for the summer Fresh Air programs. By 1958, the site at Hillsburgh was no longer adequate— too small for the increasing number of young people, poor access to swimming and uncomfortably close to the centre of a growing town. Consent for the move had come from the board, and then Morris was stricken with another bout of colitis. Annie and their younger son, David, took over the search and found a well-situated spacious 96-acre farm in the heart of Caledon township. Alex tells us that his father had some objections to the choice, "partly because he had not been directly involved in its purchase,"[1] but it soon became a well-loved setting for staff and campers alike.

158

Any buildings from the Hillsburgh campgrounds that could be moved were hoisted onto trucks and transported to the new grounds. In late spring 1958, during final preparations of the site, Morris relocated to Caledon, where he finished convalescing. Afterwards, he continued giving regular attention to the summer programs. On weekends he'd bring up supplies so that he could lead the Sunday worship service—a special time in the chapel when many gave their hearts and troubles to the Lord.

The following year, 1959, the board invited Alex to take the position of managing director and appointed an official building committee. One of their priorities was approaching city and provincial officials to assist in erecting a new building. The last time that Morris had approached the city was back in 1942. He was no longer a controversial figure, apart from his willingness to give a free meal to the hungry every day. The man who delivered a real miracle every Christmas planned to succeed this time, not by arguing with city hall but by praying for them.

Here are selections from the letter sent May 20, 1960, by the treasurer of the building fund committee, Mr. Allen T. Lambert, president of the Toronto Dominion Bank:

> We are not making any spectacular public appeal. We are not employing professional fundraisers, agents or solicitors. Every dollar contributed will go to the creation of a Refuge for the Poor.
>
> It is estimated that a new building will cost $750,000. Up to date, we have received from friends of the Mission $150,000. They have responded generously and sacrificially, but we are still short $600,000.
>
> If the Metropolitan Municipality gives us a grant, the Provincial Government will most likely follow the example. This we pray will solve our problem. We also wish to point out that this is the first time that we have ever made such a request...
>
> With your help we will be prepared to render service to this community in its present and future demands.

Among the distinguished individuals listed as the Mission's "Council of Reference" were Frederick G. Gardiner, the chairman of the Metropolitan Toronto Council, Mayor Nathan Phillips and the

Very Reverend George C. Pidgeon. The eventual recommendation sent to council by its executive committee stated,

> It should be recognized that the Scott Mission Inc. is operated by the Reverend Morris Zeidman and his family, that it receives no support for its current expenses other than from a substantial number of voluntary donors who give it very broad support.
>
> The services provided by the Scott Mission actually relieve the Municipality of Metropolitan Toronto from very substantial operating expenses which would have to be provided in some other fashion.

The official sod-turning took place on June 1, 1960, and construction was well underway by the time that the council of Metropolitan Toronto approved their request (December 2, 1960) providing a grant of $100,000 toward the new building. The provincial government also assisted, which included provision for temporary quarters for a nominal cost at 696 Spadina Avenue. Unhappily, that location was far too small to maintain their usual services and uncomfortably inadequate for clients, who, on most days, only got sandwiches in place of a hot meal.

The premier of Ontario, Leslie Frost, laid the cornerstone on April 16, 1961, the official date on which the new building was opened. Margaret recalled the wonderful response from the crowd as Morris stepped to the podium and opened with a few impromptu lines. He spoke of the long nights spent awake, worrying about the rent for the Mission's first storefront. "Then, I thought," he said, "why should I worry? The landlord should worry."

Morris added more sober comments as he thanked all those who made the moment possible and urged others to join the cause:

> "It is gratifying to us that during the erection of this new building the charitable work of the Mission has been going on as usual and if anything the numbers have been increased this year. Just visualize 4,000 hungry men being fed every week of the year. And over 1,000 articles of clothing distributed weekly to men, women and children. In addition 175 families receiving emergency orders of groceries every week and furniture, bedding, beds and other necessities of life given free to those who are in need…

"What would all these needy ones do but for the Scott Mission? One elderly gentleman supplied the answer the other day as he left after being given a lunch. He turned to me and said, "Reverend, the Mission is our salvation. If it weren't for the Scott Mission we would starve to death…

"This building project, however, is an unprecedented burden that we were forced to assume because of the growth of Metropolitan Toronto and the increased demands upon us. I therefore humbly and earnestly ask all those within my hearing to pray that the Great Burden Bearer may in some way or other lift that burden from us…so that the unemployed and needy men will not have to line up outside in the coming cold, near zero weather."

Mica Markovic was still relatively new on staff—he and Elaine had not yet married—and he experienced the transition into the new facility with feelings of relief. "The Mission was in temporary quarters up the street when this building was being built," said Mica. "It was a miserable time to work and to be a client; I will never forget the conditions. Clients had to line up in the snow and sleet to get a sandwich and cup of coffee. My heart was aching when I had to deal with the people.

"When the cornerstone was laid for this building, I was the first one to move in the building to get it prepared for the clients, arrange all the furniture [and] equip the kitchen. It's amazing how we were seeing the immense number of people, 900 people a day: 300 chairs in the dining room and 300 in the chapel waiting to eat. They were completely full. People would be coming in all conditions.

"I recall one man in February; he walked in the mission with no shoes, just socks turned into ice. He could walk because his feet were frozen. I took him aside, thawed his feet, dressed them, and I think his feet were saved. In those early days, Morris wanted to have a hostel for single men here, and that's how that area [for personal services] was provided. In those busy first years, we started to get a lot of single women with children coming for help. We set up separate tables for the children. Morris realized at that time that there was more need for a daycare than a hostel. He was the first one in Metro Toronto to open a daycare for working families."

161

Elaine remembered the rush of excitement at walking into the finished building—"This is all the space we could possibly want." As it happened, Morris didn't think that there was quite enough room to meet their future needs, and he told the family that he fully expected them to add a third floor. In fact, when they did make that addition in 1975, they were surprised to find that the original builders had already put in a stairwell, anticipating its construction. This was just like Morris, Elaine noted, continually looking ahead and saving some extra expense.

The building's capital campaign attracted the attention of the *Toronto Telegram* and the Progress Club of Canada. They jointly named Morris as Canada's "Citizen of the Year" in 1961. The *Telegram*'s front-page story featured a glowing Morris surrounded by the family. An elaborate dinner in his honour was given at the Royal York Hotel.

One of those present at the official opening was Dr. J. S. Glen, principal of Knox College. Some weeks later, during spring convocation, Dr. Glen and the college faculty conferred on Morris an honorary doctor of divinity degree, which, according to Alex, "perhaps pleased him most of all."[2]

I WIPED A TEAR (1950)

By Annie A. Zeidman

I wiped a tear once from my brother's face,
And suddenly God spoke, and gently smiled,
"Thank you, My child;
Some day I'll wipe the tears from every face,
'Til then, you take My place."
Now since that day, these hands of mine are His
Who formed the world, the stars, and all that is.
My hands, so frail and weak, O wonder grand!
Are deputy for God's almighty hand.

*And the Lord GOD will wipe away tears from off
all faces.* (Isaiah 25:8)

CHAPTER 16

"See You in the Morning"

Soon after Morris's 70th birthday in June 1964, his colitis flared up again. The pain forced him to take to his bed at home, and by late September he was placed in the Toronto General Hospital. Alex took charge of the administrative duties at the Mission and gave pastoral oversight.

The family's spirits lifted considerably on October 4 when Alex and Maureen welcomed their first child, a baby girl, and Morris suggested the name Anne Sherwood Zeidman. His health wasn't improving, and by Morris's third week in hospital, Annie and the children began keeping a constant vigil. At least once a day his longtime friend Dr. Nelles Silverthorne would walk over from Sick Kids Hospital to visit.

On October 27, arriving at the bedside, Dr. Silverthorne could tell that Morris was in discomfort, yet the greeting was as warm as always. Morris took his hand and, the doctor recalled, "spoke words similar to these: 'I feel very happy today. I am improving, and it is wonderful to be with you.'" As he left, Morris's face was lit up "with a smile that pain would never defeat."[1]

"Little did I realize," wrote Silverthorne, "that it would be our last time together." Elaine, too, had been confident that this was just another episode—longer than usual, but surely her father would recover and retire to enjoy many years surrounded by his grandchildren. Arriving at his bedside that afternoon, she saw that Morris was much weaker. Immediately Elaine called Dr. Markowitz. As the family gathered around, she wished they could take him home.

The hour was growing late when Elaine had to leave. "Even as I was saying goodbye that night," she recalled, "I felt the lingering spiritual note in those words, 'I'll see you in the morning, Daddy.'"

Alex, David and Mica stayed with him through the night. The next morning, when Dr. Silverthorne returned, Morris had lapsed into a coma. Dr. Markowitz was called and later described the scene to Elaine, almost with awe. "I saw the *shekinah* glory on him," he said, and in his last moments Morris reached out his hand as if to greet someone. Then he was gone.

As she walked into the hospital room, Elaine saw for the first time a dead person. Looking at the body without its familiar dynamic spirit, she could only say, "That's not my father." Alex and Elaine drove to the Mission, where Annie was sleeping in Morris's office. After gently waking her, they explained what had happened. She accepted it quietly. Then Alex prayed, "Lord, You have said that You are a very present help in a time of trouble, and we are in a time of trouble..."

Remembering that prayer, Elaine considered just how difficult their prospects seemed at that moment. Losing Morris had caught them all by surprise, and there was, as always, so much to do. There was no time to reflect on their loss, because the work of the Mission had to continue, even while they were making funeral arrangements. Of course, the deeper question—one that no one dared to speak—was at the centre of Alex's prayer. Could they go on? Would the Mission continue to receive the blessings they'd come to expect under Morris's prayerful guidance, his faith in miracles?

The funeral was held on October 28, 1964, in the chapel at the Mission. Every seat was taken as a member of the board, Rev. Dr. Alan Farris, professor at Knox College and future principal, spoke on the 23rd Psalm. "Through the dim fog of our grief," said Elaine, "his words were a great comfort, especially as he emphasized that we would surely pass '*through* the valley of the shadow.'"

In Elaine's memory, the day was marked by a series of curious incidents. An elderly Jewish man came and sat in the front office, reminiscing about Morris. They had grown up together in

Czestochowa, and he described seeing Morris ride into the town square on a bicycle and announce that he was going to Canada. A prank caller said that a bomb had been planted at the Mission, and for safety's sake, the auditorium was briefly cleared. A ringing phone interrupted the service—someone calling to express condolences. Sadly, Morris's sister Gertrude arrived a day late for the service, and this was very hard for her. In the midst of the family's exhaustion, Mrs. Evelyn Leuty, a former board member, made them a large quantity of beef broth, which was gratefully received. "Many of us," Elaine said, "had barely eaten for three days."

In the days after he was laid to rest in Mount Pleasant Cemetery, the city extended its tributes, including the following eulogies in the pages of two major daily newspapers. The remarks were eloquent and grateful for a life that had been so well lived for the sake of others.

SCOTT MISSION HEAD HELPED POOR 39 YEARS
(The Globe and Mail, Friday, Oct. 30, 1964)

Three hundred men stopped talking and clattering the lunch dishes yesterday at Toronto's Scott Mission when they heard the news: Dr. Morris Zeidman was dead...

He spent 39 years helping the hungry and homeless, often without knowing where he would find the next meal for himself and his family. He died Wed. [Oct. 28] at Toronto General Hospital.

Mr. [Mica] Markovic...announced Dr. Zeidman's death in the dining room at lunchtime yesterday.

During Dr. Zeidman's time with the Scott Mission, it has served 4,000,000 free meals, all of them without a means test.

Dr. Zeidman's family will continue to run the mission, which draws its $100,000 a year budget from the small cash gifts of well-wishers—some of them men who were saved from starvation and who later paid for the kindness with what money they could spare...

He worked 10 hours a day in a machine shop while going to school at night...

His wife sold her wedding and engagement rings, and he cashed in his life insurance to get money for his family's living expenses and for the mission.

In 1948 the mission outgrew its quarters, and the Zeidmans scraped together a $10,000 down payment on a $32,000 building at College and Spadina.

Dr. Zeidman later recalled how he lay awake at nights fretting about the $22,000 that the mission owed on that building.

In 1961, the mission opened a new $750,000 building constructed with municipal and provincial aid.

The mission now feeds a free noon meal to between 700 and 750 unemployed men each day, in two shifts. About 1,000 persons a day come for various kinds of help.

A tenth of the mission's visitors are alcoholics or ex-alcoholics. Dr. Zeidman, a bespectacled, kindly man, became known for his tact and his ability to gain the confidence of hard drinkers and those who were depressed and emotionally disturbed.

When some critics suggested that some of his guests took advantage of the mission, he answered, "They can't cheat me of much. What can they take from me? A bowl of soup?"[2]

THE COMFORTER

(Editorial Page, *Toronto Telegram*, Fri., Oct. 30, 1964)

Rev. Morris Zeidman, who died yesterday, was a rare combination of wisdom and humanity, warm-heartedness and love.

He defied any sort of routine classification. The Scott Mission he operated on Spadina Ave. served soup and comfort. Perhaps this describes him best: He was a comforter extraordinary.

The many thousands who knew him and loved him and mourn for him today have lost a sympathetic and understanding friend.

The helpless, the hopeless, the downtrodden, the dispossessed found balm for body and spirit in the nourishment he dispensed.

This modest man's disarming simplicity of manner veiled a deep sense of social service backed by the firm resolution to make this community a better place because of his being here.

He never spared himself to help anyone who needed him because, as he once said, kindness cannot be confined to humanity in the abstract.

In a world of sharp edges and harsh pressures he chose to be kind. And this is how Toronto will remember him.[3]

The future of the Mission was now in the hands of the board of directors, which declared its intentions with these final words on the work and legacy of their friend and colleague, almost certainly penned by the chairman, Dr. Jim Hunter, editor of *Evangelical Christian* magazine:

> Under his hand and with the blessing of God he saw the work grow from a small beginning to its present proportions as one of the largest evangelical missions on the American continent. God buries His workmen, but His work goes on. In that assurance we face the future confident that He who so wondrously guided in the past will continue to lead and to bless until the day dawns when the work is done and the kingdoms of this world have become the Kingdom of our Lord and Saviour Jesus Christ. Such we believe would be Dr. Zeidman's most ardent desire could he speak to us from the realms of glory today.

CARRIED ON HIS SHOULDER

Words and Music: Elaine Markovic

Carried on His shoulder, hidden in His wings,
Saved by the blood of the Lamb.
Named by Him and sealed, through His word revealed.
I'm a new creation by His grace.
Healed and restored by His love outpoured,
And I will see my Jesus face to face.
Kept by His power, every day and hour,
Travelling to the new Jerusalem.
Saints around are singing, hallelujahs ringing,
No more night, no tears, no poverty.
The Lamb is the Light in the city bright,
And we will see our Jesus face to face,
And we will see our Jesus face to face.

CHAPTER 17

The Good Samaritan Wears Horn-Rimmed Glasses

Behind the reception desk in the front office at 502 Spadina, there's a stained-glass portrait of the Good Samaritan wearing black horn-rimmed glasses: the unmistakable image of Alex Zeidman. Typical of his understated modesty there's no inscription, no explanation. Viewed by hundreds daily, it's a subtle, poignant reminder of his continuing influence. Although Alex has been gone for more than a quarter century, without his spiritual depth and considerable administrative and visionary gifts the Mission would be a very different place today.

After the decades of Morris's inspiring, determined guidance, Alex would bring the Mission renewed momentum. He expanded the staff, empowering them to follow his lead by innovating and seeking out new models of ministry. Meanwhile, he patiently maintained the traditional front-line work of sharing the gospel with homeless and transient men daily, the face of care and concern to families whose English language skills were often limited, and encouraged the staff to provide for the needs of clients without judgment.

At first, he had to put up with constant comparisons with his father. Physically, he was a striking contrast to Morris; taller and reedy. Like his father, he projected an even-tempered, reserved presence. His passions were focused on caring for people. One of his first decisions was to relocate his office downstairs, near to the clients, a move as symbolic as it was reflective of a hands-on approach to ministry.

"Kind" and "gentle" were common first impressions. Alex personified the gracious church pastor that he might have become in a more traditional pulpit ministry. An excellent, thoughtful speaker, he knew how to engage an audience with vital insights from Scripture. Many, including Elaine, felt that he'd have found greater prominence on a wider public stage, ranking with the leading Presbyterian clergy of his day. Instead, he spent as much time as he could with men of the street community—his unconventional congregation, and they came to have great affection for the man they called "the Rev."

That calm, peaceful character, the hallmark of a deeply felt inner spiritual life, was also a familiar trait to those who knew Elaine. They were often considered matching personalities. She knew that his love for people, particularly the men at the Mission, was integral to his faith. "He saw people as being made in the image of God," she said. "That makes a difference in the way you treat them." She often saw him reaching out to those "who had nothing; who had run out of resources."

From her post at the reception desk, Elaine watched as Alex stepped into his father's role. Alex knew that for some of the clients, his presence alone could be provoking. "He would approach a man, keeping his hands in his pockets," she said. "If he was intimidated, he never showed it. But then, he didn't stand for nonsense." That last phrase—something of a byword among those who work with the Mission's homeless men—is the ability to confront a person before any situation gets out of hand. Not everyone can do it.

"Even when a client would approach him angrily," she said, "he just spoke quietly and kept his hands in his pockets, even if he got his glasses knocked off a couple of times. There was a gentle manliness about him. And he didn't take himself too seriously."

During his three decades of leadership (November 1964 to October 1986, 22 years in total) Alex was addressing Toronto's toughest needs as it grew into Canada's largest city. The issues were often beyond logical solutions: the 60s drug culture, rising numbers of single parents, increasing crime rates in the downtown core, the influx of homeless youth to the inner city. Added to all of these challenges was the unpredictable arrival of newcomers from such widely distant regions as Eastern Europe, North Africa, South Asia and Central and South America.

Fortunately, with Annie and Elaine's depth of experience, they could identify the signs of a new wave of immigrants before they arrived in larger numbers. The Mission was often on the leading edge of assistance and became early responders, seeking out those who could help with translation and resolve the inevitable problems of serving people who had unique fears and different ways of relating and had been traumatized by their arrival in a new culture.

Under Alex's leadership the Mission grew to respond to changing circumstances while remaining spiritually grounded—even as others expected the work to become more of a social service organization. That spiritual focus stayed at the centre of the Mission's vision and daily life while Alex expanded the programs—building around himself a strong ministry team that included family members and faithful new personnel.

Elaine saw in Alex the rarest type of Mission leader, a "wise shepherd," the compassionate pastor who could also be a capable, self-effacing administrator. Later, Alex summarized his ethos of care into a declaration that was circulated among the staff. This "mission statement" expressed his total dedication to a ministry built on unconditional love:

THIS PLACE IS FOR PEOPLE
by Alex Zeidman (1984)

> *This was written with the intention of reminding all the employees why we are here and to approach serving people with open hearts and minds.*
> *This place is for people.*
> *Some of the people who come to us may be dirty, crazy, sniff solvents, drink to excess, but they are people, and this place is for people.*
> *Staff are important, and without them we wouldn't be able to do our work, and they are people, and this place is for people.*
> *Some people don't do things the way we would do them. They may be slow, naive, devious, lazy, sickly, argumentative, but they are people, and this place is for people.*
> *Some of our clients may be annoying, cloying, demanding, exasperating, frustrating, shiftless, lazy, ne'er-do-wells, but they are people, and this place is for people.*
> *Equipment is important, it is expensive and enables us to do our work well and efficiently, and we must be good stewards of these gifts of God, but this place is for people.*

*We must be careful not to forget that most of the gifts made to
the Mission are for the ministry to the people who come here, not for
the staff or for the Mission as an organization; they are for people,
and this place is for people.*

Elaine called it "a good reminder—the most important thing is
to remain sensitive." It could be difficult, she reflected, to maintain
the right attitude, but crucial. "You don't know what meal is going
to be their last."

That attitude became more meaningful during the 1960s and '70s,
when the Scott Mission seemed less relevant. People expected that government bureaucracies would take responsibility for administering
public welfare programs, and there was a growing skepticism that questioned the effectiveness of faith-based services. Elaine recalled how Alex
responded to queries of that era with the same patience that he gave to
his clients. "When people asked, 'What is your success rate?' he'd say,
'God doesn't call us to be successful; He calls us to be faithful.'"

***

THE BIAFRAN SECONDMENT

In July 1967, a civil war broke out in the West African nation of
Nigeria. The southeast region of the country, which held major oil
reserves, attempted to secede and form the Republic of Biafra. After
peace talks failed, the Nigerian military government began a military
invasion. The new republic had limited military resources, but
regional ethnic and traditional differences with the rest of the country
were a major incentive for Biafrans to assert their independence.

While there was international sympathy for Biafra, both the
United Kingdom and the Soviet Union were supplying the federal
Nigerian forces with weapons. Despite a larger army, air force and
greater firepower, the Nigerian military couldn't deliver a decisive
blow against the breakaway republic. In 1968, as the war drifted into
stalemate, a massive blockade of food and medical supplies was set
in place. By mid-year, a humanitarian disaster was taking place.

Every news outlet began displaying the horrific images of mal-
nourished Biafran adults and children. There was widespread alarm

across North America and Europe. Alex Zeidman was genuinely affected by the coverage and spoke with missionary colleagues who had worked in the region. He wondered if he could be of use to help ease the suffering and made inquiries. Eventually, a request came from the Presbyterian Church in Canada for a secondment from his position at the Scott Mission to serve with the World Council of Churches in the war zone.

"Separation from my wife and two small children was the most painful experience," he wrote in an article for the *Presbyterian Record* (June 1969).[1] He was a bit more reticent to write that he had begun by approaching Annie and Maureen to ask their blessing and releasing him to go. He was leaving behind an 18-month-old son and 4-year-old daughter.

Alex's determination convinced the highly reluctant members from the rest of the family and the mission board to let him go. To smooth the way for his Mission colleagues, he prepared his office by working on the administrative tasks six months ahead of schedule, the estimated time of his return.

Maureen sensed how important this was for him, but the dangers of a war zone were a genuine test of her own faith. None of this was allayed by newspaper accounts of the Nigerian army's slaughter of Biafran relief workers. Repeatedly she claimed a passage of Scripture that she sensed the Lord had given her for comfort, the opening verses of Psalm 41:

> Blessed is he that considereth the poor: The LORD will deliver him in time of trouble. The LORD will preserve him, and keep him alive; and he shall be blessed upon the earth: and thou wilt not deliver him unto the will of his enemies.

Of course, a lot of the Nigerian bombings and attacks were happening at the landing strip where the air shipments were received, and Alex assured her that he wouldn't be working there. As he left for the airport on the morning of October 15, 1968, Annie's memorable last words stayed with him: "You'll see how the Lord sees you through this time."

Alex flew out of Toronto to Amsterdam and then boarded a flight to Sao Tome, an island off the African coast. The normally sleepy tropical isle had been jolted into action as one of the major air links to the Nigerian conflict. His first flight into Biafra was turned back because of poor weather; a second attempt succeeded.

Soon after landing, Alex confronted the dangers of a war zone. While he was being driven into town to receive official clearance, "sentries jumped onto the road with lowered guns and asked us to identify ourselves. Between the air strip and Umuahia [the nearest city] there were at least nine such checkpoints."

After a few days of orientation he was assigned to assist Dr. Herman Middelkoop, the organizing secretary of the World Council of Churches (WCC). He travelled to every corner of Biafra, gathering information on provincial food and aid distribution centres.

The news pictures he'd seen were not exaggerated. "It was with some trepidation that I paid my first visit to a children's ward in a hospital and viewed the hunger-wracked little bodies with swollen tummies and with legs cracked and oozing from accumulated fluid...I inevitably compared these pitiful little children with my own happy and healthy youngsters at home."

The area where Alex worked for the WCC was responsible for feeding more than two million refugees. He was pleased to see the success of the program in alleviating hunger. "In the few months that I was in Biafra a remarkable change took place...The supplies moving in had meant the difference between life and death for thousands."

In December, Alex was assigned the task of setting up immunization clinics, vaccinating children for measles and providing vaccines for children and adults against small pox. It was a pressing need, and the medical authorities were extremely worried about the diseases becoming rampant when the population was vulnerable. Clinics were set up, and the campaign still ongoing when Alex left in April.

There had been continuing interest from the Toronto media in Alex's story since the Mission had first announced the secondment. The *Toronto Star*, for example, ran a few stories of the director's "mercy mission" overseas. On March 1, almost the entire religion page of the *Saturday Toronto Star* was dedicated to Alex's photos from the region and a feature written from Umuahia. He spoke of the heroic relief efforts by a diverse international collective of individuals and organizations working to stem the twin challenges of hunger and disease. "Everywhere you go," he wrote, "you hear enthusiastic testimony to the effect of this food on the condition of the people...I have seen the remarkable effect of a very few weeks of proper nutrition."

His article included touching details about the many hundreds of thousands of refugees he'd witnessed, starving children and adults too enfeebled from hunger to move, the aching loneliness of a newly orphaned girl with no family and no hope in the midst of a refugee camp. He also spoke of his co-workers, those he had joined in a "fellowship of common purpose and of Christian brotherhood that makes this a rich experience... Faith has seemed to grow stronger in the face of adversity." With no end in sight to the war between the federal Nigerian army and Biafran troops, Alex reported, "Morale is high, and the will to resist and survive as a nation is strong."[2]

The final two months were busily spent at the central receiving airstrip and storage facility—yes, the place that Maureen had most feared. Alex described the experience in the *Record* of relief flights arriving, usually at night: "in darkness broken only for a few seconds by the landing lights." As many as 44 planes made their drop in a single night. "It is an indication of the need that the central store is always empty," he wrote. "The food received at this air strip is immediately sent out to the provinces where it is desperately needed."

In his low-key way, Alex described the scenario as "the most exciting part of my experience there because of the regular visits of the Nigerian air force bombing and strafing and otherwise attempting to hinder the flow of supplies into Biafra." He was especially proud of the brave and efficient relief flights of the Canadian crew of Canairelief.

As agreed, Maureen planned to join him wherever he returned in Europe. She knew the time would be around Holy Week, and finally he sent her a telegram from Amsterdam. She arrived to find him utterly exhausted. One of his last assignments was the evacuation of a hospital. Despite the long months of separation, Maureen had felt all along that Alex was where he felt called—and where he belonged. She knew this would be a highlight of his career.

His arrival in Toronto on Sunday, April 20, 1969, was widely reported in the media, and he addressed the local news outlets at

Pearson International Airport.[3] Alex reported that "there doesn't seem to be much hope," either for the breakaway state or the two to three million innocent refugee civilians living in barely subsistence conditions. The *Star* coverage included a picture of him embracing his young children, Anne (four) and Andrew (two).[4]

"Time and time again," Alex wrote in the *Record*, "I was approached by Biafrans who expressed gratitude for my being there...they were grateful that the church overseas had not forgotten them, and one felt humbled by being able to strengthen faith in the very simple act of being at a certain place at a special time."

PRAYER OF THE GOOD SAMARITAN (1967)

By Annie A. Zeidman

Oh, stony is the Jericho road, Jerusalem's road is steep,
But up and down, from town to town, there travel on weary feet
The wanderers, the sinning ones, the humble and the proud,
The pompous and the pitiful; and hid among the crowd
Are heartaches past all telling, wounds beyond all care.
Grant, Lord, that I may bring Thy love to those who suffer there.

The Parable of the Good Samaritan (See Luke 10:30–37)

CHAPTER 18

"As for God, His Way Is Perfect"

The busy Christmas season was well underway in December 1969 when Elaine began to notice that she was having trouble swallowing food. A check of her temperature showed a fever. She called in sick at the Mission on December 12 and within a few days was feeling even weaker. When she saw her doctor, he suspected that she had tuberculosis (TB), a rarity in Canada. He happened to have a test in his office, and two days later it came back positive. She thought that the infection had most likely come from an immigrant client out of Europe, where the disease remained a continuing problem.

Two days before Christmas, as hospital patients were being sent home for the holidays, her doctor was able to get Elaine admitted into Toronto General. She was immediately placed in isolation. With her lungs filling up with fluid and her weight down to 94 pounds, Elaine lay physically and mentally incapacitated. She remembered having no strength at all.

At first, the doctors were undecided about a mass located in her lungs; was it only fluid or a tumour? Elaine was told that she'd have to undergo a series of tests. "We're *hoping* that it's fluid" was all the doctors would say. She heard a note of uncertainty in their voices and feared the worst. The specialists were able to aspirate the lung, extract fluid and send it away to be examined. Days would pass before she knew the results.

While she lay in bed waiting, there was lots of time to think. For some reason, Elaine had been prepared early for the holidays, so there was no concern about presents for the children. Visitors were few and couldn't stay long. Like in that episode of scarlet fever so long ago, each one had to take the precaution of dressing up in a full gown, gloves and mask. Mica came by every day after work. Alex was there on Sunday morning and Dr. Silverthorne on Sunday evening. Returning to the same hospital where Morris had died was still too hard for Annie.

The Bible lay closed on the bedside table next to a few magazines that friends had sent. Worn out after weeks of illness, Elaine lacked even the strength, let alone the interest, to pick them up. A couple of Scripture verses kept coming into her thoughts without prompting, and she began to cling to these, especially this one: "As for God, His way is perfect" (Psalm 18:30 NKJV), and then "The LORD will perfect that which concerns me" (Psalm 138:8 NKJV).

She had no idea where the passages were from or how she knew them. Perhaps it was part of the great wealth of Scriptures that her parents had shared over the dining room table or from Principal Trotter's Bible class in the sitting room at Moulton.

Elaine recalled looking back, reflecting on so many past decisions, considering again "what if." One evening, lying in bed, she found herself at peace and contemplating the possibility that the illness might take her life. She thought of her girls. Lois was only six; Sera not yet three.

As her mind sifted through the prospects for her little family it occurred to her, "If I die, Mica is still young. He could marry again." That was the moment when something rose up in her. "Not exactly anger," she said, "but some energy." A willful rebuke: "No! I want to do their hair. I want to iron their clothes. I want to be their mother."

Even in her weakness, she felt the power of that resolve urging her to stay alive. "An electric shock that I needed," she said. It had activated "a little switch." At the time, it didn't seem so powerful. "It wasn't a big switch; I didn't have the energy."

For the first time in weeks, Elaine understood how fragile her condition had become. Day after day she'd not been eating or sleeping properly, and there was constant discomfort: "After that, you don't even care—much." The decision to live for her daughters' sake gave her new momentum.

"I needed to want to pull out of this. I began thinking, 'Let's turn this around.'

"It was a breakthrough," she said, "and I just kept remembering that God would perfect all that concerned me." Then the results came back, and there was no tumour.

Soon she was able to speak to her children over the phone every evening before they went to bed, which was a great comfort. The family rallied round to support them. Mica struggled every morning, getting the girls ready for daycare at the Mission. The teachers didn't mind helping with combing the girls' hair and making pigtails—little things that a harried dad could barely manage.

Events outside the hospital were adding to the family's problems. The neighbourhood was under redevelopment, and their home had been sold to the developer. Earlier, he'd assured them that they could stay until spring. On January 19, a letter arrived saying that the company had acquired all the necessary properties in the neighbourhood. The family had one month to get out before workers put up boarding around the house. For a week, Mica searched for a place to move. Taking a full precious week away from work, he found nothing, and he had to take another week to locate a suitable home. Now all their belongings had to be packed up.

The family needed her, and it was a great motivator for Elaine. After leaving Toronto General, her extended treatment was continuing at West Park Hospital, the former sanatorium in the west end of Toronto. Her doctor interceded with the head of the chest clinic so that she could return home on a daily basis.

Elaine was permitted to supervise the packing—no physical work. And she was still contagious. Family members were forbidden to have any direct physical contact. Annie was there with the girls; their grandmother repeatedly warning the little ones that they couldn't touch their mother. Of course, the rules felt heartless. Elaine longed to feel her arms around them, just as they wanted to be held. Little Sera showed poignant restraint by choosing to sit nearby, as close as she could get to Mom.

Months of clinical treatments followed, and by the end of August, Elaine had made a full recovery, finally returning to work. "It was a shock to see that things were still running. What a blow to my ego. I wasn't indispensable at all," she said, not without laughing. In the period before the illness, she'd been spending more time doing office work. "When I came back," she said, "I was on the front lines again, which was fine by me."

The effects of the disease had passed; the profound changes in her perspective lasted much longer. A new maturity had come. Her view of God, her ministry and her faith had all been affected by those days of clinging to the promises of Scripture while her life hung in the balance.

She didn't want to be the same person when she resumed working with the clients. "I felt that I understood them much more than I had previously." For months, she'd been a regular patient of the chest clinic attached to West Park Hospital. She noticed how it was crowded with the poor, the homeless and those at the lower end of society. Without proper nutrition or basic hygiene, they were vulnerable to the disease.

The clinics were well run, she thought. She was the only woman she ever saw in the clinic's waiting room and was better dressed than most of the men. Everyone was treated equally. Yet after many repeated experiences there, she began to appreciate the awkwardness of those around her. Most of the men arrived from shelters without the same benefits she enjoyed, including a shower and change of clothes. Those things made a huge difference for one's sense of dignity. Elaine had a new awareness of their daily struggles, the challenges to maintain one's self-respect.

Another profound difference before and after the illness was her concept of time. "Time took on a new dimension for me," she said.

"For far too long I had been impressed with my own busyness," Elaine said. At first, the waiting room experiences at the clinic made her feel the affront of having to wait. But she was no different from anyone else. She realized how the clients at the Mission must feel going from one agency to another, one waiting room to another. She understood how this, too, was one of the indignities of those who weren't allowed to control their own time. She became a slower, more thoughtful person. "I had a better appreciation of the people around me."

Finally, Elaine accepted that she needed to make some personal adjustments. "There was a reconsideration of priorities—they were in disorder. I had always known that the Mission could become an unrelenting giant in one's life," she said. "It was beginning to be that for me. But after God, my family needed to come first."

There was a certain surprise, too, when she returned to the Mission. She recognized many of the clients. They weren't just familiar faces but had been her fellow patients at the chest clinic. "Now," she said, "we had something in common."

ONE GRACE MORE (1971)

By Annie A. Zeidman

Thou who hast given so many gifts of priceless worth to me,
Salvation, and the inner grace to hear Thy voice, to see Thy face,
To love, adore,
Grant one grace more:
That I may greet each soul I meet
As Thou wert meeting me.

CHAPTER 19

Alex in the Pulpit and in Print

Every day at the Mission, Alex was used to speaking with discouraged, hurting people. The authentic quality of his preaching inspired listeners with the message that God's grace was still present in their lives, whether they could see it or not. A recurring theme was that our troubles aren't an obstacle to blessing. So the ultimate sign of God's sovereignty remains the cross—a defeat in the world's eyes that precedes the Lord's ultimate victory of life over death.

Here are two of Alex's sermons, the first based on the carol "Silent Night," and selections from another called "God's Mistakes and Our Mistakes."

A MEDITATION ON "SILENT NIGHT"

The carol "Silent Night" is one of the best known and yet the simplest of our Christmas carols. Although it is very unadorned and easily memorized, it has a number of lessons to teach us, particularly at this holy Christmas time.

The first lesson is from the way that the carol originated. In a very small town of Germany, when the pastor and organist were preparing for the Christmas services, it was discovered that a little mouse had gotten into the organ and chewed away at the bellows, so it would not work. This was a great tragedy, but it stimulated the organist to write a little tune that could be played on a guitar and the pastor to write the now familiar words of "Silent Night," and together they produced the much loved carol.

The lesson we get from this is that so often God can bring a blessing out of trouble or tragedy. All of us experience troubles to one degree or another, some many and severe and some not so many and not so severe. It's helpful for us to remember the lesson that God in His mercy and love can bring a blessing out of our trouble. As the old hymn puts it, "Behind a frowning providence He hides a smiling face."

The very simplicity of the carol reminds us of the plainness of the gospel message. Even the smallest child can understand that Jesus loves him. And in the simple, clear, uncomplicated words of this carol, we have the good news of the gospel that Jesus Christ was born. Although there is that in the Bible that will challenge the keenest minds, the good news of God's love in Jesus Christ and His saving grace is not complicated. One of the most profound theologians of recent time was the late Karl Barth, who once was asked how he would sum up his faith. This man, who had written many volumes of very deep and complicated theology, said, "Jesus loves me, this I know for the Bible tells me so." It is not for nothing that Jesus said it was for those who had the faith of a child that the gates of heaven were opened.

This carol, "Silent Night," reminds us that the Christmas event was a special moment in history. When it says, "Silent night, holy night" it refers to a specific time in the calendar. A special place in history. This story of the birth of Jesus Christ is not a fairy tale. It doesn't start with fairy-tale type of words "Once upon a time," but it begins "That night." And it is important to remember that when we are sometimes assailed by unbelievers who try to downgrade the Christian faith, it is grounded in historical fact. What was special about that night? What was special about that moment in history? Why is it called "holy night"? It is holy, it is special, because that night God entered history. While we believe that God is always present and does order our lives, from time to time He enters history in a specific way, and certainly this is true of the birth of His Son, Jesus Christ. The carol testifies to this when it describes it as a "holy night," when it speaks of the "virgin mother," when it talks of the "holy infant." Even the little phrase "all is bright" refers to the shining star and the visit of the angels. All of these things are encompassed in the simple words of the carol, that God has entered history.

The words of the carol also tell us something about Jesus Christ, that He is both God and man, holy and infant. This is the way that God chose to tell us of His love. He came himself in the person of His Son. This is why we call Jesus "the Word." Words are used to communicate, and Jesus, the Word, is the way that God communicates with us.

Listen to some of the words of this carol: "silent," "calm," "tender," "mild," "sleep," and "peace." These words remind us that the one whose birth we celebrate at this season is known as the Prince of Peace. How much we need His calming, comforting spirit in our troubled world, our troubled homes, our troubled lives, our troubled minds. As we look out across our world and see trouble almost everywhere, our prayer is that the Prince of Peace might reign. As we look within ourselves we often see trouble. I sometimes think of the old spiritual "Nobody knows the trouble I've seen, nobody knows but Jesus." And that is a great comfort for any of us who do suffer trouble of any sort or another, either in our own lives or in the lives closest to us. It is a comfort that Jesus knows, and He who is the Prince of Peace can bring peace to our troubled minds and hearts.

The final thing that we might remember from this carol, "Silent Night," is that it reminds us that God is in control. On that night so many years ago, He was working out His plan of salvation in sending His Son, Jesus. Although the carol doesn't tell of it, we must remember that the cross is behind the cradle. The calmness of the stable in Bethlehem is a prelude to the chaos of Calvary. But it looks beyond that turbulent scene of execution to another time of great calmness on Easter when, in the quiet of the early morning, the disciples discovered the empty tomb and the risen Christ. As we sing the Christmas carols and rejoice at this season of the year, let us sing them with understanding and insight as they bring to us in a different way the good news of Jesus Christ.

FROM "GOD'S MISTAKES AND OUR MISTAKES"

All of us make mistakes. We can look back on our lives and see that perhaps we have made many of them; some of them very serious. And then, when we look around at the world around us and see some of the tragedy, injustice, sorrow, pain, we sometimes wonder, hasn't God made a mistake? Aren't some of these world tragedies His mistakes, where the divine plan has gone awry, where God's goodness has become twisted and distorted?

We want to look at a couple of examples in the Bible this morning, some of the most familiar ones of Scripture. The first comes from that incident when Joseph, the object of great jealousy by his brothers, was first of all thrown into an old well and then later sold into Egypt. The second incident is the story in the Gospels where a young man is brought to Jesus for healing. He had been blind from his birth, and some of the people were asking some difficult questions. The third incident is the time when Paul and his friend Silas had been preaching in the town of Philippi, and they were both thrown into prison after being beaten and whipped. From all of these incidents it would seem that maybe God was making a mistake. Had His love and mercy gone astray? Were His purposes being diverted?...

In these three incidents, Joseph as a slave, the man born blind, Paul and Silas in prison, we have the advantage of being able to look at the whole scene...And having this kind of perspective we can see that God was using these incidents, these so-called mistakes, for His greater glory. God used the mistakes of those who were involved to work out His purposes.

So, in the story of Joseph and his brothers, Joseph, looking with an inspired eye at what had happened to him and his brothers, at the moment of revelation when he is the prince of Egypt and his brothers come begging for grain for their starving families—when he lets them know who he is and they are dreadfully worried about what is going to happen to them—he comes out with this generous and perceptive statement: "You thought evil against me, but God meant it for good." ...Because Joseph was sold into Egypt and by God's sovereign purposes was elevated to a place of power and privilege, he was able to provide for his family, and they all moved down to Egypt and were cared for.

So, also, with the young man who had been born blind. Jesus tells us that this was not any mistake of God's, but it was in His sovereign purpose...Jesus says, "Neither has this man sinned, nor his parents: but that the works of God should be made manifest in Him." He wasn't being punished; his parents weren't being punished. It wasn't a great mistake by God. It was in God's plan, so that at this time he could be healed and God be given the glory.

In the story of Paul and Silas in prison we see what happened later—the doors burst open; the jailor almost committed suicide and then heard the gospel message from his captives. "What must I do to be saved?" he asked. And they answered, "Believe on the Lord, Jesus Christ, and you shall be saved." And he was. And his whole household believed with him...

In these stories, we see three principles of God at work. First of all, God sees. The very concept of God means that He is sovereign, that He is all-powerful, that He is all-seeing and He sees what goes wrong, He sees our sin. He sees the overall plan. Not a sparrow falls to the earth, we are told, but He sees it. The very hairs of our head are numbered. He sees our mistakes.

These incidents in Scripture also teach us that God sees with compassion. Where there is sin, He forgives. Where there is pain and suffering, He heals. He enters our pain. He intervenes in our mistakes and works out His purposes.

He sees. He sees with love and forgiveness, and He uses our mistakes. Just as He used the mistakes of the brothers of Joseph. Just as He used Paul and Silas in the life of their jailor in Philippi. Just as He used the blindness of the young man.

Just think for a moment of our own situation. As we sit here this morning God knows, and we know, that we've all made mistakes, wrong decisions, wrong turnings. We've yielded to temptation. We've done things we shouldn't have done, and we've not done things that we should have done. As the Bible says, "All we like sheep have gone astray."

Maybe we have made a mistake, or a series of mistakes, and it's like having made one mistake or a series of mistakes in a long arithmetic question. There doesn't seem to be any going back to put it all right again. The wonderful thing is that God sees our mistakes. We might not think that that's so wonderful. We might be filled with guilt—a horror of judgment. But if it brings us to a place where we confess that we have made a mistake, then put our trust in Him; that we acknowledge that He sees, and we repent? That is good. Remember, God sees, and He sees in compassion and love. He can forgive our mistakes, and, strange as it may seem, God can even use our mistakes.

Some of you may remember the blind pianist Alex Templeton, who in the course of his act would ask for several notes from the audience, and at random people would shout out various notes on the scale. Played together they might be a discord. And yet, Alex Templeton with his talent would take those notes and immediately weave them in to a composition and out of chaos and disharmony would bring music and harmony.

God's mistakes and ours. Let us think just for a minute of the Cross of Calvary. Surely to the outside eye this would seem to be God's greatest mistake of all. The Son sent to bring the message of love is arrested, beaten and killed on a cross. This tragic mistake is all part of God's plan. It's through that "mistake" that death and sin are conquered, life everlasting is accomplished. In God's sovereign way His so-called greatest mistake becomes His greatest means of bringing harmony into our world of mistakes, of sin, of disharmony, of discord. May He, by His Spirit, help us to leave our mistakes before Him, whatever they are, that He can take them and weave them and us into that harmonious composition in which the whole of creation raises its voice in praise to His glory.

In 1983, Alex prepared a magazine article on the Mission that serves as an excellent summary of the work as it had grown under his leadership. That text is largely quoted here:

FROM "THE MIRACLE ON SPADINA AVENUE"

For many persons, the Scott Mission is a place that acts as a refuge to the denizens of skid row. What many people do not realize is how many people come each day looking for assistance. This past July an

average of over 600 people came for a daily meal. That so many people could be looked after without government assistance or any
assured source of supply is in itself a miracle, and yet, each day
promptly at 10 o'clock that number of hungry people files into the
dining room to be served an ample, nourishing meal. Some of the
food comes as donations from bakeries, food companies and individuals. Some of the food is purchased with gifts of money, but everything that appears on the table (and these days it is literally from soup
to nuts, the latter being supplied by a whole truck load of peanuts) is
a miracle of God's supplying grace.

Clothing, haircuts, razors, soap, shoelaces, band-aids—the needs
of the homeless people on the streets of Toronto are almost endless,
and seven days a week the staff at the Scott Mission endeavours to
meet those needs. The spiritual needs of these "wanderers in the
storm of life" are also met in private conversations, in worship services each Sunday morning, and in weekly Bible studies. Attendance
at the "spiritual" activities of the Mission is not compulsory; however,
the chapel is almost always full for its weekly services, and there is an
active participation in the weekly Bible studies.

Contrary to its public image the Scott Mission also ministers to
women and children. A new phenomenon is the appearance of some
women in the "soup line." These are so-called "bag ladies," who wan-
der the downtown streets with all their earthly possessions contained
in a shopping bag or two. Most women, however, are cared for in the
Mission family department. There, in a separate area, they are sym-
pathetically interviewed, and if their needs should be groceries or
clothing or furniture, they are referred to the appropriate department
and there are given assistance to overcome the crises that have
brought them to the doors of the Scott Mission. Again, the miracle on
Spadina Avenue is in operation. Some days over 100 women apply for
groceries to tide them over until their next welfare cheque comes. As
with the meals for the homeless, the food is supplied by donations or
purchased with donated money. Clothing for these needy families is
distributed through a "free clothing store," the racks and shelves of
which are supplied almost entirely by donations from interested
householders. Occasionally the supply of children's clothing and

shoes runs short, and so purchases of the necessary items are made from wholesalers and manufacturers. The spiritual needs of the women and children are not forgotten either. On Thursday afternoons a large group of over 100 women gathers for what must surely be a unique gathering. After a time of praise and prayer this enthusiastic group of women breaks up into four different Bible studies reflecting the cosmopolitan area in which the Mission finds itself and also reflecting the rich variety of peoples among whom it ministers. One Bible study is in English. Others are conducted in Hungarian, Portuguese, and Italian. On Tuesday mornings a smaller group of 15 to 20 young mothers gathers for a Bible study and fellowship group that ministers to their particular needs.

Ministry to children and teens is carried on in six different groups throughout the week. For example, on Saturday mornings from 10 a.m. to 12, the primary age children gather for their time of Bible stories, of games and handwork. Other age groups are conducted at times through the week. In the summer months an innovative extended vacation school called "Summer House" operates for eight weeks in July and August, and over the same period there is an evening programme four nights a week exclusively for teenagers. Another area of ministry to children is the day nursery programme. On the second floor of the Mission building, 50 children, many of them from broken homes and with all the variety of the United Nations, come to spend their days in a wholesome, Christian atmosphere. In games and crafts; in Bible stories and song times; in outings and at meals the love of Jesus Christ is expressed.

Older people are not forgotten either. Each weekday some 240 meals are delivered to shut-ins through the Scott Mission Meals on Wheels service. The serving of the meals is backed up by a regular programme of pastoral visitation to these older folk, who are often lonely and worried. A cassette tape ministry is also exercised among these older folk.

In addition to activities in downtown Toronto, the Scott Mission conducts two summer camps, one near Caledon, Ontario, where some 400 boys and girls age 7 to 12 and 60 to 80 mothers with infants are accommodated. At the Collingwood Lodge seniors representative from the women's and men's fellowships, and also teenagers, all at different times and with programmes designed to meet their different needs, enjoy the blessings of a summer camp experience. Still farther afield, near the town of Kenora in northwest Ontario, 16 children are cared for in the Scott Mission group home called "Homestake House." These children are orphaned or are victims of neglect and so need a special measure of Christian love and care.

Over one thousand people a day pass through the doors of the Scott Mission to be ministered to in the name of Jesus Christ. It is indeed a miracle of God's Providence and His sustaining and saving grace.

SUBMISSIONS TO "THE GOOD SAMARITAN CORNER"

Alex had a true gift for sharing with readers of "The Good Samaritan Corner." He helped them see the tragedy, irony and humour of his world and shared a grounded sense of God's grace. Added to this sampling is the last one that he prepared.

DECEMBER 1, 1984

Roast beef was served at the Scott Mission the other day to 600 appreciative hungry men and women. Such an elegant, not to say expensive, meal is not the usual fare in our busy dining room. In an around about way, we have to thank a certain restaurant reviewer who writes for one of our Toronto newspapers. She came to visit our dining room not long ago and apparently found the contrast between the dining room at the Scott Mission and her usual haunts too much for her sophisticated palate. As a result she made some unflattering remarks about our simple but hearty meals...[he explains that the meals are often dependent on food donations, which are "unexpected gifts"]...No less than the manna that fell in the desert, we regard the food that is given us as from the hand of God...A supporter of the Scott Mission was annoyed by the newspaper article to the extent that she got together with some of her friends and made a donation to provide a roast beef dinner for our guests from off the street. And so it was that a meal fit for a king, or even a restaurant critic, was served in our dining room. "Miss Food Columnist," we wish you had been there.

SEPTEMBER 15, 1984

The telephone call from a distant city carried with it its own message of tragedy and sadness. The young woman at the end of the line was desperate for news of her father. There was indeed a bond of love between the two, whose relationship was "illegitimate" in the eyes of the law. Separated by distance and the bondage of alcohol, their contact had been infrequent. Then the father died. Somehow the daughter, estranged from the rest of the family, had heard the news. Still later she gleaned some rumour that he was still alive, and half hoping, she called the Scott Mission to see if the rumour was true. We had to tell her that her father was indeed dead. We had seen him dragging himself around the streets in a courageous effort. We remembered his coming in for a bowl of soup, so sick he could hardly eat it. We had visited him in hospital in his last illness. And we paid our respects at the funeral home before he went to his last resting place. We told all this to the little voice at the end of the line as gently as we could and went on to say how well loved and respected her father had been in the community of the streets. We were also able to tell her the location of his grave so that if she ever came to Toronto she would be able to visit. We hope she does and that she will come to see us.

OCTOBER 6, 1984

The letters H.A.T.E. were tattooed across the knuckles that he used so often. His violent nature meant that he probably spent more time in jail than outside, and he was barred from most of the missions and hostels in Toronto. And yet there was a tenderness that was well hidden under the scars and encrustations of his life. He once confessed to weeping in his penitentiary cell after he had been visited. At the Scott Mission there is a little children's plaque with the words "Things go better with friends," which he had given in a heartfelt expression of appreciation, simply because we had written letters to him while he was in prison. This violent, virtually friendless man was found dead in a laneway in downtown Toronto not long ago. We suspect that he will not be mourned or even missed by many people, and yet we have to admit to a real sense of loss and regret at the waste of this

196

comparatively young man's life. There is also a sense of gratitude that this person who had almost no friends and whose acquaintances were coerced into closeness called us a friend. To him and to other lonely ones like him we point to the "Friend that sticketh closer than a brother."

> "I've found a Friend, O such a Friend! He bled,
> He died to save me;
> And not alone the gift of life, But His own self
> He gave me."
>
> G.C. Stebbins

NOVEMBER 17, 1984

It was like a junior version of "The Angelus." We saw them at prayer as we poked our head around the corner of the Scott Mission Day Nursery last week. There they were, three or four small children in our care, with hands folded and heads reverently bowed in prayer. The scene, now preserved in our memory, lasted but a moment, and then the little ones went on about their playtime. We do not know what prompted the brief devotion for their teacher was off in another corner of the large room. The special little time upon which we were privileged to eavesdrop reminded us once again of the holy responsibility we have for the lives, young and old, that we have in our care.

In a few short weeks we will be conducting our free toy store at the Scott Mission. Here mothers may choose toys for Christmas for their children that otherwise they might have to disappoint. Prayer and toys. They seem to be at opposite ends of the spiritual spectrum. But surely He of whom we read that He makes the mountains sing for joy and the trees to clap their hands desires His children, especially His littlest ones, to be happy as well as prayerful.

> "So the little moments,
> Humble though they be,
> Make the mighty ages_
> Of eternity."
>
> Carney

OCTOBER 18, 1986

This edition of the "Good Samaritan Corner" concluded with the following note: Prepared by our late director, Rev. Alex Zeidman, one week before his tragic passing from us.

Among the many myths about the inner-city missions and the people who frequent them is that they have no interest in the "finer things" in life—art galleries for instance. Like many such myths this one also is untrue. The lie was put to it by a trip that a group of women from the Scott Mission made not long ago. The members of the group wandered the halls of the art exhibit with appreciation and enjoyment. At lunch afterwards, one of them said, "You know, if it were not for a group like this I would never be able to have this experience." It is not for a lack of interest but rather a lack of opportunity that many of our inner-city friends do not participate in the rich cultural life of our city. "What has a mission got to do with art galleries?" you might ask. "What does the Group of Seven have to do with either material or spiritual need?" While material need is a major need, it is not the only one, and we believe that it is important to meet the needs of the spirit as well. Material need begets a feeling of isolation. Particularly when that need is experienced in the midst of an affluent society like ours. A trip to an art gallery enables some of those who would otherwise be unable to share in our "culture" to do so. From a spiritual point of view we believe it is good theology to be interested in the whole person, and by participating in shared experiences, a sense of community is formed. In that community the sharing of things of the spirit is more natural and meaningful than a "preaching" divorced from the rest of life.

SHE

By Elaine Z. Markovic

She is sometimes tormented,
Bangs her head against the concrete,
Tears at her clothing,
Pulls at her hair.
But today,
She saw her reflection in the window
And she began to sing to herself.
Sad.
This lovely voice is secreted away
Like a fine old tablecloth
Displayed only on occasion.

CHAPTER 20

Losing Alex

B y 1979, when Alex received the City of Toronto's Civic Award of Merit from Mayor John Sewell, its highest award of service, the Mission had a special place in the hearts of Metro residents. It was commonly accepted as a spiritual institution meeting some of the city's most challenging, practical social service needs. After a decade and a half in charge and doubling the staff from about 40 to 50 part-time and full-time staff to over 100, Alex would not take any credit for that achievement. He gave the glory to God and recognized the tremendous goodwill that had been nurtured through his parents' many decades of ministry.

"The Scott" had now successfully expanded to serve a much wider clientele through a variety of services—food, clothing and furniture distribution and various children's and teens' ministries throughout the week, including daycare and a busy Meals on Wheels program delivering to some 240 housebound clients, many of them elderly, throughout the city. The summer camp programs at Caledon continued to be filled, and at the Collingwood Lodge there were unique programs for seniors and teens. Each spring, Alex also would take up to Collingwood a select group of men who were trying to move off the street. The results weren't easily identified, but the intention was clear—to equip the men for a better life and not simply sustain their situations by providing the necessities of life.

Each annual report carried the familiar "Miracle on Spadina" motto and was filled with inspiring evidence of God's enduring blessings for the homeless, the needy and inner-city kids, parents and seniors. In person, Alex remained an open, caring pastor to hundreds of transient men who depended on the Scott Mission for a daily meal, even if he was now the Rev. Dr. Zeidman with an honorary doctorate from Knox College, granted in 1974. His patriarchal appearance was further enhanced by a thick salt-and-pepper beard.

The Scott wasn't the only setting where Alex's vision for ministry would mature. In 1976 he pursued his interest in the ministry of the deacon by spending his sabbatical—seven months of study—in Kaiserswerth, a small German town on the Rhine River north of Düsseldorf. A 19th century pioneer in training deacons, Pastor Theodor Fliedner, had established a remarkable institution in the mid-1800s dedicated to training men and women in caring for the poor and sick. Many women trained by Fliedner became nurses, including his most famous trainee, Florence Nightingale. Fliedner's original institution continues to thrive as a centre for diaconate training through various educational facilities and provides care through a hospital, group homes for orphans and a primary school.

Alex gave a full description of the resources at Kaiserswerth for an article in the *Presbyterian Record*.[1] He wrote, "The extent of the present day institution as well as the history of Theodor Fliedner is an inspiration to all as to what God can do through a dedicated servant of his." Looking back over Alex's life, one can see the imprint of Fliedner's personal attributes of energy, determination, practical focus and dedication to the most vulnerable in society. The German pastor's motto could easily be taken as a watchword for Alex's life as well: "He must increase, but I must decrease" (John 3:30).

Morris had been the determined visionary; Alex became much more consultative in his approach. A man of few words, he had developed a talent for drawing out the best efforts in those around him to build an effective, functional and sustainable organization. His genuine concern for individuals and the personal integrity that he instilled into ministry relationships were models for the staff. According to his wife, Maureen, Alex would circulate to build those relationships. "He called it 'encouraging the troops,'" she said, "and he was also encouraging everyone else." His ministry peers admired him as an exemplary "servant leader." (A good friend, Dr. Donald Page, a former dean of Trinity Western University, wrote a book on leadership that named Alex as a leading example of leadership in his own life.)[2]

One of the most innovative and satisfying ministry developments at the Mission started in the fall of 1978. The late Dr. Stan Skarsten, a board member and close friend of Alex, suggested that the work might benefit from the services of Diane Marshall, a trained family therapist and counsellor. Initially, Diane served as a staff consultant, but then she became involved with a weekly women's group that Maureen, Alex's wife, had started. Everyone in the group had been assessed by the Women and Family Ministries department as having special needs.

The program started out as a Tuesday Bible study, but in the ensuing years, as issues in the group were better understood, more components were added. Maureen and Diane became a strong team, and many of the women, who were immigrants, eventually revealed to them shocking histories of physical and sexual abuse. "They were wounded people," said Diane, "who only wanted to raise their children with love." Isolated and emotionally insecure, they were trying to maintain families in public housing. Some had already lost their children to Children's Aid Society (CAS); others feared it would happen to them.

Immediately, Diane saw how Maureen's close relationship with Elaine helped to strengthen the program. Elaine wasn't a program leader, but she'd show up to play the piano. "Elaine had a very joyful way of playing and singing," said Diane, and they made song sheets—that eventually grew into a songbook for the group.

After the sessions, the leaders went into Elaine's office to brainstorm on what they'd learned. "Elaine was incredibly encouraging and supportive," said Diane, "and if we had a problem person, she would be praying. She was an encourager." They noticed how the women in the group seemed collectively depressed by a lack of sunlight and dismal surroundings at home. There was a need to add a measure of personal dignity and allow the clients to experience beauty in their lives. So the refreshments were served with cups and saucers on tablecloths; decorations included potted flowers that participants were encouraged to take home. Bible studies emphasized a message of God's enduring love for the poor, weak and vulnerable. "Some of those women," said Diane, "were hearing the gospel for the first time."

Elaine would make program suggestions like having the women do a day trip in the spring to the Mission site in Collingwood or to Caledon for a special weekend. In the fall, they went into the countryside to pick apples while their children were in daycare. After gathering baskets of fresh fruit, they were invited to enjoy apple pie and tea. One of their fall outings had 30 women take part. Diane recalled how healing it was for the women in the program to be in nature since these were the only times they could get away from the city.

The clients responded by revealing how disempowered they felt dealing with the problems at home. This led to life skills development and more educational programs, including nutrition and parenting classes on "discipline without punishment." Diane was talking about the Tuesday group with the founder of Citizens for Public Justice (CPJ), Gerald Vandezande.[3] He invited them to join a public submission to city hall on issues related to social assistance.

Women from the group delivered a stirring presentation explaining their unique challenges—that without money for healthy food, many were suffering from diabetes, and their struggle to get proper nutrition. They showed how single mothers could live with more dignity and respect if they had safe housing, healthy playgrounds adjacent to public housing and support for children's programs. The commissioners at city hall were impressed, and the group got a standing ovation. Diane's involvement with the Mission continued until 1991. She recalled, "Someone at CAS said it was one of the longest standing groups for abused women in the city."

Still in private practice, Marshall is currently the director of the Institute of Family Living, a centre for family counselling and personal therapy founded by the late Dr. Skarsten.

Around the time that he turned 50 (1980), Alex made a slight change. His office on the first floor was moved upstairs. That didn't stop him from being available to the men who came to the Mission, and they were often looking to have a word with "the Rev." By all appearances, Alex seemed as actively engaged as ever.

The office move was a minimal warning sign of a private matter—a secret that Alex shared within a discreet circle of family members, friends and colleagues. He'd been diagnosed with a blood disorder—*polycythemia vera*—a thickening of his blood caused by an abnormal increase of red blood cells. Patients are vulnerable to blood clots, heart attack, stroke and other painful conditions. Regular blood-letting provided some relief, but over the long-term, the disease was terminal. His doctors warned him that he couldn't expect to live with the condition more than ten years. With the increased risk of a heart attack or stroke, and as a concession to his wife, who asked him to ease some of his daily stress, the office was moved.

Alex and Maureen considered buying a cottage where they might go away and relax from city pressures, but they balked at the cost and inevitable work to renovate a property. He settled instead on purchasing a small boat that was moored in Pickering. After taking sailing lessons, he and Maureen frequently went out together. All in all, Alex continued to function well. In 1985, he even joined a short-term overseas mission project in the Sudan to assist in food distribution. Before leaving, as always, he scrupulously prepared reports and contributions to "The Good Samaritan Corner." While Alex was gone his brother, David, provided the necessary managerial oversight, and the Mission programs appeared to continue seamlessly.

Alex's closest friends saw that the growing awareness of how much he was going to miss of his family's future life was depressing. And he carried another major concern, the continuing success of "the Scott"—which meant the future of his closest family members and colleagues. That would be in the hands of the next executive director, and he was resolutely forming his private opinions about who might fill that role.

Quietly, Alex approached David Cross, a newer board member who was familiar with the issues of generational transition and leadership succession in business. Alex understood that the increased size and complexity of the Mission would require someone more professionally trained, with wider experience, capable of leading the ministry through the critical changes that would come as they prepared for a new century.

Cross was enormously impressed by the quality of ministry that he witnessed at the Mission, not simply the care and effective work going on, but the spiritual character of faith evident in so many answers to prayer. He recalled one of his early meetings where the board had made the tough decision to spend $52,000 to put in a new pool at Caledon, and the news seemed to arrive almost immediately that a single, unexpected gift of $52,000 had been given from a donor who knew nothing about that particular need. Elaine often called board members to keep them updated about "the miracles on Spadina."

Cross understood that it would be very difficult to bring in someone from outside this setting and expect them to maintain the ministry as it was currently functioning. Any new leader would work to reshape the Mission according to their priorities and agenda. He explained to Alex that only a family member could be expected to sustain the values of the founders. He advised that whatever succession took place, it would be crucial to ensure that family members— those who had been raised with the experience of absorbing from an early age the Mission priorities, standards and procedures—not be driven away by a new leader. This was a common problem with succession plans. The most committed managers in any organization were those who had personal ties to the operation, and these were often family members. But they were also the ones most likely to leave or be replaced once a transition took place.

Although the issues of succession continued to loom large—and Alex made a series of efforts to address the problem—six years after the diagnosis, his health appeared to be stable. During the board meetings in early October 1986, there was a general sense of confidence in Alex's ongoing leadership. Everyone thought there was still time.

On the evening of October 5, Alex didn't come back from the marina in Pickering where he'd been sailing out of Frenchman Bay. Late that evening, Diane Marshall got a call from Anne, his daughter. She was in Ajax at a hospital with her uncle, David, who had just confirmed to police that a body found in the water near the shore of Lake

Ontario was her father. She asked Diane to go and tell Maureen in person what had happened. Diane rushed over to be close to her good friend—especially through the night, as the phone kept on ringing. Nothing, of course, could have prepared them for this.

❧

Alex had a lot on his mind in the days leading up to the tragic boating accident. The previous week, the mission board had travelled up to Kenora to review the program of Homestake House for First Nations youth. Among the various matters of discussion, they'd come to the conclusion that the program was sound and doing good work, but it shouldn't be run by the Scott Mission. As they prepared to return to Toronto on Friday evening, the weather had turned stormy. Because of a local emergency, another couple had received priority seating, leaving Alex and Maureen to stay over for the next flight out.

Saturday, October 4, was Anne's birthday, but the family planned to celebrate after church on Sunday. In the morning, Alex drove Anne and a friend to church, then returned home to pick up Maureen so that they could attend services at Knox Spadina. The family then enjoyed Sunday lunch together. Afterwards, Alex dropped off Andrew at work, went home and had a phone conversation with his niece Jae, then left for Pickering.

Maureen remembered that it was "a glorious, sunny fall afternoon." Only later did the winds pick up and the sky cloud over. There were showers forecast for later in the evening. Alex drove out to the marina at Frenchman Bay, where he kept their small, 18-foot craft. Usually he went out with Maureen, but she already had other plans. Although conditions weren't ideal, with some strong wind gusts, Alex was now reasonably experienced and was wearing a life jacket. Much later, a police spokesperson described the water on the lake as "rough."[4]

When he hadn't returned by 8:30 p.m., Maureen called the police. An immediate search was started with three Metro police marine units called out and eventually a Canadian Forces helicopter. Durham Regional Police located the capsized boat at the foot of Harwood St. in Ajax.[5] At 11:40 that night, they found Alex's body in shallow water near the shoreline, some 400 metres east of his boat, and he was taken to the nearby Ajax and Pickering General Hospital. Anne was there with her Uncle David, who identified the remains, a task that he remembered as one of the most difficult moments in his life.

Later, Elaine and Margaret went to the Mission to tell their mother, but they'd come too late. Annie had already heard about his death on the radio. "She was very stoic," said Margaret, "but Alex was so precious to her. Because the doctor had predicted that he wouldn't live long, there was a special bond."

The question of whether Alex had died as a direct result of his disease was difficult to assess. Officially, the coroner listed drowning as the cause. In private, Elaine and her mother were told by their doctor that almost certainly Alex had experienced some form of stroke. As Elaine recalled, the doctor suggested, "He was already gone before he hit the water." In hindsight, Maureen recalled that the doctors had given him ten years and that he lived for six.

David Cross later recalled how leaving Maureen and Alex in Kenora on Friday night had left him uneasy, and when the phone rang on Sunday night, he was wary of bad news. He described Maureen's call as "devastating." As much as he knew that Alex didn't have long, this seemed to have happened all too soon for the Mission and his family.

A quiet funeral for family members was held on Wednesday, October 8, in the afternoon at Mt. Pleasant Cemetery. That evening, more than 1,000 mourners crowded into the sanctuary of Knox Presbyterian Church on Spadina to honour the memory of Alexander Morris Zeidman. Cross was astonished as he looked around the great circular hall. In addition to the many he knew who were passionate about the Mission, he saw an equal number of accomplished business people and professionals, some known through family connections, and even the unexpected presence of good friends. He'd never been so aware of how strongly the community felt about the Mission. That included the mayor of Toronto, Art Eggleton, and other leading politicians, who crowded the podium. On the steps leading up to the church doors were numerous transient men from the street, old acquaintances of Alex, some too shy to come inside.

Among them all, rich and poor, loyal donors, staff and grateful clients, there was a shared overwhelming grief that Maureen understood too well: "A lot of people wondered," she said, "why God would allow this." Dr. Skarsten echoed those words. "We are all in a state of shock. He certainly was the heart and soul of the mission."[6]

The senior minister, Rev. Don MacLeod, surrounded by the faculty of Knox College, gave this tribute to an esteemed friend and colleague: "The inner city was written on his heart. And that heart could be characterized by one word: love. Many of you are here tonight because you knew that love in your need."[7]

During the evening, David Zeidman was introduced as the interim director, and he promised to do his best to carry on the ministry. Thoughts of Alex were still very much on his mind when he told a reporter, "A tone of sadness pervades the place, but we believe he is safely in the hands of Christ and there is no reason for us to stop doing our work."[8] On the morning of October 17, the board met to mark the passing of Alex. After considering their options for a new executive director, they gave the position to David.

ALEX

By Elaine Z. Markovic

"Here comes the one who fed the poor,"
The angels whispered at the door.
They garbed him in his robe of white
And led him into glorious light.

His tongue was loosed from earth's restraints,
He joined the chorus of the saints.
In joy that's only heaven-known
The Lord embraced him at His throne.

October 1986

CHAPTER 21

An Unexpected Turn

After Alex's funeral, Elaine struggled to apply herself to the work of the Mission, unable to relieve the persisting ache of grief. From her place on the front lines of the Mission, she had watched in the previous two decades as Alex had quietly set the tone and pace of their ministry. Tactfully he'd manage the staff's personnel issues and eased clients through the daily programs. With his low-key approach, he maintained the traditional strengths of the Mission and allowed the capable men and women around him to develop their gifts, reinvigorate the familiar ministries and expand into new areas. His patience and dependability were so consistent that he'd become the rock at the centre of everyone's demanding schedules. Until he was gone, it was hard to appreciate how much he accomplished in a day.

The loss had exposed just how much everyone else had leaned on him. As family patriarch and director of the Mission, Alex didn't seem replaceable. Despite his medical diagnosis, Elaine had genuinely expected him to be spared—just as she'd expected Morris to enjoy old age. She wasn't alone. A close friend, one of the few to whom Alex revealed the grim nature of his disease, also had seemed incapable of talking with him about the possibility of being taken at any time.

At first, Elaine recalled the feelings of crisis she'd experienced after her father's death—that an indispensable spiritual force supporting the work was gone. Alex, though, had been ready by then, groomed with the full expectation that he'd take up his father's mantle. The current situation felt more like a crisis than losing Morris had. So many of the family's problems seemed larger, and in many ways the hidden challenges were greater. Elaine and her siblings' families had been struggling to cope with all the competing demands of family and ministry.

"I used to work 40 days straight at the Mission," said Mica, "weekends, too. And then change the weekends with Alex and David." This meant working every third weekend. "You don't have much time for your immediate family. But there was that mutual commitment, and every member of the family knew where our priorities lay. I never thought of it as a sacrifice. I accepted it as my duty."

Underneath the contented appearance of the various branches of the Zeidman family united in ministry, each couple was coping with the frictions of approaching middle age and having teenage children in crisis or transition. All those vulnerabilities, too, seemed even more exposed.

Elaine had been extraordinarily close to Alex. They had always been well matched in temperament and after years of working together, shared a profound commitment to their parents' values and to those who depended on the ministry. Shaken to the very roots of her faith, it would take a long time for Elaine to fully recover her spiritual balance. "When he was taken, it felt so unfair," she said. "And— it's hard to admit feeling this way—unwise of God."

Confounded by the loss, Elaine compared her instability to the Mission's most troubled clients trying to turn their lives around. "They're right when they say, 'You have to hit bottom before you can recover.'" For the first time in many years, she stopped going to church. On occasion, when she forced herself to attend services, she was overcome by grief and anger. None of those moments gave her much solace. "I got tired of crying," she said.

The crisis brought other aspects of her life into clearer focus. She began to see even the most familiar things in a new way. In time, that would lead her back to a new perspective on the meaning of faith. "I've learned so much about the faithfulness of God," she said. "I've seen Him being faithful even when I wasn't aware that He was there. I've come to realize that when I don't see Him, it's not that He's moved: it's my problem and a matter of perception."

She tried reaching out to family members whose feelings of loss were equally profound. "I was concerned about my children, my mother and [our] elderly aunt, Gertrude, who needed care. They all missed him in their own way, and I was trying to make sure that they were okay and ignored how I was doing." If her own feelings were buried, the larger problems emerging at the Mission were more than enough to demand her attention.

The issue of Mission leadership had taken an unexpected turn. Only a few months before, David had quietly submitted his resignation to the board and began preparing to leave the Mission. The board could not guarantee that he would be the next executive director, although they assured him that he was welcome to apply at the right time.

In the immediate crisis after Alex was gone, every member of the board was caught up in the urgency of the situation, including David. In order to keep the Mission functioning, they felt that a decision on the next director was needed almost immediately. As they talked over the questions of succession, a consensus emerged. Things being as they were, David should be offered the opportunity.

Elaine had always seen him as a capable administrator, a hands-on ministry partner who wasn't afraid to get his hands dirty or work hard to solve the logistical problems at the various Mission sites. David was also much more decisive, and that would be a contrast to Alex.

Anyone who took on that role would face tremendous issues. Every member of the staff was experiencing some measure of grief at losing a close friend. In the first few months, Elaine saw David, in the midst of his own grief, doing his best to hold things together while they all tried to get used to someone new being in charge.

David had worked closely with Alex in many areas of Mission management: finances, maintaining the growing number of Mission properties (Spadina, Caledon and Collingwood) and the development of a facility in Kenora for Native children. David himself appreciated how different he and Alex had become. He didn't have the same relationships with clients.

Years later, reflecting on the situation, David said, "We were entirely different. He was the pastoral clergyman. I was more the businessman: getting my job done and accounts balanced and conversing with business people." Of course, numerous business people had connections with the Mission as donors, supporters and members of the board. This is where David had become most comfortable.

Board member (and future chair) David Cross understood that the very nature of the job was overwhelming. "Working in a mission, there's always a crisis to deal with," said Cross, "and compelling reasons to keep working. There's even the guilty feeling that if you don't stay a little longer, someone will suffer." Cross realized that a mission leader had to learn when to get up and walk out of the office. Instead, he saw that David was working longer and longer hours.

David also sensed the rising tension as he became overworked. "Being young and tired, I made wrong decisions," he said much later; "I didn't have the guidance that would have helped."

After a year and a half, the board was aware that David was not able to sustain the role of director, and by their April 5, 1988, meeting when the decision was made, he'd been absent for a month.[1] The consequences of his departure were equally devastating for David's wife, Elizabeth—who decided to leave her position with the Scott at that time—and for their children, who had been involved with the Mission.

"I can't put into words the effect that it had on me and my family," said David. "The kids never spoke to me about it. They were upset for their father."

In addition to the difficult situation, David was now pressed to find work. Eventually, he went on to have a successful career in commercial real estate. A specialist in retail and small commercial properties, he later expanded into industrial and residential properties for corporate purchasers. "It's been tough," he reflected, and then, "I have enjoyed it."

Much later, Elaine reflected on David's tenure as director. "Because of the long-standing history of the Mission," she said, "and the role of my parents as founders, there was an unspoken assumption that the new executive director would be a Zeidman. Of course, our family did not have any entitlement to the leadership of the Mission. But after such a long period of family leadership, neither David nor the board could be faulted for that expectation. His purpose, as always, was to respond faithfully to the needs of the Mission."

David Cross agreed with her assessment. "The job was clearly overwhelming him, and he was struggling. It wasn't the lack of wanting to do a good job," said Cross, "or willingness to sacrifice."

Through all this, Elaine felt equally tested to her personal limits. "I don't believe that God had forgotten us," she said, "or was looking the other way." However, the Mission would begin moving in new directions. As Mica said, "None of us were prepared for those changes."

Elaine believed that the Zeidmans might still provide leadership, even if it wasn't from the position of executive director. Whatever changes might come, she would not lose sight of the Mission's spiritual character, the ingrained knowledge of the ministry's roots she'd learned first-hand from Morris and Annie and worked so hard with Alex to sustain. Mica described what others also saw: "Elaine was the thread that held the Mission together after Alex's death."

In the years to come, there would still be many blessings and challenges in store. A younger generation of Zeidmans was about to emerge. New leadership at the Mission would require Elaine to make even greater demands on her spiritual reserves, and in time, she'd rediscover how to depend on God's faithfulness in every situation.

LET US SEEK OUT
A QUIET PLACE (1986)

By Annie A. Zeidman

Let us seek out a quiet place, and sheltered there
Think only upon Thee, my Lord.
Yearn past the symbols of this holy time,
The lights, the carolling, the joyous chime,
And glimpse in one sharp ecstasy
Thy love's compassion, Thy majesty's humility.
The covering glory of Thy grace.
And then, and then, O dearest Lord,
Thy face.

CHAPTER 22

Praying Through

The transition to new leadership was much harder on Elaine than she could have foreseen and very taxing on Mica as he watched her struggle. "Things at the Mission were extremely difficult after Alex," said Mica. "Every new director who came wanted to shape the Mission in their image, to leave their own footprint. We had to go along with it up to a point."

The person who was most capable of helping Elaine cope with the changes was Maureen, but spending time at the Mission was too painful. She stopped coming. "I was struggling to find my way," Maureen said. Only occasionally during this period did they have time together.

"We were companions through life from our late teens. I think she was like a sister, a soulmate. I was one of the few people she could confide in," said Maureen, "but I wasn't by her side in the aftermath."

Executive oversight was given to Christian directors with a sincere personal faith: Garnet Martin (1987–89) and Margaret Cheung (1989–96). Their focus was on meeting administrative goals—maintaining the efficiency of public programs and providing financial stability—so the essential work of the Mission for needy families and transient men continued to function well. Pastoral oversight and spiritual programming, particularly for staff, became a secondary concern.

The executive directors were no longer engaged with the spiritual development of front-line workers. That was disorienting for many of the long-term staff. Mica watched Elaine trying to maintain continuity with the ministry that Alex had led. "She was at the front desk, on the firing line, having to convince the employees that things hadn't changed."

"I felt very much alone," said Elaine, and she frankly admitted to "disappointment with God. He wasn't doing things the way that I would like to have them done." She understood, as few could, that the Mission's unique vision of non-judgmental care is based on the development of spiritual discernment and a sensitivity that demanded continual pastoral support.

Pastoral care at the Mission had not been an added program; it was essential to the quality of care. Clients were used to social service agencies that assessed them on the basis of the resources they had available. Elaine saw her task as retaining the Mission's relationship with clients based on a biblical model of God's love for every individual. Her staff training continued to emphasize a genuine understanding of clients and giving without judgment (although there was an assessment process for handing out groceries and clothing). One of her trainees described it succinctly: "to give and not judge; to err on the side of giving." Another long-time staff worker, who had begun working under Morris, described Elaine's growing importance: "When the EDs no longer gave [us] encouragement in Christ, she always knew when the staff was going through a hard time."

Although she was uncomfortable in front of crowds, Elaine began leading the weekly staff meetings that served as a chapel for biblical teaching and prayer. She'd bring inspiring devotions, going to great lengths to become an accomplished storyteller for her messages. Keeping up morale was essential. If she sensed the ministry employees were unhappy or feeling half-hearted in the work, she'd organize a day of encouragement, a talent show or Watermelon Day to lift their spirits.

Her long-time friend Marilyn Nelson witnessed Elaine's struggles. "Elaine was very private. She was one who never cried over spilled milk—just go on. When I got her prayer requests, I knew she was in trouble. She was distressed when people in charge were not leading them as they needed," said Marilyn. "She knew God was not going to let it go."

Marilyn and Elaine began to actively share together in prayer. "We prayed for each other, sometimes on the phone, mastering the power of prayer," said Marilyn. "We both had mothers who prayed for us and for our children. We realized that we had to take up that mantle.

"Through her personal troubles she grew stronger and grew in her prayer life," said Marilyn. "She grew because of the difficulties in her life. Alex wasn't allowed to carry on the legacy. Elaine was chosen. She suffered a lot, and through all of that came spiritual growth." Although she felt isolated, Elaine wasn't alone. Mica was faithfully working at the Mission; Annie was still nearby, and Elaine's younger daughter, Sera, had also joined the staff.

Sera, like all of the grandchildren, had been exposed to the Mission from her earliest years and became very involved. There was some hesitation from the second generation—Morris and Annie's children—to invite their children to make the Mission a full-time career. It wasn't Elaine but Sera's Uncle David who opened up a place for her on staff.

Alex had died in the year she graduated from high school. Sera, who had singing and drama gifts in the arts comparable to her Aunt Margaret's, felt a compelling sense of call to the work. The grief and weariness she saw in the family and staff didn't discourage her; she wanted to join them as they pressed on. David asked Sera to assist in the mailroom and offered her a permanent job. She remains grateful for that opportunity.

In time, Sera could see the contrast between the current and previous styles of leadership. "There were executive directors who weren't relational and didn't like a culture of family," she said, "so we clashed."

Why did Elaine stay? "It was duty," Sera said. "Her personality was that if you see a need you try to meet it. It was ingrained in her to watch over the ministry until it became healthy again. If we don't do this, who will?"

Addressing that feeling of being "alone" became a necessity for Elaine. At one point, she called Diane Marshall, who was still working at the Mission, to assist her after experiencing a very powerful dream. "We met and talked about it," said Diane. Then they approached Rev. Fred Crook, the rector of Little Trinity Anglican Church, where both were members. "The three of us prayed for God's healing of things in the Mission," said Diane, "including a communion service and anointing for Elaine."

Rev. Fred Crook became a familiar figure at the Mission, providing ministry to Elaine. "He was a priest to her and a confidant," said Sera. Diane was pleased to see him lending support.

"It was an indicator of her spiritual depth and wisdom," said Diane. "She needed people outside the Mission to help her respond. She stayed a steady rock and never lost her beautiful qualities—such a faithful person and so gracious. She never got flustered in her inner spiritual life, even when things were very distressing."

Apart from the Mission, there were family problems that Elaine couldn't ignore. One of the most troubling was the impact of Alex's death on his son, Andrew. There had been some of the normal tensions that many pastors' children experience with their parents. After the accident Maureen could see that Andrew was devastated. He reacted by trying to put more distance between himself and the family.

"I felt as if I had lost both of them," Maureen said.

After a couple years of futility, Andrew had a spiritual awakening. "I recommitted my life to the Lord," he said. The renewal brought a new sense of purpose. He took a year off to spend in serious personal reflection in Tucson, Arizona. Andrew came to love the area and considered it a second home. On his return, he felt a very powerful calling to the ministry of the Scott.

"Initially, when I was younger, I didn't see myself working at the Mission," said Andrew, reflecting on his surprise to find such great satisfaction. "I felt like I was coming home." Andrew shares more of his story in a later chapter ("The Next Generation").

Looking back at the years that followed the loss of Alex, Elaine and Maureen often felt that the events and experiences could not have been harder. Added to this, their elderly mentors in ministry were in decline and passing away. It took time for them to grasp that another generation was rising up to take on new roles in the story of the Mission.

FROM ANNIE'S DESK:

It is God's will that I should cast
My care on Him each day:
He also asks me not to cast
My confidence away.
But, oh, how stupidly I act
When taken unaware;
I cast away my confidence
And carry all my care! (Author unknown)

Annie never forgot where she was from or lost faith in where she was going. Her mother's family—the Aitkens, who generations before had been jewelers and clock-makers in Dumfries, Scotland—have a crest that bears the motto *In Crucis Salus Est*—In the Cross Is Salvation. The crest and motto are imprinted inside the cover of her popular book of poems, "The Love and The Gift," published (and expanded in later editions) by the Scott Mission.

Through the difficult years following Alex's death, Annie remained devoted to encouraging her children and grandchildren. Instead of moving into a retirement home, she occupied a small apartment on the second floor at 502 Spadina. She was not only the Zeidman family matriarch; Annie remained an inspiration to the extended Mission family.

In addition to receiving numerous visitors, Annie answered many of the ministry's letters, wrote out copy for "The Good Samaritan Corner," stayed in touch with donors and prayed for the needs around her. Family often came to visit, especially her grandchildren. They still gratefully remember her wisdom and candour while they were puzzling through the challenges of life and faith. A number of local publications featured her remarkable story and lifelong connection with the Scott.

Alex had kept a close watch on his mother, and after he was gone, Elaine saw her at least three times a day, with a visit first thing in the morning. "She was wise, and I miss that," Elaine reflected later. "She would give an opinion about something, and I might not always have agreed, but I could always see that what she said was valid. She was coming at the advice with tremendous experience. And she prayed for us all and those at the Mission."

Her care for people remained a model for Elaine. "Sometimes we would have a client who knew better days, so she would set something aside for them," said Elaine. "I know that she took care of people in a way that made them feel comfortable."

That included the way that Annie chose to use her musical gifts at the piano. "She loved to play," said Elaine; "she was a musician at heart." As a young woman, Annie's family couldn't afford to let her take the conservatory's final vocal exams, so she became a piano teacher. For decades, she played the piano during the Portuguese church service at the Mission. She didn't understand a word of the language but could play all the music. "That was church for her," Elaine said. "She couldn't get to the services at Knox."

Elaine was reminded of another quality that she saw in Annie: an unflinching dignity. "I think it was a spiritual gift. She knew difficulty," said Elaine. "She would have been at home with anyone. Annie was a lady in bearing and manners. But she would not have made anybody uncomfortable." The comments are even more poignant because others often applied that description to Elaine— a talent for treating everyone, whatever their background, with such respect.

On the other hand, Elaine recalled with laughter Annie's compulsive thrift: "She never bought anything that wasn't on sale." The late Gordon Sinclair, a Toronto media personality for many decades (and a proud Scot unashamed of his financial success), once commented, "Morris Zeidman is a Jew married to a Scot, and you can't lose with that combination." Elaine didn't think of that as a compliment.

Annie's unflagging work ethic also won Elaine's admiration. She knew from her earliest recollections that her mother's workday had always started in the morning, as soon as she sat down on the streetcar to the Mission. That's when she'd begin writing. Each December, Morris urged her to have a poem ready for the calendar that was mailed out by Christmas, usually with a seasonal theme.

"I remember asking her if she was thinking about a poem for the calendar," Elaine said, recalling one of their last conversations. "I've got one in my mind," Annie had said, "'but I'm still working on it.'" As Elaine noted, "She was very alert up to the end."

Whether it was her life habits, opinions or poetry, all were thoroughly rooted in Annie's studious love of the Bible, which only increased with the years. "She pored over the Scriptures," said Elaine. "She'd be sitting at her table with her Bible open." Annie enjoyed Psalm 103:

Bless the Lord, O my soul: and all that is within me, bless his holy name (Psalm 103:1)

and Psalm 121:

I will lift up mine eyes unto the hills, from whence cometh my help. My help cometh from the LORD, which made heaven and earth (Psalm 121:1–2).

That wasn't all that she read, of course. Annie's wide-ranging curiosity allowed her to enjoy all sorts of reading material, especially a good mystery, but she never could stand watching TV. As Elaine said, "She just wasn't all that interested."

One major difference between them was that Elaine, who had experienced so much illness, had watched her mother persevere through the years with such persistent good health.

"She'd only been in the hospital," Elaine said, "for the birth of her four children. Once she broke her thumb up at camp and didn't do anything for it."

Annie was almost 90 when her hip broke. Elaine found her the next morning on the floor. "I knew she was in rough shape. She just said, 'O Laine,' and after that she became incoherent. She had no recollection afterwards about what had happened."

Her rehabilitation took place in a separate facility over Christmas, where the family gathered around her and brought a trifle. At the time, she did something that Elaine found quite profound. Annie went around the room, asking every person if she had ever hurt them and asked for their forgiveness. When she recovered, Annie still wanted to live on her own—"to keep up her writing and make hot chocolate in the evening," said Elaine. The break in her second hip brought a doctor's warning: most patients die from the complications. Annie had it replaced and carried on.

Then her eyesight began to fail. Annie's cataract surgery in February 1992 was unsuccessful. "This was devastating for us and her.

Without being able to read, it became difficult." Annie's 97th birthday was March 8. "We had a wonderful birthday party," said Elaine, "and I don't know how she blew out the candles." Shortly afterwards, her health began to decline severely, and she couldn't take care of herself.

Annie was placed in the Toronto General Hospital, and by March 31 she was declining. Before many of the family gathered at her bedside, Sera was there alone and saw Annie turn her head toward the window. "As if someone had called her," said Sera, "although the drapes were closed." Sera spoke to her, saying, "Nanny," but her grandmother didn't turn back.

Rev. Dr. Stephen Farris, a member of the mission board and professor at Knox College (son of the late Rev. Dr. Alan Farris), joined the family. He'd been Annie's frequent visitor along with Rev. Don McLeod from Knox Church, who happened to be away. Elaine recalled that Dr. Farris opened his Bible and began reading from the opening verses of Romans 8. "She took her last breath between verses 23 and 24," said Elaine. "And not only the creation, but we ourselves, who have the first fruits of the Spirit, groan inwardly as we wait for adoption as sons, the redemption of our bodies. For in this hope we were saved" (Romans 8:23–24 RSV).

Rev. Dr. Farris and Rev. McLeod conducted the funeral service. "Annie was very meticulous," Elaine said. "She wrote out how she wanted her funeral—at the Mission." Annie's instructions came with a final admonition to them all: "I don't want you to grieve. I will just be on the other side waiting for you." One of her last requests was later honoured in a special version of "The Good Samaritan Corner."

Despite her mother's words, Elaine grieved all through the service, even as she was playing at the piano. "I can hardly remember it," she said. "It was the end of an era for us. The good thing was that we just had to follow her instructions, and I used a hymnbook that Alex had used." On April 2, 1992, Annie was buried next to Morris in Mt. Pleasant cemetery near Alex. The *Toronto Star* ran a modest obituary notice that began as follows:

> Annie Zeidman pawned her engagement ring to help her husband start Toronto's Scott Mission in 1941.
> She continued doing volunteer work for the mission until just before she died Tuesday in Toronto General Hospital...

Mrs. Zeidman wrote the poem for the mission's Christmas calendar each year as well as the Good Samaritan Corner once a week from September to June.

She had written the corner…for more than 50 years.[1]

And underneath the notice for Annie Aitken Zeidman, "Co-founder Scott Mission," was the Aitken family motto: *In Crucis Salus Est.*[2]

THE GOOD SAMARITAN CORNER
May 16, 1992

Most of our readers will know by now that Annie Zeidman went to be with her Lord on March 31st. Among her wishes was to have the following hymn printed to her friends after she died as a farewell message and comfort for us.

God be with you till we meet again,
By His counsels guide, uphold you,
With His sheep securely fold you;
God be with you till we meet again.

God be with you till we meet again,
'Neath His wings securely hide you,
Daily manna still provide you:
God be with you till we meet again.

God be with you till we meet again,
When life's perils thick confound you,
Put His loving arms around you:
God be with you till we meet again.

God be with you till we meet again,
Keep love's banner floating o'er you,
Smite death's threatening wave before you:
God be with you till we meet again.

Till we meet, till we meet at Jesus' feet.
Till we meet, God be with you till we meet again.

Jeremiah E. Rankin

ELAINE'S CONTRIBUTIONS TO "THE GOOD SAMARITAN CORNER"

After Annie passed away, Elaine often prepared the text for "The Good Samaritan Corner," although that title was eventually no longer used. These examples were printed in the *Toronto Star* over an eight-year period from 1994 to 2002. Like Alex, Elaine was an astute observer of human nature, who gave us insights with a light touch, gracious humour and genuine concern for the people we meet in her stories.

JUNE 25, 1994

On the Jewish feast of "Shavuoth" or Pentecost, one hundred years ago in the Polish city of Czestochowa, when Ziskind Zeidman returned from synagogue, he found he had a new son. The child was named Morris. This unremarkable baby had a remarkable God whose hand was upon him from the beginning. Seventeen years later, in the providence of God this Morris Zeidman arrived in Toronto, alone. Still later, in the providence of God, Morris Zeidman accepted Christ as his Messiah through the ministry of the forerunner of the Scott Mission. He furthered his education and by 1941 was director of the Scott Mission. This month is the 100th anniversary of Morris Zeidman's birth. Unremarkable babies are still being born and are becoming men and women who come to the Scott Mission. God still places His hand on them and uses each one of us to help them become members in the Kingdom of Heaven. Thank God for each new little life, and thank God for the life of Morris Zeidman.

MAY 14, 1994

Sometimes in the midst of the poverty and tears, we at the Scott Mission are blessed with unexpected humour and laughter. It was so when someone we thought was soundly "sleeping it off" suddenly came to life and asked a most piercing question, which sparked immediate participation from an up-until-then unresponsive group. We laughed. Then there is the fellow who visits us in the afternoon asking if his electric golf-cart is in yet. He laughs and so do we. A certain grumpy individual asks for toothpaste, but we notice she hasn't a tooth in her head. We all laugh, she in particular. Another asks for a hairnet and laughs until he wheezes. He is completely bald. Thank God for those who share their good humour with us. Thank God for laughter.

SEPTEMBER 17, 1994

The old song "What a Difference a Day Makes" came to mind one evening this week. Our day started with a young mother collapsing to the floor while she waited for groceries. She had not eaten for three days. Then Bill fainted as he was choosing some clothing in our men's department. An ambulance took him to hospital while we notified his doctor. Next, we received a call from the father of one of our guests asking us to forward her mail because she had recently taken her life. As we tried to deal with the emotion of that call, the dining room was filling with hungry homeless men and women. Ron was at one of the tables, and upon our enquiry for his brother, Ron mumbled to us that he had died just hours ago. He could not speak further, got up and ran down the street. As families were being interviewed for a multitude of requests, the tots in our nursery school, chirping like so many little sparrows, trouped out the front door for a walk. We offer up the day and each soul to God.

JANUARY 28, 1995

Incidents occur at the Scott Mission which delight and encourage us. We prefer not to see them as coincidence, but rather providential. For instance, last week a children's group was cooking upstairs. A donor arrived with a carton of bagged treats, exactly enough for the 25 youngsters! We remembered the noon hour we had run out of desserts for the dining room with several tables still to serve. While we were fretting about what to do, a bakery brought in the exact dessert we had been serving to the others, and the exact number required! Thanks be to God.

MARCH 18, 1995

Susanne comes to the Scott Mission Camp each summer. Her favourite times are at campfire and after lunch when there is singing. It did not take us long to notice that Susanne has a lovely voice. To encourage her, we suggested she join her local church choir. How proud her parents must be to know that Susanne has been chosen to sing a solo in the Easter pageant! She practices diligently, but her parents do not hear her. They are both deaf. However, the delight of their daughter as she sings is mirrored in their faces, and so, her joy becomes theirs.

"Yea, we know that Thou rejoices o'er each work of Thine; Thou didst ears and hands and voices for Thy praise combine" F. Pott.

NOVEMBER 21, 1998

What kind of gift moves us to tears? An expensive one? A romantic one? Poor Angela was moved to tears today by our gift of diapers. "You will never know what this means to me," she said, as tears slipped down her face. How tender is the comfort of the Scriptures to our fragile ones. "He tends his flock like a shepherd…and carries them close to his heart; he gently leads those that have young" (Isaiah 40:11 NIV).

JANUARY 5, 2002

T. was a very active child, the one who jumped on the desks in our offices when he came to the after-school clubs. His parents had difficulty choosing to pay rent or to eat. And that is where the Scott Mission helped, providing food and even clothing to wear to the father's funeral after his untimely death. But now this grown-up boy is bringing his New Year's donation to the place that, in his words, "kept us alive." For a New Year, and the One who makes all things new, thanks be to God.

FROM ELAINE'S CORRESPONDENCE

Elaine sent a note to encourage the well-known writer and media personality June Callwood in mid-1992 and got this reply that follows. No copy of the original was attached, only a rough handwritten draft, which begins,

Dear Ms. Callwood,

In considering all the benefit my city and my country has received from you and the encouragement you have been to me, personally, I felt I must write a note of support to you.

The single-page response is dated August 18, 1992, under the letterhead "June Callwood."

PRAYING THROUGH

Dear Elaine Markovic:

That's a wonderful and wonderfully kind
letter you wrote me and I'm hanging on
to it forever. In my home-made theology,
there is divinity in acts of comfort
between people. I've been hurting
sorely but when all of this mess at
Nellie's is well behind me, what I'll
remember best is the good stuff, like
your letter. It will be a bulwark
against the blues...
I keep reminding myself "This, too,
shall pass." What solace that thought
brings.
Gratefully,
[signature: June Callwood]

HE CARRIED HIS OWN CROSS

By Elaine Z. Markovic

He carried His own cross,
That ugly load of wrongs,
The secret you have sheltered
all these years,
A shame unmelted by your
tears.
He knew,
And carried it that dreadful day
All
Away.

CHAPTER 23

The Gracious Hand of the Lord

It took some practice, but Sera and Lois began to recognize when their mother had written a new song. Elaine would be playing the piano in the living room of their parents' Etobicoke home, and they'd notice an unfamiliar melody. As soon as someone asked, "Is that something new?" she'd say, "Do you want to hear the words?"

For the longest time, Annie was the family poet, and she had even composed a book of children's original Bible songs (with Margaret's piano accompaniments). In the years after Annie passed away, just as Elaine had taken up her mother's mantle of prayer, she began writing songs of praise and worship. Her lyrics revealed a passionate, mature faith full of heartfelt devotion:

> The gracious hand of the Lord is upon me,
> Merciful and true all His ways,
> Righteousness and peace are from Him,
> Kindness and grace reign from above.
> Though I walk through the valley of shadows
> Even there His presence is with me,
> I am not afraid for He's promised,
> Never to forsake His child.

Leading in worship with the Mission's lively praise and worship team—guitars, drums, violin and many voices—moved Elaine out of the awkwardness that she felt in front of crowds. The songs spoke of the authentic devotion that she personified to those around her:

Like a rushing, mighty wind, or the whisper of a breeze
As a flame of holy fire, Holy Spirit, You come.
On the wings of a dove in the word from Your heart,
Holy Spirit, You come down to my soul.
We were not left as orphans, the Counsellor has come.
Moving within the hearts of those who love Him,
Even the Spirit of Truth.
("Holy Spirit," Words and Music by Elaine Markovic)

All of this helped her to cope with executive leaders who rarely appreciated her role of providing spiritual and emotional counsel for the staff. The concerns that David Cross had expressed to Alex years before—that family members in an organization were likely to leave or be replaced after a transition to non-family leadership—were all too real in Elaine's experience.

Recalling those years, Mica recoiled visibly at some of the memories. "I tried to help her as much as I could," he said. "Psychologically, it was very difficult for her to deal with, and for me, too." Sera recalled that Elaine's advice was so frequently sought out that it became a source of inevitable resentment. Every family member was affected, and at some point in the ensuing years, each one felt compelled to ask themselves, "What are you doing here?"

None of this diminished the growing love and affection that Elaine received from the staff and donors. The family was encouraged to see her cultivating new creative outlets. "She blossomed in her spiritual gifts and leadership when some of the directors who came and went 'didn't get it,'" said Maureen, Alex's widow. "Elaine had the endurance through the ups and downs of different administrations."

Maureen remarried in 1989 to Bob Topp, a congenial widower with grown children, who supported her continuing involvement in ministry. She eventually returned to the Mission, briefly working under Graham Barnes, and then served as a member of the board. She and Elaine grew closer again, taking some vacations together.

The power of Elaine's prayer life was a noticeable inspiration to those around her. "As you mature spiritually, prayer matures you," said Marilyn Nelson, her long-time friend and prayer partner. They put a special focus on each other's extended families. This was crucial for Elaine, said Marilyn. "It was important that her children have a close walk with the Lord."

During the year that Annie passed away, Sera renewed ties with a Greek Orthodox Christian she'd gotten to know while travelling in Greece several years before. Sera had spent three months on the island of Paxos, where she met Thanasis Rousalis. Later, getting to know each other again, Sera and Thanasis became certain of God's blessing on the relationship, and they were married in 1994.

Thanasis, with his naturally warm, engaging personality, developed a close bond with his mother-in-law. "Elaine welcomed him into the family like a son," said Marilyn Nelson. He became a source of joy and encouragement during the difficult times of her illness and gave practical assistance, often driving her to medical appointments. He held a number of positions after his move to Canada, both in and out of the Mission. Currently, Thanasis directs the food services department at the Scott.

Added to her delight in finding a fellow bird-watcher (Elaine and Thanasis liked doing morning devotions and birding afterwards), there was the pleasure of taking family vacations in Greece. Elaine's diary records wonderful times spent there by the sea—where she described colours that "range from indigo to royal blue to turquoise blue to turquoise green to pale green"—and vacation photos show her entirely relaxed.

Around this time, Elaine was encouraged when her eldest daughter, Lois, applied for a position at the Scott and came on staff. Lois had trained in social work at Ryerson University and worked extensively in other settings. Despite growing up in the Mission, Lois hadn't envisioned working there. The decision emerged from a lengthy personal spiritual journey that brought her back temporarily as a volunteer.

"My grandmother was still alive, and she was a positive connection with the Mission," said Lois. A restored feeling of professional satisfaction and the opportunity to develop a spiritual connection with people have made Lois a long-term employee, and she's now a department head. (Her story is told with greater detail in chapter 25.)

Like Morris before her, Elaine was open to a fresh personal revival in the Holy Spirit. Her daughters had become members at the Toronto

Airport Christian Fellowship (now called Catch the Fire). They invited Elaine to join them in services, where she experienced some profound and beautiful worship experiences. Elaine didn't give up her Anglican Church membership, but the Holy Spirit was never far from her thoughts. As she said, "Personalities certainly affect any ministry but the person of the Holy Spirit is primary—if He's running the Mission, we'll keep going."

Lois and Sera saw and heard their mother's inner struggles over the Mission's increasingly secular direction. The years of coping with insensitive administrators were taking a toll, and Elaine frequently wondered if she ought to leave—questioning if her status had been reduced to "a thorn in the side" of the director and the board—yet was equally resolute that someone must sustain the Mission's spiritual character.

As her challenges continued, Elaine's daughters saw their mother grow into a new mindset of spiritual authority. "She did evolve and come into her identity as an individual child of God—a new place of intimacy and confidence in that relationship," said Lois, and Sera added, "She would minister to people confidently, speaking words of truth." They could hear that certainty in her prayers, which became expectant and insistent that God would assert His sovereignty in a place that had been dedicated to Him.

A lingering question remained. Why didn't she apply for the position of executive director? In the periods between executive appointments, she successfully served as interim director and would do so a few times in tandem with Peter Duraisami, whom she had trained as a staff member in men's ministry/front office (as it was known at that time).

Her lack of self-confidence was occasionally cited, and her daughters agreed that she was self-conscious that she'd never earned a university degree. According to David Cross, who served during this period as chairman of the board and held Elaine in the highest esteem, the board was obligated to find leaders with strong managerial skills who could balance the conflicting demands of programming and budgets. Although he recognized her as "the Mission's voice of faith," candidates for director were measured by their potential to oversee both the spiritual leadership of the Mission and the complex details of maintaining services and finances.

Mica gave a more nuanced insight. "She never had the ambition to be the head of the Mission. She didn't want that. Elaine achieved a lot in her life and at the Mission through faith, trying to implement the teaching of Christ in her everyday life as much as humanly possible. This was her guide. A lot of people didn't know about that. We all make mistakes, but she tried more than anybody I knew. She was very humble."

Elaine's role in the life of the Mission was thoroughly evident to those around her. "She was the spiritual head of this place," said Maureen, who watched her carry forward the Mission's spiritual legacy. Elaine would direct the staff to set aside days of prayer, of fasting and also of celebration, leading by example and surrendering herself to God as she'd seen her parents do so many times before. As Maureen said, "Elaine embodied the faithfulness that Alex spoke about."

In 1999, Graham Barnes became the executive director, and Elaine found in him the qualities of the "wise shepherd" that had been missing in Mission leadership. David Cross also admitted that the Mission had been perilously close to becoming "an average charity instead of a Christian witness." Barnes began to heal the divisions between long-time staff who were focused on faithful ministry and those who were much more private in their faith.

"He got everyone back on track," said Cross, "and did a wonderful job of turning it back around into a Christian mission." A sign of the renewed ministry, according to Cross, came in a series of extraordinary blessings.

A serious fire affected the production at a McCain's plant in eastern Ontario, and the company offered to donate truckloads of frozen vegetables. Mica was put in charge and rented a refrigerated warehouse. He contacted missions around Ontario, inviting them to take what they wanted. Afterwards, the Mission still had a year's supply of frozen vegetables.

A fur company on Spadina was closing down and had to dispose of old fur coats left in storage. Through the Meals on Wheels ministry, the Mission gave out the mink coats and stoles to elderly women who could truly appreciate the gift.

While going through his late father-in-law's library, a man randomly pulled down a book from a shelf. Inside was a will, leaving all his assets to the Scott Mission, an estate worth well over a million dollars. The handwritten will had been signed at a time when such wills didn't require a witness. "This honest man was the source of blessing to many," said Cross. All these events were an inspiration to the staff.

Unfortunately, Barnes's ministry was shortened by the cancer that ended his life in November 2001, barely three years into his appointment. The pews of Yorkminster Park Baptist Church in Toronto were packed as the congregation and the Mission mourned their loss. Afterwards, Elaine and Peter Duraisami did an outstanding job in holding things together until a new executive leader took over, but once again, the Mission struggled to move forward. That director lasted 10 months, and it wasn't until 2003 that the board decided on a replacement, the late David Smith, who held the position until 2010.

In an interview in 2009, while he was still executive director, Smith remembered his first impressions of Elaine as "kind, understanding and welcoming." Recalling her spiritual impact, he remembered how Elaine led in worship: "She was on fire for the Lord, a combination of old and new music, humour and gravity. There was that presence of the Lord through her. I experienced true worship," he said.

"When I think of Elaine, I always think of what she left with the Mission: a longing to be with the Lord, a longing to serve, to be cheerful and welcoming and warm. That spiritual hunger is something that she bequeathed—to reach people as God sent them and to impact them meaningfully."

He also recognized the tensions between the spiritual and economic priorities that were bound up with the position he held and that he had not always succeeded in making the right choices. "It's hard to discover we weren't all that people expected," he said. "It doesn't begin with others but me."

When he entered her office, knowing that her door was always open to everyone, he would privately think, "Who am I to head this place?"

"That mantle has been placed on the members of the family who work here," said Smith. "It's not always fun. There's prejudice and judgment on them, but they keep going on and they are determined that the evangelical roots and ethos of the Mission are preserved."

In the years after Annie's death, Elaine tried to give more attention to her elderly Aunt Gertrude. Originally named Gitel, she'd come from Poland while Morris was in seminary but arrived in Toronto during his severe illness. She was only 14 at the time. The college's New Testament professor, William Manson, took her in, and she became part of his family. The Rev. Dr. Manson was widely admired as an outstanding scholar, author and teacher of his era and eventually received an appointment on the faculty of Edinburgh University. By this time, Gitel had developed such an affectionate relationship with the family that they officially adopted her and she became Gertrude Manson, happily moving with them to Scotland.

Morris had sponsored his sister to Canada to fulfill her desire to become a nurse. The Mansons helped her achieve that ambition. Gertrude spent most of her life in Scotland and became a colourful figure for her Canadian relatives. They remembered her as dignified, quite short, though always wearing very high heels, and an excellent cook. A story circulated in the family that while she was in nursing school, Gertrude fell in love with a doctor. Her adoptive parents ended the romance, and she never married. For decades, Annie would send the grandchildren—when they reached 16—to visit Gertrude and experience a bit of Scottish culture.

In her senior years, Gertrude's loss of vision became a serious problem. Alex arranged her return to Toronto in the 1980s so that the family could help her manage. Sometime later, Elaine and Maureen went back with her to visit Scotland.

After Alex was gone, Elaine regretted that she didn't see her aunt more often and encouraged the family to visit. Gertrude enjoyed a good love story and became fond of Sera's husband, Thanasis. Unable to recall his name, she resorted to calling him "the Spaniard," "the Greek," "Cincinnati," until he finally said, "Just call me Sam." She chuckled at that.

Gertrude quietly passed away in a Toronto retirement residence on September 5, 1999.[1] Like her brother, she'd been a faithful Hebrew Christian and never forgot her heritage. In the drawer of her night table, the family found the Hebrew prayer book she'd received as a child.

Housecleaning isn't usually a defining moment in a ministry. The Scott Mission staff happened to be cleaning out some old cupboards when someone found a set of Hebrew Bibles. Andrew, Alex's son, had long been fascinated by the Mission's history. He was surprised to see what looked like evidence of a Hebrew-speaking congregation. After investigating in the Mission archives, questioning the family and seeking out other resources, he learned about the Mission's Jewish origins. He also discovered that Morris had been quietly leading a Hebrew Christian congregation until he passed away in 1964.

The events reminded Andrew of the biblical story of King Josiah, whose servants were cleaning out the temple when they discovered the Torah scroll. "His people found the book of the Law and a revival started," said Andrew. "We were just cleaning up—it was uncovering the roots."

"Several years ago, I started to feel called back to my Jewish roots," said Andrew, "my own roots as well as the Mission's. Growing up, I remember having a Jewish identity through my name, and we would hear stories about my grandfather." Just as Morris had led the annual Passover at the Mission, Alex had celebrated the traditional festival meal—the *Seder*—with the extended family every year.

Andrew's memories of those times led to a new awareness of his heritage and identity. He began attending City of David, a Messianic Jewish synagogue, and sharing Messianic music with the family and staff. During the same period, Andrew felt called to attend Tyndale Seminary, where he completed a master of theology degree.

Andrew also encouraged Elaine to participate in Messianic celebrations of the feasts and festivals. She'd never lost her sense of Jewish identity—and was in close contact with their extended Israeli family. Now there was a new avenue to express herself, like this piece, marked with the notation "Flowing Middle Eastern feel."

Unto us a child is born, unto us a son is given
And His Name shall be called
Wonderful, Counselor, the Mighty God...
Everlasting Father, Sar Shalom, the Prince of Peace.
Hallelujah, hallelujah, Sar Shalom, the Prince of Peace.

As a result of uncovering the history of the Mission, another development took place, with Elaine's support. On the afternoon of November 9, 2008, she welcomed a large crowd of board members, staff, donors and supporters to the chapel of the Scott Mission. They were celebrating a remarkable milestone: it was a century since the ministry of the Christian synagogue had begun in Toronto under Rev. Sabati "Ben" Rohold.

Yet there was something unspoken that day. While she extolled the ministry of the Christian synagogue in reaching her father with the gospel, Elaine didn't mention that for over half a century, since 1953—a remarkable 55 years—she had dedicated her life to the work. With selfless devotion through six decades she'd upheld her parents' vision, grounded in the integrity and faithfulness taught them by Rev. Rohold. That was also ample reason to celebrate.

CLAY

By Elaine Z. Markovic

There was clay near the shore.
She put some in a small pail
And carried it to the house.
Next time I saw the clay
It was a graceful bowl,
Shaped, glazed, fired, used
To hold green grapes and nectarines.

CHAPTER 24

Elaine's People

In recalling a conversation with Annie about the legacy of those who were gone, Elaine had been reminded of the well-intentioned impulse to recall only the good things a person has done. "They were just people," Elaine said. "They're not the ones to emulate. If we see God in there, that's what we're to emulate."

Those who were touched by Elaine's life saw "God in there." Melida, a Scott Mission staff member, described a common experience with Elaine: "I felt like I was the disciple she loved. And then, it was as if my eyes were opened and I saw that this is how she was with everybody." Everyone felt that they had a special relationship with Elaine, and they did. When the Mission staff and her colleagues speak of her, she's still inspiring them.

Here are some of the colleagues whose lives she changed.

MARIA'S STORY

Maria Oliveria was born in Portugal and arrived in Canada at age 10 with her mother and baby sister. The family eventually grew to 10 children, and her mother started coming to the Mission to get clothing that she would cut down to fit the young ones. In 1963, Maria was only 14 and decided to help out her family by finding a summer job. Together with her mother, she went to the Mission and spoke to Morris Zeidman.

"He was a very loving man," Maria said, "and knew what hardships were and how hard it was for my mom." Her mother was concerned about her daughter's safety around so many homeless men. Morris promised, "Don't worry. I will look after her." (She choked up.) "He did look after me as if I were his own child. I quit school that year and asked for a steady job so that I could help out at home."

Maria began doing custodial work in the dining room while most of the Zeidman family members were working at the Mission. All of them were supportive at a time when she was very shy and worried about making mistakes.

"We used to have morning devotions, and Alex would encourage me to read. He'd say, 'I'll ask you to read this passage for next week.' Eventually he asked me to lead in prayer. He was also a wonderful man."

As the family and its financial burdens grew, Maria's father turned to alcohol, and the conflicts between her parents became intolerable. Maria found that she had an extended family at the Mission. If she had to leave home, Elaine and Mica took her in until the uproar passed.

"I found love, care and acceptance. It didn't matter to them that I came from a family that was poor. What mattered was my well-being and the well-being of my family. The turmoil at home went on and on. Finally, I got engaged at 18. The young man was in Portugal, in the army. We met when I was 16 and on vacation with my grandparents. We corresponded until we got married. I was 19 when I got married in Portugal.

"Elaine and the family here at the Mission gave me a shower. Those were the only wedding gifts that I got. While I was waiting, Elaine had Eaton's deliver a toaster. That was so precious to me.

"I was young, and my mom had taught me as much as she could. One of the people I looked to was Elaine, to imitate her loving, gentle ways and to be the lady that she was. Elaine was very special to me. She always knew how to encourage us.

"I worked with another lady in the office. Both of us would comment on how Elaine was a mentor and how we copied her. She was the one who inspired us. That's how I chose the type of company that I wanted to keep, the type of clothes that I wore. Elaine taught us how to be ladies right to the very end. She was the one we all admired. She taught us not to be ashamed in front of anyone for who we are.

"After my first child, I went through depression, and Elaine called me every day to make me laugh. Later, my son was very sick and had to be admitted to the hospital. Elaine sent a teddy bear and some flowers in an ice cream bowl. He still talks about it.

"When I went for my Canadian citizenship papers, Elaine went with me, and the woman doing the interview asked Elaine if she was my mother. From that day forward, Elaine and I were mother and daughter. I used to call her Mom, and she would call me Daughter.

"As she grew in the Lord, we all grew. She loved the Lord in such a way that it was always a joy to be with her and talk about the Lord. She spoke about what she read in the Bible, so that you just got it. She always knew when the staff was going through a hard time and she'd organize a celebration, crafts displays, or we'd have lunches together."

"Elaine held things together. She let us know that the work that we were doing was for God and not for anyone else. Then we would have the courage to keep on doing what we needed to do.

"She encouraged me at every turn; I knew that I could talk with her and she would pray with me. We always just prayed about it. She did that when I was going through hard times when my daughter was born."

Maria no longer works at the Mission, but she feels assured that the legacy of the Mission, and Elaine, will go on.

"She was instrumental in moulding me, and her gentle and kind ways stayed with me, and that's what I want to be like: kindness, gentleness, forgiveness, and generosity."

(In addition to her reflections on Elaine, Maria added another story. One day, Alex was working alone when he propped a high ladder up against the glass wall at the front of the chapel. After he had climbed to the top, the ladder began slipping. Maria was alone in the dining room when she heard him call for help. She rushed in as it was falling away beneath him. Grabbing the inside rungs, she held on until Alex had come down.)

PAULINE'S STORY

Pauline Murray came to the Mission in 1988, soon after her arrival from Jamaica. A position came available in the mailroom for a week, and she left the Scott 19 years later. From her very first months—and with a young son joining her only six months after she had arrived—Pauline found herself constantly seeking Elaine's help.

"She became my confidante and finally became my 'mother.' Being mothered by Elaine was the best. She understood my struggles with the culture. The way I did things was so different. She had so much grace with me. The language here was different. I watched her closely and wouldn't make a move until Elaine made a move. I would always ask myself, 'What would Elaine do?' That woman had tact, and it rubbed off. Talk about fruit of the Spirit.

"I was in my 20s and she would coach me in a gentle way. It was more than just work. If I had to attend an occasion, I'd ask her how to dress. We all learned to be ladies from Elaine.

"I always grew up knowing about God. We would say, 'I'm a Christian.' I didn't truly understand what that meant. I didn't plan to work in a Christian organization. I didn't know what it would require. She guided me through it.

"When I was pregnant with my second child, we didn't know if the child would make it. I would say to Elaine, 'How am I going to do this?' and she'd say, 'One day at a time.' She would pray with me. I could confide in her and talk with ease."

"Sometimes you don't understand how much you miss her. When the time came to leave the hospital with the baby, the nurse said I needed a car seat. So I called Elaine, and she said, 'Mica is on his way.' My son is at the [Scott Mission] camp working with the youth—he's a counsellor—it is well.

"I watched Elaine—she was God-sent. I decided, 'I want that. That's the kind of mother I want to be.' I wasn't surprised that she was this way with me and others. She wasn't doing it; she was just being it."

Pauline's last position with the Mission was director of occupational health and safety. Her transition from the mailroom to management came through a long process of personal change, and Elaine had a key role in fostering that personal growth. Pauline explains, "I had difficulty reading, and as I started to get to know God, I felt strongly that I should read the Word. I started to read the Bible aloud at home. Things happened inside me, and I started to feel alive.

"I was still in the mailroom, stuffing envelopes and aware of my limitations. I was asked to lead devotions, and I'd never done that before. I was so shy that I wouldn't make eye contact. I had to stand before the staff and speak. I said to Elaine, 'I can't do this.' She said, 'Of course you can. Speak from your heart. You have a lot to tell.' As I read and spoke, I became quite articulate. I realized that I had an understanding of the Word of God that was extraordinary.

"I grew, got wings and decided that I love the air under these wings. I went to Ryerson University. I had an incredible memory that took me places. And I decided that I loved learning. When different directors came and there were transitions, opportunities presented themselves. I thought, 'I'll be the best of what's required of me.'

"My son grew with me. When we came here he was five. That was one of the reasons I took this job. I was told there would be a daycare. This was his playing field. He had access to every office, and he called Elaine 'Auntie.'

"When my husband, Charles, joined me, everywhere he went he was told he needed Canadian experience. He was a motor vehicle mechanic. He got experience at the Mission for a few months, and then he found work in his field.

"Ten years after we got married, I felt compelled to renew our vows. I wanted to truly give thanks. I needed a menorah [a seven-branched candlestick] so that we could have seven blessings but didn't know where to get one. Elaine said, 'I've got one.' A year and a half later, Charles fell ill, and within a few weeks he was gone. She was there for me and helped to organize the funeral" (said with tears).

"Elaine taught me how to be grateful. She would say little things that I overlooked at first. Things about God's provision that I took for granted. In the late '90s, the Mission used to host gospel night events. The kitchen staff had food for the event, but twice as many people came. Seeing all those people there, she would have prayed about that—and she'd regularly remind the staff about the words of the sampler: 'The Lord will provide.' It was quite unusual for food to arrive so late, but then a truck pulled up with all this marvelous pizza. They had prepared it for a fancy event, and when they arrived it was cancelled. We were asking, 'What will we serve?' and Elaine could say, 'The most beautiful gourmet pizza.'

"Sometimes Christians have no balance; Elaine was well-balanced and well rounded. If somebody needed a word, an embrace or a smile, she wouldn't just pray for them and leave. She would ask, 'What do you need?' And when she saw God at work in our lives she knew how to celebrate His goodness. Henry Blackaby says, 'When you see God at work, join Him.' She'd join Him."

PETER'S STORY

Peter Duraisami is the current chief executive officer of the Scott Mission. Born in southern India and raised in a Christian home, he trained as an accountant. While at university, Peter began to seek God and experienced a new sense of His reality: "Being in accounting," he said, "I needed proof."

After early success in business, he entered Christian service with the Evangelical Fellowship of India, working in relief work as a director of operations and finance. Then in 1989 at age 32, he followed a "call to the nations," coming to Canada as a student at Tyndale Seminary. He and his wife, Sheela, learned about an opening at the Scott Mission for weekend dishwashers. They worked together until she became pregnant, and he later moved into the men's ministry.

"Elaine was my supervisor. She was in charge of the men's ministry. As a new immigrant I was thrown into the culture downtown, and she guided me. She was like a mother figure to me and to the Mission. I learned what to do, what not to do and the culture of the Mission.

"There were differences between the Mission and where I had been. Here you were to give and not judge, to err on the side of giving. You can't be judgmental. And you must really get to know the men.

"Elaine was not afraid to confront people. But I saw how she was able to maintain order with respect, love and dignity. That was one of the key things I had to learn, that grace can only go so far. She didn't draw a line between herself and the men we served. And she cared for us as staff. While I was there, we had our firstborn, Yohan (studying at Tyndale). She cared for us in practical ways."

Peter took on the role of director of finance unexpectedly and made the shift from front-line worker to management, where his appreciation for Elaine grew further. In time, they worked very closely. On three occasions, between the appointments of executive directors, they shared the role of interim director together.

"Elaine guarded the Mission in many ways, in her relations with the staff and with donors. It was very important for her that we were a faith mission. She was always giving glory to God and saying that a faith element had to be preserved. I learned that from her.

"She had such a deep commitment to the staff. When she came to know about a need she'd go above and beyond. If she found out something about a staff member, she'd call and bless them. It wasn't just giving things; her acts of kindness were amazing.

"We were both part of a prayer and intercessory group, and I saw how she was so consistent in prayer and went through a prayer list. She was constantly praying."

Peter developed an appreciation of her songs as well as her power in prayer. "When she prayed or wrote her songs, the words came down from heaven: 'Let me hear your voice in the morning...' So many were powerful, so simple, and moved the hearts of the people." What was her legacy?

"People are more important than programs. She had such a heart for the people she served, a high call of service and a high level of excellence, the godliness of prayer and devotions. In all this there was joy. The songs were so joyful; she was a person of fun and laughter and joy.

"No one can fill her shoes, but we can carry on what she left behind. My hope is that for years to come we will not let go of the founders' legacy and the principles on which the Mission was built.

"It was real when she said, 'For me to live is Christ and to die is gain.' Her life was Christ. She was there in every single element living Christ. You see people who can pray. Elaine could live it. People called her the 'Mother Teresa of Spadina.' You want something more real, and she was very real."

BENEDICTION (1968)

By Annie A. Zeidman

May the Lord grant you
Special grace to love Him, special strength to serve Him,
Special peace in Him to rest, special faith to know Him best.
May no war alarm you, may no evil harm you,
May your sheltered dwelling stand, roofed with
Joy, beneath His hand.

Abide under the shadow of the Almighty. (Psalm 91:1)

CHAPTER 25

A New Generation:
Jae, Lois, Sera and Andrew

JAE FRATZL

Jae is Margaret's daughter, and although she's not currently involved with the Scott Mission, she's certainly left her mark. She crafted the stained-glass image of the Good Samaritan in the front window, that unmistakable image of her Uncle Alex in dark glasses. Her profession as an art therapist also reflects Jae's family roots.

The Mission held a central place in her life from the beginning. "It was the other place I called home," Jae says. "My mother and I lived with my grandparents; I have recollections of Elaine and David still living at home—people who ran the Mission."

Being the child of a single mother in the 1960s was difficult. Jae's biological father ceased to be part of her life when she was around the age of two, yet she says, "I feel very grateful for having been raised in [those] circumstances because I had multiple parents. They'd all take turns picking me up from school." Jae describes herself as "thoughtful" and "painfully shy as a child."

It was a unique family life. "Christmas didn't begin until 6 p.m., because the whole family wouldn't be home by then. I remember waiting for my grandfather to come home because then we could have Christmas dinner." The relationship with Morris was affectionate. "He loved me very much, and I loved him," she says.

Like many children, sometime around the age of four or five Jae decided to run away from home. "I packed my suitcase and got to the stop sign, and I remember thinking, 'I don't know where Children's Aid is'; then my mother came out and invited me home for lunch and to put it off 'til after."

During those years, Margaret worked at the Mission and sang in a choir. When Jae was about age eight, Margaret went back to school. She enrolled in the Royal Conservatory of Music and received a bachelor of music degree with a focus on opera.

All through Jae's early years, the Mission remained a special part of her life. "I was very proud, and it gave me an acute sense of being privileged. I think back to things like the camp," she said. There was also a unique view of the work behind the scenes. She knew that Annie kept a section of the attic for children's clothing that was needed when young campers arrived without summer outfits or a bathing suit. It was also a window on a harsher world—"the kid in the nursery who came in and his father had beaten him, and you realized there's a lot of suffering in the world."

A high achiever in school, Jae ranked in the top three students during her years at Branksome Hall. She also had musical talent, singing in choirs and learning how to play guitar from Alex. Her relationship with Elaine was close, and Jae has memories of her aunt as a young woman. Often, it was Elaine who comforted her when she came home crying for not fitting in. She still recalls Elaine's remarkable gift of expressing care, "going above and beyond."

Her grandparents' home was a place where Annie maintained order, and she advised young Jae to be careful about the image she presented. People might be watching her behaviour. Those expectations created some barriers. "It took until my late teens to see how loving and caring [Annie] was. I saw mostly the good old Protestant work ethic."

Then, when Jae was around age 13, her mother remarried, and Jae followed her parents to Europe and then South Africa. At 18 she returned to Toronto to enter the Ontario College of Art and Design, planning to be a medical illustrator. By her second year, she was exhausted and frustrated. She left, and she now reflects, "It was God's way of getting me out of being pigheaded, which He's done before and since."

Alex arranged for counselling, and Jae started to bring paintings to the sessions, which led to the suggestion that she consider a future in art therapy. It was a natural outgrowth of the converging interests in her life. She went on to receive an extensive professional education for her work, but she hasn't forgotten where she started.

"Alex is the reason I'm here today," Jae says, and she thinks she may well have been one of the last to speak with him before his accident. They'd had a long conversation on the phone before he left to spend time on his boat. She also appreciates the assistance that she received from her Uncle David. "He would do his level best but did not always get recognized. I relate to David." As Jae notes, she may not be involved with the Mission, "but the Mission is part of me."

As a side comment, Jae explains that she began life with the more conventional name of "Janet." "I thought it was an unpleasant name," Jae says. "'Janet' did not sound melodic to me. I was complaining at the Scott Mission one day to someone who had been a camper, about the same age (19–20). He made the suggestion that I shorten it."

While working at another summer camp for kids, Jae met her husband, Gerald Fratzl, and they've been together since 1989. After studies at Concordia, York University and the University of Toronto, she completed her qualifications as a therapist in 1992, and has been working in the Barrie area since '94. Jae has a thriving private practice where she provides services in both art therapy and counselling.

Jae doesn't see her work within a formal religious context. "The Mission has a very strong identity in that way. I don't. I consider myself to be a Christian with a specific faith. I do see myself as clear about who God is. When I was with my grandmother, we would have long conversations." Many of her clients, she said, have been "turned off by organized religion." Yet spirituality is a meaningful component of her work. "A number of people," she said, "have gone back to their religious roots as a result of counselling."

Jae maintains a strong sense of connection with the aims of the Mission in reaching individuals. "Without a measure of mental health you can't help but be poor," she said. As an example, she refers to individuals recovering from addictions. Speaking of one, she said, "It was gratifying to see this person recover a sense of self. That's the kind of moment that I relate back to the Mission. That's what this family does best: giving people a hand up—lives saved, not just religion for religion's sake."

LOIS MARKOVIC

Lois, Elaine's eldest daughter, sometimes feels as if her memories of the Mission began before she had a memory. So when she says "I was born here," it's because the same hallways where she once went running as a toddler to look for her grandfather, Morris, are where she now has her office. But Lois wasn't attracted to working at the Mission. "It took a long time to appreciate how God used my family," she said. Above all, she promised herself, "I'll never work [there]."

Of course, as a young person, that's exactly what she did. In her mid-teens, she joined an innovative summer outreach program from the Scott to the Lawrence Heights area. She learned how to cope with difficult kids, took a leadership role and discovered something about herself. "There was something in me that loved serving people and being generous," she said.

She entered Ryerson and prepared for a career in social work, with no intention of practicing at the Mission. But one constant in her life was a close relationship with Annie. "I used to love visiting my grandmother." By the time Lois was 27, she was a professional in clinical social work. During a transitional period, she decided to come back to the Mission as a volunteer.

"I really liked it," she said. "My grandmother was still alive, and she was a positive connection with the Mission. I wound up getting hired." Lois found a new level of satisfaction coming back into her work, along with acceptance from her clients and support from colleagues.

Her approach to her professional life changed. "It's not about social work; it's about God. I connect with people. I want them to feel what I felt [in] a relationship with God." In time, that connection blossomed into the discovery of her spiritual strengths. "I love praying for people," said Lois, who now facilitates a prayer team at the Mission. Prayer has become her key to connecting with people and coordinating the work of her colleagues to seek His best for their clients. Currently, she's a department head.

"What I learned from my grandmother, mother and father was generosity. They were very generous on the front line," she says. Lois sees her place at the Mission with satisfying clarity. "I feel like I'm supposed to be here."

ANDREW ZEIDMAN

Of all the family members who were severely affected by the death of Alex, none was more crushed than his son, Andrew, who was 19. "I didn't see myself working at the Mission," Andrews says, but after several years, including one spent away from Toronto, he came back. He enjoyed working in the men's ministry and intuitively connected with the street population.

Not surprisingly, it also helped to resolve the relationship with his late father. There was added satisfaction when Andrew began using his musical gifts for ministry, especially on the guitar. He became a leader of the Mission's praise team for worship services. Returning to school as a mature student, he graduated with a theological degree from Ontario Theological Seminary (now Tyndale University). The education helped to equip Andrew for ministry leadership, and one of his current roles is leading Sunday morning worship at the Mission.

Andrew also had an interest in the history of the Mission and was surprised to discover that a Hebrew congregation had been affiliated with the work at the beginning. "A few years ago," he said, "I started to feel called back to my Jewish roots—as well as those of the Mission." He remembered stories of his grandfather and the annual celebrations of the Passover. That led to a budding Messianic Jewish identity that influenced Elaine and his cousins.

After spending some years involved in a Messianic Jewish congregation, Andrew felt called to establish Tallit, an independent Messianic ministry that has led short-term missions to Mexico and South America. Under the auspices of Tallit he's also been establishing a downtown Messianic congregation.

As a parent, Andrew sees his father differently. "I certainly understand him more," he says. "We did do things together, but he was very dedicated to his work. Being called to the Mission, there's a level of sacrifice. You're called to go beyond."

SERA MARKOVIC ROUSALIS

Elaine's youngest daughter, Sera, was immersed into life at the Mission from an early age and, like Elaine, was surprised to find her life's calling there. As a child, Sera's first loves were drama and music. She thrived as a performer, singing in the Canadian Children's Opera Chorus and taking children's roles in operas, including *La Bohème* at the Hummingbird Centre. The family encouraged her talent. Aunt Margaret provided voice training, and Sera won leading roles in school plays and musicals.

Taking part in the work of the Mission was also expected, beginning in the childhood years and through high school. She saw that at some point all the grandchildren were involved. "We helped with the mail, packing food hampers and assisting the children's programs," she said. Annie wouldn't let them serve adults until they had turned 18.

They were taught to be responsive. "We weren't even allowed to bring a cup of coffee purchased outside to an area with clients. It was something many of them couldn't afford," said Sera. "We were expected to be alert to needs and ready to serve immediately," she said. "We had to make ourselves useful or get out of the way."

Some of those experiences were not easy to witness. She and her cousins endured some very difficult episodes, despite attempts to shield them. There was violence between clients, some of it directed toward the staff—including assaults on adult family members. "It was, at times, a frightening atmosphere," she said.

Despite her talents and strong inclination to the arts, an inner voice was saying "You have to be where you're needed." And Sera—who had given her heart to the Lord as a young child—was led toward a life of service. As she contemplated her future, the Scott seemed more meaningful and realistic than a career in performance. Yet, like Elaine, there was an inner resistance, a strong ambivalence about the demands that the ministry had made on their family life.

In the year that her Uncle Alex died, Sera graduated from high school. Despite the heart-rending grief that surrounded her, Sera could see the ministry pressing on. Her Uncle David asked if she would assist in the mailroom. "That was my first full-time work experience at the Mission. It was in the midst of family and staff trying to carry on while grappling with shock and grief." She still appreciates that he made it possible.

Annie, who Sera called "Nanny," was also influential. "I knew the Mission was of utmost importance to Nanny," said Sera. "When I was going to school, I saw her every day at lunch." The noontime visits continued after she began working.

"One day at the table, Nanny asked, 'You will stay, won't you?' It took me aback. I didn't know she felt like that," said Sera.

In hindsight, she identifies with her mother's decision to work at the Mission rather than enter university immediately following high school. "I'm most comfortable when I'm doing things—responding in practical ways to the needs around me," she says, recognizing another trait shared with Elaine. This explains why she postponed her education to work full-time at the Mission (although she'd been accepted at the universities where she applied). Though there was some regret in deferring higher education, she's currently enrolled in an MBA non-profit leadership program.

Following her first year at the Mission, Sera wanted to see more of the world. She enjoyed travelling in Greece and explored the island of Paxos (where Gaios, a disciple of Paul, was exiled and is buried). "Greek culture was so similar to my father's Serbian culture," she said. "I connected with others my age right away and felt safe and accepted." She met a young man, Thanasis, and stayed for more than three months before returning to Canada. Annie would refer to that year as Sera's "running away period."

Five years later, she and Thanasis were in contact again and began to feel certain of God's blessing on their relationship; two years later they were married. Thanasis held a number of jobs (in and out of the Mission) before advancing into his current position, directing the food services departments at the Scott. His warm personality and sense of loyalty have proven to be a great support and encouragement for Elaine, family members, Mission staff and leaders.

When Sera was asked to take over the personnel department (now human resources), her view of the Scott began to change again. "Moving into administration," she said, "I began seeking the Lord in new ways related to the financial needs and corporate identity of the

255

Mission." Sera has been working at the Scott Mission for 27 years and has overseen the human resources department since 1992. Her increasing concern for the spiritual life of the staff and their ministries and the Mission's overall direction, service culture and identity has added to her own spiritual growth.

SERA'S REFLECTIONS

These are some of Sera's personal reflections as a long-time Mission staff worker and observer:

On the Mission

After Alex passed away, while working at the Mission through the 1980s and 90s I watched the declining influence of Christian faith among the leadership at the Mission. We began to gradually drift away from the centrality of faith (and all that comes with it). Once the shift had taken place, the Mission's core beliefs were no longer a driving force. It was frustrating to see hiring decisions made outside of my influence in the area of human resources. The Zeidmans, who were on staff and serving on the board, knew that the direction was wrong but had no authority to bring change.

By the late 1990s, the disunity around hiring qualifications had become a major issue. We needed to do more than value the professional skills of our candidates; we had to emphasize the importance of character and Christian faith. I was encouraged by the board vice chairman, Dr. Stephen Farris, to prepare a philosophy of ministry statement. In 2000, the executive director, Graham Barnes, completed that document and led the leadership team through the development of our core values.

We learned to articulate the Mission's core Christian beliefs and values. We understand now that you cannot depend on one single personality to bring forward the core Christian beliefs and identity and Mission culture. Christian principles and practices have to be integrated and engaged through everything we do. We've come to corporately recognize the value of community and strong Christian relationships among the staff and board to expand our vision. That's critical to accomplish our mandate and promote the best possible culture for staff and clients. I can't put enough stress on the necessity of having key leaders who have a strong, sustained personal faith at work in their lives.

When the Mission is served by individuals with a meaningful and shared faith on staff and on the board, especially in our current secular North American climate, we're able to exert our energy on bigger issues, not disputing fundamentals between ourselves.

Many of us gathered in those days for prayer and fasting, throughout the 90s, and we saw situations turn around. Had we not gone through this struggle, I believe we would certainly have become a secular non-profit organization, perhaps only with a nod towards our Christian heritage. Our faith wouldn't be a living, vital part of our work, as it is now.

On Family and the Mission

Growing up at the Mission has been a unique blessing in many ways. This community has been a place of support, strengthening and Christian growth for many people, including family members, and God has used our family to build and be part of leading this ministry. It has also been difficult having one's life on display: "growing pains," familial relationships, marriage, and especially grief.

We are reminded of our family's legacy and loss every day—where they served for years, the effects of their work—and hear their names and examples mentioned all the time. It's wonderful; it also pricks the heart each time. As my mom would say, I am starting to get more of a "Teflon coating" now. But I do understand why others have stepped away from the work for a while. It's a huge emotional load, until you can come through the larger grief to a place of peace and gratitude. For now, it's still a bit tender and even bittersweet.

The Mission is a part of us—it's in our hearts—and we want to see it thrive and be a generous blessing to many in need. We've also learned through tough experiences that the Lord and our walk with Him is our priority. There has been a process of embracing our full identity in Christ and letting go of an unhealthy enmeshment with the Mission. The ministry is to be the outflow of our heart-walk with God. We ought to be just as fervent in our service even if we weren't in the Mission, and I think that we have arrived at a place now where we would be, no matter where we served.

FAMILY

By Elaine Z. Markovic

In a long white gown
As water was placed on her head,
Quietly
She was baptized,
In the Name of the Father
And of the Son
And of the Holy Spirit.
"The Lord bless thee and keep thee,"
We prayed.
Some years later, now,
I see, in spite of my mistakes
And hers,
God is keeping His word.

CHAPTER 26

Learning to Pray for Herself

After more than four decades working in the front office, in 2003 Elaine was asked to take a position in public relations. A note in her diary records the private frustrations at moving away from direct contact with clients. Her new place on the second floor had once been part of Annie's apartment, and Elaine knew exactly where she was located—the bedroom "where I found her March 10th, 1992, on the floor and went with her to hospital, where she died March 31. My office has been [the] main floor since 1961—big change. Many emotions—mostly feeling overwhelmed at the packing-unpacking job, at which I still had much to do…I let myself get drawn into the chaos instead of viewing it from a healthy distance. 'How important is it?'"

A year later, Elaine confronted a new health crisis. During interviews in 2008, she spoke about being diagnosed and treated for cancer during a time when Mica was also facing major surgery. These reflections, made at different times and arranged in a single monologue, reveal Elaine growing open to receive her own personal miracles.

❧

How could I have not seen my own needs? I have been in the helping community for so long, and you tend to think of others first. My experience with TB had taught me how to properly set my priorities, and I thought that I had them straight. And that seems like the scriptural and Christian thing to do. But I needed to be praying for myself as much as I do for other people.

I need to attend to myself. That gives my spirit peace and the proper focus. Even now, when I go to hospital, I've learned that I need to pray for myself, although I will find myself praying for everybody else. That's something that I can slip into very easily, and when it goes beyond a certain point, it's not healthy.

Over the years, the ministry has gone from one crisis to another. There doesn't seem to have been any time when there wasn't a challenge of one kind or another. It has taken a heavy toll on my immediate family, and my husband's illnesses have been difficult. He's had his own health problems with his back, related to when he did heavy labour as a child during the war years. Many of his crises have stemmed from that.

There were many changes at the Mission over the years, and these were difficult. I tried not to take them home, but I probably wasn't aware of the toll it was taking on my health. In 2004, after I had gone for my annual general checkup, I received a personal call from the doctor that evening. For years, my health had been fine. But they had seen something, and they thought they ought to take another X-ray, and that led to a biopsy. It showed there was a cancer, a very aggressive one, and they referred me to a surgeon. That took the wind out of my sails, and I remember feeling very angry. This is interrupting my life, I thought. I don't have time for this. On top of everything, the surgery was scheduled for May 5, my wedding anniversary, and only a week before my husband was scheduled for back surgery.

I had to prepare for a lumpectomy. The cancer was so insidious that it couldn't be felt. They had to insert a wire into the lump using X-rays and apply green dye to show the surgeon where to operate. Sera and Lois found a little waiting room at Women's College Hospital, where they prayed for me all through those difficult hours. I didn't have a chance to tell them about the full procedure and how it would make me look after the surgery. But I clearly recall how I felt when I woke up.

Lois and Sera came in, and their first reaction was shock because I was pale green from the dye, until the nurse explained what had happened. And I recall them asking, "How are you, Mom?" Without thinking, I answered, "I'm blessed." I hadn't yet heard anything from the surgeon, but that's how I felt.

It was not some drug-induced high from the anesthetic. Lying in the recovery bed, I was perfectly conscious of what I was saying. I had such a wonderful awareness of being at peace with myself and an inner joy. Somehow, I knew that I was being well looked after by God, which I hadn't felt for a long while. And my daughters had to laugh, seeing me look green as I spoke about being blessed.

The next week after my surgery, on May 12, my husband had his first spinal fusion surgery for his lower back. He reacted violently to the anesthetic during recovery, hallucinating and even crawling out of the bed. The staff called me to come to the hospital and assist in restraining him. I had to explain that I was recuperating from my own surgery and couldn't help.

As I made progress through recovery, the doctors urged me to begin chemo and radiation therapies. It had to begin within eight weeks of the surgery. But I really didn't feel at peace about taking either of those treatments. I wasn't afraid, but I didn't know how I would manage looking after my husband, who was now in rehabilitation and needed me.

I felt that if I was to proceed with the treatment, then I would pray about it and have peace, yet I had no peace. Finally, a decision had to be made, and I cried out to the Lord that I needed Him to let me know.

There have been times before when I've tried opening my Bible at random in order to get a helpful verse. Some people can do that and get the most wonderful insights. Usually, all I get are genealogies. But this time God must have known I was desperate. I opened my Bible to those words from Psalm 139: "I am fearfully and wonderfully made" (14). At that moment I knew—it was like a physical moment of relief—*this is not the time*. So I called the hospital and said I wasn't going to be able to have the treatments.

That summer, my husband had a serious fall. He got much worse and finally had to go back into the hospital. His sacrum, where the screws were anchored, had fractured, and the doctors had to repeat the surgery. He lost a lot of blood but eventually did recuperate, and the following year he had a hip replacement. Then, in 2006, the fusion surgery in his back had to be extended further up his spine.

In October 2006, during the course of post-operative cancer care, my blood tests showed a dramatic increase in tumour activity. I requested a mammogram from the hospital that month—my regular checkup was not scheduled until February. In late November I had a biopsy, which confirmed the recurrence of cancer. When I walked out of the hospital it was dark and cold; there had been an ice storm. My car was at the back of the parking lot, and I wasn't even dressed properly for the weather. It was a miserable evening, and I was shaking.

But after I got myself home and into bed, I felt a rush of joy that started me singing this song that came from inside me. I was singing it all night long: "You are so good to me, Lord, You are so good to me. You are my strength and high tower; under your wings I will trust." The feelings were so strong that I had to get out of bed and write them down. Later, I shared it with Sera.

The diagnosis came a few weeks later, just before Christmas. I had developed a very rare cancer that was likely to spread. I urgently needed to have chemotherapy. The doctors assumed that I had already been treated with chemo after my last surgery and said it was too soon to be repeated. Of course, I explained that I didn't have those treatments. They scheduled my first appointment on December 27, 2006.

This time I had great peace about receiving chemotherapy and fully understood why I wasn't comfortable having it done before. As my mother would have said, this was a moment when the "big guns" were needed. It was a miracle of godly intervention.

Every time I went for treatment, Sera and I would sit together and sing that little song I'd been given. Her husband, Thanasis, would drive me; on a few occasions Lois would come. Things didn't get better right away, but I survived the chemo and the radiation.

My family was so supportive; it hurt me to see what I was putting them through. My husband would do anything to get me to eat, and sometimes he did. It wasn't easy for him. I lost my appetite. I couldn't bear the smell or even the thought of toast, or anything with yeast in it. I have the greatest admiration for people battling this disease. And there were, and are, God-appointed people looking after me. I have very good care.

God knows what he is doing. I'm often reminded of the story of Gladys Aylward as told in *The Small Woman* by Alan Burgess. Gladys grew up in England and didn't like the way she looked. She was dark haired, and she prayed as a child every day to be changed into a blonde. Later, Gladys knew that she was meant to be a missionary in China, but she was poor. She went to work for a wealthy family of Christians, who paid her way through Bible college. The moment Gladys stepped off the train in Shanghai she looked out at the sea of black-haired people, the ones to whom she had come to minister, and she said, "My Lord, You know what You're doing."

God has done very special things for me during those difficult times. My niece (Jae) painted a picture inspired by her memories of the woods up at Caledon where the mission has a camp. She filled it with trilliums, which is my favourite flower. At the centre of the picture is a clearing where there's a glow, which is why I call it "The Glory of God." I had it hanging on the left wall of my bedroom. Every morning, when the sun comes in through a crack in the drapery, it shines on the right wall. But one morning, the sun was shining across the ceiling and down to that picture. It stopped at the place in the picture where I imagined "the Glory of the Lord." I kept looking at the right wall, where the sun should have been, and then back to the picture. That helped me know that God saw me. He sent that experience to say that He saw me.

Then another thing happened. One morning as I prepared to go for treatment, I was getting my bag ready. I remember that I was packing a special shawl that a congregation in Niagara Falls had prayed over. I liked to put it on while I was getting chemo, and it reminded me that there were many people praying for me, even people I didn't know. And as I was putting that and some other things into the bag, I saw a feather. When I saw it, I exclaimed, "That's a feather. There's 'healing in his wings'" (Malachi 4:2). I still have that feather. A few months later, my nephew Andrew was sitting in a restaurant with one of our board members, Joe Nemni, who was asking, "How's Elaine doing?" Andrew was about to answer, and he looked down. There was a feather on the table.

Another time, I was crying in bed during the day over some very bad news from the hospital. I hadn't cried a lot, except perhaps during the middle of the night, the time when we're all most vulnerable. Even then, I would only shed a few tears. But this time I was crying a lot. At the end of the bedroom there appeared a kind of light. I thought it was just the light of the sun off my tears. But my tears had stopped; my eyes were dry. Every time I blinked it moved across the wall, until it had crossed the room and came up to my shoulder. I felt that it was an angel. Once again, I knew that God sees me.

Whatever happened, nothing in my situation was taking Him by surprise. He had it all in hand. If someone else were telling me that these were their experiences, I might not believe them. But God knew that I needed to have something special to believe Him—this kind of experience—to be able to trust Him completely. Not only "If all else fails, try God" or "If all else fails, try prayer." He's not the last resort. He's the first resort. It was gracious of God; He didn't have to do that for me.

I've come to appreciate that when the Bible says "by His stripes we are healed" (Isaiah 53:5 NKJV), it's not only a promise of spiritual healing. Now I see that it also provides for my physical healing, and I see it as a package deal. When Jesus was on the cross, He took not only our sins but our diseases, including my illness. I have no difficulty in believing in miracles now. I admit, I was skeptical, because I had never experienced such dramatic healing. Now, it seems that I've become aware of them going on every day. I'm so much more aware of God's miracle-working presence. As my parents taught me, Jesus is the same yesterday, today and forever.

RUNNING AND RETURNING

By Elaine Z. Markovic

Last evening
Our dog ran away.
She ran because she heard a dreadful noise
and was filled with terror.

She ran far away.
We searched well into
the night, praying.
We longed to comfort her,
warm her, give her water.
But she was hiding.

While it was still dark,
she returned.
Made a gentle noise at
the door.
And with head hanging,
fur matted and dripping with dew
she came into the house
and was loved.

One evening I fled.
I fled because I
heard such dreadful news
and was filled with horror.

I stayed away;
hurt, angry, sad,
perplexed, filled with mistrust.
He longed to comfort and assure
that He was in control.
But I was hiding.

So with words and memories,
through the dark
He found me.

CHAPTER 27

Reflections on a Life in Ministry

On a sunlit day in mid-July 2008, Elaine took time to ruminate on the spiritual insights she'd gained in recent years. She described the changes that had come into her life through her illness, the cost of her calling and how the character of the Mission was still rooted in the spiritual values of her parents. Finally, she considered her experience under recent directors and what it means to be "a Zeidman" at this stage of the Mission's history.

HOW HAVE YOUR EXPERIENCES WITH CANCER CHANGED YOUR PERSPECTIVE?

I'm more grateful for small things. We were always taught to say grace at home; we didn't have meals without saying grace. We were always taught to be thankful for what we had. But I'm so grateful for every meal. For so long [during the illness], food was repulsive to me. It's not that I didn't have an appetite; I did, but even thinking about it was repulsive. Now, I eat with more enjoyment and thanksgiving.

I'm aware of breathing. I'm more thankful to be alive. I don't think I was ever thankful for the years I was healthy. I probably took my health for granted. It's just made me very much more thankful—and for the people that God put in my life during my treatment and the facilities He used. I'm just more thankful.

WHAT PRIORITIES HAVE SHIFTED?

The Bible says, "Take no thought of what you put on." Every woman likes to look nice. Well, when I lost so much weight and could hardly put on any clothes that didn't fall off—really, that's minor. Losing my hair was minor, when you think about it. When they said I'd lose my hair, I didn't expect my eyelashes and eyebrows would fall out. That's minor. I knew it would grow back. And it did. I just put a scarf over my head, and that was fine. I thought it would be a devastation to have my hair fall out. It fell out, and so what? I just gathered it up and threw it in the wastebasket. I wore my scarf, and my niece knit a little cap for me with a nice design. Someone else crocheted a lovely cap. I got through it. "This too shall pass" is a good word to remember. And it passed well. [Elaine enjoyed a warm chuckle all the way through these comments.]

Somebody was trying to give me advice. If I encounter someone with cancer I won't give advice unless they ask for it. The advice was to not take chemotherapy, and yet I think God was encouraging me to do that. The other thing this person said was "The worst that can happen is that you die, and then you just go to be with Jesus." Well, I wasn't ready to die, and it won't be a bad thing to be with Jesus, but I didn't feel He was ready for me; nor was I ready for Him. I don't want to be irreverent, but I think that when that time comes, I'll be in another space spiritually.

Some people I respect said to me, "This is not your time." That was a tremendous encouragement. I just hung on to the fact that the cross is a package deal; it deals with my sins and my sicknesses.

When I was a child in the Sunday school at the Scott Mission, we sang those old gospel hymns that people don't sing anymore. Those were the hymns I was raised on. The message to the poor is the same as to the richest person on earth: What can wash away my sins? Nothing but the blood of Jesus. What can make me whole again? Nothing but the blood of Jesus.

HAS THERE BEEN A PARTICULARLY DIFFICULT LESSON TO LEARN?

As a family, we were other-people oriented and Scott Mission oriented. Everything else paled in priority. But when your health is compromised, you don't have control. You can't just take an aspirin so that the cancer or the TB goes away. It takes time. You are forced to look at all kinds of priorities.

One phrase that I came across recently was from Jan Karon's book *Home to Holly Springs* [from her Mitford series of novels]. The main character [an Episcopalian priest], asks God in a prayer to forgive him for being impressed with his own busyness. That hit me between the eyes. I've not always been aware of being impressed with my own busyness. Busyness can take over, especially if it's taking care of other people. That's not a bad thing, to care for other people, but then you're faced with yourself: I'm the person who's sick here.

In desperation, I began to pray for myself. There's only so much another person can do for you. I've had so many wonderful people pray for me and with me. My own family prayed with me and for me. But there comes a time, around two in the morning, when I'm faced with being alone. Maybe I'm weeping and frightened and all kinds of things come into my mind. There's nothing else for me to do but to pray for myself. I'm learning to do that. It's not a bad thing to pray for myself, to finally realize that I have a responsibility to look after this temple. A lot of people know this lesson. I'm not saying anything new. But it was new for me.

IN RETROSPECT, HAVE YOU CHANGED THE WAY YOU SEE YOUR CALLING AT THE SCOTT MISSION?

I knew, from the beginning, that God was calling me here, but I didn't realize the strength of that calling or what the calling was going to cost: what it would look like; what the calling was going to put us all through; what it would put me through. When you want to take a trip, you know the places you want to go. Then you have to figure out what it's going to cost and—can you afford it? I didn't know what it was going to cost. That's probably a good thing. With a spiritual calling, we're more aware of what we're putting into it, not—

What am I going to get out of it? But there's another side to this. It's probably a good thing that that we usually don't know what our calling is going to cost. The calling of God is expensive. It's not cheap, because the gospel isn't cheap. We've been redeemed, not with silver and gold. It's beyond that.

Working at the Scott Mission is a good thing for me. I'm thankful for my job. Yes, it's been really hard and brought me to my knees. But, that's not a bad thing. Any of the difficulties that we've had were used by God to bring us closer to Himself, to get a better perspective on ourselves and the work of the Mission. God used everyone who was here.

God knows how hard-headed and stiff-necked—and all the rest of it—that I can be, and He knows what it takes to teach me. He only deals with us in love. It's fine to discipline a kid and say, "It's for your own good." We can't see that it's for our own good. It hurts! The discipline has always been awesome. The hardest lessons are always taught in love, and there's always a treat at the end. He's more than a good parent. God goes beyond a good parent.

HAS THIS AFFECTED YOUR VIEW OF THE PEOPLE YOU MINISTER TO HERE AT THE MISSION?

What still bothers me is the way that people talk down to the poor. And I think that sin is sin, but I believe God is more merciful to the poor because they don't have the same hang-ups that impede others in their faith journey. I'm not saying it's a sin to be rich. It's a great blessing when God blesses us with material goods, and we can do so much because of that. But when people have nothing, it makes them unencumbered.

WHERE DO YOU SEE THE MISSION MOVING IN THE FUTURE?

I look forward to the Scott Mission going from strength to strength and watching God bless the work. That's not just in terms of finances but in programs, seeing how God will move the Mission to change people's lives.

Did Rev. Rohold envision that this would be celebrating a hundred years? Did my parents envision it going on for 60 years? I don't envision the need around us getting significantly less. People's spiritual need will always be there. Should the city open up more housing for the homeless, that would be wonderful. But the Bible tells us, "We'll always have the poor with us." We minister to those who are poor in their finances and also to those who are poor in spirit.

WHEN YOU THINK OF THE MISSION, WHAT REMAINS CENTRAL FOR YOU?

The strength of the work is the gospel. The gospel is the foundation, the four walls and the roof. We are not just a social service agency, as important as that would be. We're more than just a group of Christians doing good work. We're a group of Christians working and giving the gospel through the programs that are offered here. Many agencies have started off like that, and then the gospel part has somehow fallen away, even among Christians.

It is hard work to maintain the original mandate. The staff loses its focus, or the administration doesn't maintain the vision. It can happen very easily and perhaps not very deliberately. It just weakens. It could happen here. We have to intentionally maintain the gospel in the Mission and within the programs. The encouragement comes when you see men, women and children being brought into the kingdom of God through their decisions.

YOU MUST HAVE A GREATER AWARENESS NOW OF THE CHALLENGES THAT MORRIS AND ANNIE FACED IN MAINTAINING THE CHARACTER AND INTEGRITY OF THE WORK.

My regard for Morris has appreciated over time. He could have just written Christian literature, and that would have been enough. But seeing the way he ministered has been an example for me, my siblings and my husband. To know how he did things and to see how my mother did things was an example. It wasn't hard to follow. It was like a pattern or a map. You just saw the way to go. They did it the way that Jesus would do it. It would be wrong for us to just follow a person. We saw the person of Jesus Christ behind them. They did things with His compassion.

I remember Annie saying, "When someone dies, it's so easy to make an idol of that person." One tends to just remember the good things. They're not the ones to emulate. If we see God in there, that's what we're to emulate. She said, "When I die, don't let anybody write books about me." She was very conscious about what she perceived to be her failings. When she was 90, she had a broken hip. In the hospital, they found out that she had this malignant tumour, which was successfully removed. She lived for six more years. We were able to visit her Christmas Day evening, together as a family. With all the family around her, she asked everyone for forgiveness for any offense she had caused. She thought she may not live another day. I'm sure she was thinking about her own shortcomings. Maybe she was thinking that she hadn't been the best mother in the world. Maybe she wasn't, but she sure did something right.

HOW HAS IT BEEN SERVING UNDER A SERIES OF VERY DIFFERENT LEADERS IN THE PAST FEW DECADES?

The years have been difficult, getting used to the style of one new director after another. Each one is different. Each one comes with their own gifts and shortcomings. We need to learn to live with that and work with that. God has allowed them to come and minister in our midst until it's time for them to move on to other things. On reflection, it's good to see why God brings particular people into our path, and what we learn from them.

Hopefully, other people are looking at my life in the same way. I'm far, far, far from perfect. Hopefully, people will see that God is working on me and in me, too. There isn't any person who crosses our path from whom we can't learn something. We're all made in the image of God, and we're all unique, not that we all know Him, but because He knows us all. There's an aspect where we can learn something from each other, particularly from the household of faith, but others as well.

WILL YOU STAY ON TO HELP MAINTAIN THE FAMILY PRESENCE AT THE MISSION?

There have been times when I wondered if I should go. It's not the Zeidmans' mission. We're just like anyone else, and we can apply for a position, and we either get it or we don't. But we are here, and we do have a history with the place. Various family members have felt a calling to work here. If that makes others feel insecure, then perhaps it's their problem. When the time comes for any family member to step down, and that is God's will, then He will initiate that. He brings circumstances into play. For myself, I'm now down to working one day a week. Is that the way that I will ease myself out of the work? Perhaps I'll get the strength to work two days a week. I just don't know. I think it's dangerous when you don't know what to do that you go ahead and do something. It's much better to stand still.

E. Margaret Clarkson wrote a little chorus for children, and I remember one line: "When you don't know what to do, ask Jesus." I was in my adult years when she wrote it, but it has served me in good stead. Quite frankly, Jesus doesn't always answer me, so at those times I've had to be still and wait and see, and know.

I can be very much like Peter, who was very impulsive. I think sometimes God causes us to move quickly, but very often He tells us to sit down before we hurt ourselves, which is a line from *The Lion King*: "Sit down before you hurt yourself." As Christians, we often hurt each other, and I'm sorry for the times that I've hurt people. And I'm sure that people are sorry for the times that they have hurt me.

HOW DO YOU THINK PEOPLE SEE THE FAMILY TODAY?

It isn't always easy being a Zeidman. Others in the family have often felt as if we lived under a magnifying glass. People want to know how we live. Are we rich? No, we're not. People thought that we lived in Rosedale and that my father drove a Cadillac. This happened to my father and Alex, time and time again. Once it was said of Alex that he used the homeless people to wash his car. He said, "Well, no, my wife washes the car." He was joking.

Whoever you are and wherever you are, there will always be someone whose curiosity and imagination overtakes them. They imagine that someone is much better off than they are, and maybe it comforts them. And I don't mind if someone wants to ask me a personal question. It's always better to know the truth.

REFLECTIONS ON "LOVE DIVINE"*

By Elaine Z. Markovic

"Pure Unbounded Love" I sang this morning,
And yet,
At midnight with anxieties and wild imaginations,
I forget.
No remembrance of His goodness raining down,
No note of hymn within my mind is found.
Unbounded love in everlasting mercy covers me.
I wake to a songbird's ecstasy.

* Reflections on the hymn "Love Divine" as I drove
  home from church one morning.

CHAPTER 28

"Let Me Hear Your Voice in the Morning"

I 'll see you in the morning, Daddy." One couldn't help recalling Elaine's last words to Morris on the warm, idyllic spring morning when friends gathered for her funeral. A cloudless blue sky hung over the high peaked sanctuary of Christ Church St. James Anglican on Monday, May 4, 2009. She'd been attending the congregation for some time, not too far from her and Mica's suburban Etobicoke home.

In the front pew, facing the coffin with her picture prominently displayed, Mica leaned over his cane, with Lois and Sera on either side. Family members nearby included Margaret, her husband, Giulio, and Jae; David and his wife, Elizabeth, and their daughter, Kate; Maureen Zeidman Topp with her husband, Bob, Anne, Andrew and others from their extended families.

Close behind them sat the administrative leaders of the Scott Mission: executive director David Smith, Rev. Steve Shaw, chairman of the board of directors, members of the board and senior staff. In the surrounding pews, some were openly grieving, and many appeared distraught. The Mission had closed for the service and a bus had brought in many of the staff so that every seat was filled and some were standing at the back.

As the resonant harmonies of the organ filled the sanctuary, a large bronze cross proceeded down the centre aisle. The rector, Rev. Murray Henderson, followed in white vestments, reciting from the

Gospel of John, "I am the resurrection, and the life" (11:25)—words that Elaine had always appreciated in the Anglican funeral service. Rev. Henderson entered the pulpit, welcomed the congregation and began leading in prayer from the Anglican *Book of Alternative Services*. The congregation sang "Praise My Soul, the King of Heaven."

Margaret's daughter, Jae, read from 1 Thessalonians 4:13–18 (NRSV):

But we do not want you to be uninformed, brothers and sisters, about those who have died, so that you may not grieve as others do who have no hope.

David, Elaine's brother, read from the Gospel of John 20:1–9 (NRSV):

Early on the first day of the week, while it was still dark, Mary Magdalene came to the tomb and saw that the stone had been removed...Then Simon Peter came...and went into the tomb. He saw the linen wrappings lying there, and the cloth that had been on Jesus' head...Then the other disciple...also went in, and he saw and believed.

Between the readings, many wiped away tears as they sang Elaine's poignant hymn:

Let me hear Your voice in the morning,
Let me see Your path by day,
Let me know the breath of Your presence
In the evening
Lord, teach my feet to walk in Your way.

Even in the storm, You are with me
You have calmed the raging sea,
Death nor life, nor powers,
Nor any of creation can separate Your love from me.
Death nor life, nor powers,
Nor any of creation can separate Your love from me.

The rector spoke of Elaine with great affection and gratitude for the remarkable dedication she'd shown to the church despite illness and commitments to the Mission. Peter Duraisami, her long-time colleague, followed with a heartfelt tribute. He'd been with Elaine on the last day and described her enduring faith, courage, great love for others, and of the Lord.

In the bulletin was a special reflection from Maureen Zeidman Topp, called "Remembering Elaine":

Elaine was the third child of Morris and Annie Zeidman...She grew up, along with brothers Alex and David and sister Margaret, helping out in the work of the Mission, whether that meant stuffing envelopes and licking stamps at the dining room table, helping with cleaning chores or working at the summer camp. After graduating from Moulton College, Elaine joined her parents in the ministry they had founded and started work at the Scott Mission on a full-time basis.

In 1962 she married her dear Mica, and they had two wonderful daughters, Lois and Sera. Together they established a home that was a place of warmth and refuel for her family and others. Elaine was the loving centre of the family, always ready to listen and to lend support and comfort whenever needed. She was a godly mother who faithfully prayed for and with her children and husband, living her faith at home as she did outside its walls. She was lively and full of fun, often delighting the family with her storytelling and great sense of humour.

Over a span of more than 50 years in her work at the Scott Mission, she was at various times the camp registrar, the Christmas hamper coordinator, the office manager, a public speaker, and writer of the weekly newspaper column "The Good Samaritan Corner," which told the inspirational stories of lives touched and transformed by God through the Mission. Her creative gifts included writing poems and songs...

For her co-workers, she was an inspiration, always caring for others, tireless in her devotion in serving the Lord. Those who came to the Mission seeking help and comfort found in Elaine a tender heart, a sympathetic ear and a readiness to offer kindness and support. She was always eager to extend God's love and mercy to others. A reporter doing a story on the Mission some years ago remarked that if he was ever in trouble and needed help he would want to come to Elaine!

Her heart was open and generous to others, but more than anything else, her heart was open to God and filled with His love. All that she did came out of her deep commitment to her Lord Jesus Christ, whom she loved to worship and serve.

Many took solace in the Eucharist, going forward to kneel at the altar rail and receive the wafer and sip from the silver chalice, a reminder of what was most important for her—the body and blood of the Lord, elements "broken" and "poured out" for those who trust in Him. During Communion, the congregation sang "There Is a Redeemer" including these lyrics:

When I stand in glory, I will see His face, and
There I'll I serve my King forever, in that holy place.

The service began moving to a close with the words of the commendation:

Receive her into the arms of Your mercy,
into the blessed rest of everlasting peace,
and into the glorious company of the saints in light. Amen.

Then, out of the pews came the singers and musicians who had surrounded Elaine so many times when the Mission staff gathered for worship—the Scott Mission praise and worship team. Andrew, Alex's son, leaned over his guitar and introduced one last praise song from Elaine, starting with a strong, pulsing rhythm that she had called "Middle Eastern dance, double time."

Sound the trumpet in Zion, You singers, raise your voices high!
Clap the cymbals, blow the ram's horn!
The redemption of our God is nigh!

Wave the banners of Yeshua, He comes to set the captive free!
He comes to heal the broken-hearted,
And rejoice you blind for you shall see!

Alleluiah, Alleluiah, Alleluiah, Alleluiah,
Alleluiah, Alleluiah, Alleluiah, Alleluiah, Amen!

A surprising wave of joy revived the mourners as the cross was recessed back up the centre aisle, followed by Rev. Henderson and the family. Tears were mixed with smiles and the lingering comment heard in the pews, "This is how Elaine would have wanted to be remembered."

A generous luncheon was laid out in the reception area, where the family formed a receiving line. There were hugs, tears, kind words and so many memories of how precious Elaine had been to each one. They shared a feeling that she'd known so well at similar moments: someone has been lost that no one can replace.

Sustained by uncompromising courage, Elaine had inspired so many by the integrity of her faith and reassuring strength of her hope.

All the joy that she had poured into her life, poetry, music and those she loved was still reverberating among them as they shared their memories long into the afternoon. And there was also an ethereal reflection of grace that left everyone who loved Elaine with a greater confidence: "Lord, You know what You're doing."

THREE COMMUNION POEMS

By Elaine Z. Markovic

1 The wounded kneel with one accord
   Around the table of the Lord;
   His hands dispense the holy meal,
   The scars our promised wholeness seals.

2 "Broken" and "Shed."
   His ministering hand
   That was pierced
   Makes me whole.

   "Hungry" and "Fed."
   This ransom
   Paid for me by love
   Lifts my soul.

3 All is witnessed by that unseen cloud,
   For whom the feast in memory lies;
   Those who dwell with Christ and wait, with us
   Until the grand reunion in the skies.

We are surrounded by such a great cloud of witnesses.
(Hebrews 12:1 NIV)

CHAPTER 29

Afterwards: A Final Task

Mica was surrounded by his youngest sister, Gordana, daughters Lois and Sera, and his niece, Anne, when he passed away on Friday, January 6, 2012. They heard his last words: "It's time for me to say goodbye. I love you all very much and those who are not with us today." Many of the Mission staff and members of his congregation, St. Michael the Archangel Church, joined the family at his funeral on the following Tuesday, January 10. The event was graced by a genuine sadness, yet without the severe grief that had followed the loss of Elaine. There was a sensitive understanding that Mica had never felt complete apart from her and that to be with Elaine was the final desire of his heart. The congregation once again sang Elaine's hymns, "Let me hear Your voice in the morning," and closed with "Sound the Trumpet."

The previous summer, Mica and his daughters had gathered at the Mission's Caledon campsite for an act of dedication. Elaine had a special affection for the setting, and she'd have been pleased to see the campers happily engaged in the summer programs. Sera described Mica's preparations, which had begun more than a year before: "This was what my dad felt was his last assignment from the Lord—in fact, after getting the tree (an English oak) and a plaque made, he said, 'My work here is now done.' It's at Caledon Camp, behind the chapel, next to the tree. Buried beneath the oak is the entire Scripture of Isaiah 61."

The plaque displays a phrase taken from Isaiah 61:3: "They will be called oaks of righteousness" (NIV). The powerful opening verses, read by Jesus to His home congregation in Nazareth, had long been a spiritual touchstone for Elaine, an inspirational word sometimes shared with the Mission staff. As Sera noted, "It remains a calling on all of us"—everyone who carries on the work to which Elaine dedicated her life, a ministry that began more than a century ago with a young Jewish boy helping his pious father deliver groceries to the needy before *Erev Shabbat* (the eve of the Sabbath).

ISAIAH 61: THE YEAR OF THE LORD'S FAVOUR

The Spirit of the Sovereign LORD is on me, because the LORD has anointed me to proclaim good news to the poor. He has sent me to bind up the brokenhearted, to proclaim freedom for the captives and release from darkness for the prisoners, to proclaim the year of the LORD's favor and the day of vengeance of our God, to comfort all who mourn, and provide for those who grieve in Zion—to bestow on them a crown of beauty instead of ashes, the oil of joy instead of mourning, and a garment of praise instead of a spirit of despair. They will be called oaks of righteousness, a planting of the LORD for the display of his splendor. They will rebuild the ancient ruins and restore the places long devastated; they will renew the ruined cities that have been devastated for generations. Strangers will shepherd your flocks; foreigners will work your fields and vineyards. And you will be called priests of the LORD, you will be named ministers of our God. You will feed on the wealth of nations, and in their riches you will boast. Instead of your shame you will receive a double portion, and instead of disgrace you will rejoice in your inheritance. And so you will inherit a double portion in your land, and everlasting joy will be yours. (NIV)

ACKNOWLEDGEMENTS

There are innumerable people whose assistance was invaluable in developing this project, and I apologize if your name is not listed here. In particular, I need to thank:

Elaine, who I invited to envision a book that would honour her parents and describe her journey. Her sustaining presence has remained with me until the last words were written.

Elaine's daughters, Sera Rousalis and Lois Markovic, carried on that vision with me through their tireless efforts, contributions and personal support. I am also grateful to all the members of the family who allowed me to interview them and later helped to critique the manuscript.

My wife, Sue, and son, Jon, who sacrificed far beyond telling so that I could keep working until the drafts and edited versions were completed. Sue is always the "first reader, first editor and first critic" of all my pages. Her endless hours of dedication and tolerance made this possible.

Krysia Lear is the patient and caring editor who helped me to jump-start the project when I was stuck.

The elders and members of Kehillat Eytz Chaim/Tree of Life Congregation, who allowed me to take a two month sabbatical from congregational duties to write the first 100 pages.

Dr. Calvin Pater was my first church history professor at Knox College. His tremendous encouragement first allowed me to embrace a project on the Scott Mission, and he's never been properly thanked for telling me to get my work published.

Dr. Stuart Macdonald, professor of Canadian Church History at Knox College, looked over the chapters on Presbyterian church history.

The late David Smith, former executive director of the Scott Mission, encouraged the project to go ahead and was financially committed to getting it ready.

Peter Duraisami, CEO of The Scott Mission, Chair of the Board Joe Nemni, and the Board of the Mission (2008–2015) are due many thanks for supporting the completion of the project.

Special thanks are extended to all those who were interviewed and let their stories mingle with Elaine's. I've done my best to reproduce your love and affectionate memories of her.

This project would not be possible without those individuals dedicated to maintaining historical archives and assisting their clients. I gratefully extend thanks to the directors and staff at the Archives of the Presbyterian Church in Canada and The Ontario Jewish Archives (UJA Federation of Greater Toronto). I am particularly indebted to the PCC Archives, which has kept my undergraduate essay on file since 1980.

One last note: None of this would have happened if Rev. Dr. Alex Zeidman hadn't invited me, as a young Knox student, so kindly into his office 35 years ago. His wisdom and generosity of spirit have always remained an inspiration.

ENDNOTES

INTRODUCTION: MEETING ELAINE

[1] Jan Karon, *At Home in Mitford* (Toronto: Penguin, 1996), 139. Elaine enjoyed reading The Mitford Series, and the quote from this book, first in the series, is flagged and underlined with her exclamation mark in the margin.

CHAPTER 1: FINDING LAINE

[1] Homel Gene, "Spadina Avenue: The Cosmic Spine," *Outlook* (May/June 2007), 22ff.

[2] Irving Abella and Harold Troper, *None Is Too Many: Canada and the Jews of Europe 1933–1948* (Toronto: University of Toronto Press, 1983), xi.

[3] Anecdotal material about the family and Elaine's earliest years was taken from interviews with Margaret Kukurugya. Elaine's more extensive interviews provide the bulk of family material, and these were supplemented by interviews with other family members, as noted in the text.

CHAPTER 2: AN INTERESTING WEDDING

[1] "Zeidman-Martin," *Toronto Daily Star*, September 3, 1926.

[2] "Zeidman-Martin," *Toronto Evening Telegram*, September 3, 1926. Her daughters mentioned Elaine's aggravation with her middle name, "McNicol." Rev. McNicol, principal of Toronto Bible College, was a revered evangelical teacher in the first decades of the 20th century.

[3] In addition to Elaine's retelling of Annie's story, it was recounted in numerous publications to which Annie granted interviews over the years. Notes from an extensive, undated interview were found in the Scott Mission's archives.

4 Alex Zeidman, *Good and Faithful Servant: The Biography of Morris Zeidman* (Burlington: Crown Publications, 1990), 11. Alex prepared his father's biography at the request of the Scott mission board. This volume includes some of its contents but in no way replaces it. Readers will find stories, information and views that are not included here.

5 Sabati B. Rohold, *Missions to the Jews* (Toronto: Christian Synagogue, 1918), 4–5. Note that "Sabati" is sometimes spelled "Sabeti." The former is preferred, and other sources refer to him as as "Shabbetai" or "Shabtai," the more traditional spelling and pronunciation of this name.

6 Daniel Nessim, "Jewish Missions in Canada—A History," *LCJE Bulletin* 76 (May 2004), 10.

7 See photos in Rohold's *Missions to the Jews*.

8 S. B. Rohold, *The War and the Jew: A Bird's Eye View of the World's Situation and the Jews' Place in It* (Toronto: Macmillan, 1915), ix.

9 In 2015, the Messianic Jewish Alliance of America, the continuing organization of the H.C.A.A. (the name was changed in 1975), celebrated its 100th anniversary. With the International Messianic Jewish Alliance, the International Association of Messianic Congregations and Synagogues and the Union of Messianic Jewish Congregations, they represent a worldwide network of congregations and organizations, including many in Israel.

10 When the author spoke to Annie Zeidman concerning Rev. Rohold she emphasized his extraordinary intellectual gifts.

11 Jacob Gartenhaus, *Famous Hebrew Christians* (Grand Rapids: Baker Book House, 1979), 153–54.

12 Rohold, *Missions to the Jews*, 9.

13 Ibid., 10.

14 Bill Gladstone, "Backstory: Early 20th century missionary group sparks riot," *Canadian Jewish News,* April 22, 2015.

15 "Rev. S. B. Rohold, Excited, Says He Will Continue, Calls It 'Persecution,'" *Toronto Daily Star*, June 19, 1911, 1.

16 Rohold, *Missions to the Jews*, 17.

CHAPTER 3: HOLY CHUTZPAH—THE CHALLENGE OF A CALL

[1] Rohold, *Missions to the Jews*, 23.

[2] See post-war telegram in chapter 9.

[3] Fragment in United Church Archives, Toronto, file reference to S. B. Rohold in "Missions to Jews" [n.d.] includes materials from the pre-1925 Historical Committee of the Presbyterian Church in Canada.

[4] Presbyterian Church Archives, Minutes of the Presbytery of Toronto (November 3, 1930).

[5] See Gertrude's story in chapter 23.

[6] Gartenhaus, *Famous Hebrew Christians*, 157.

[7] See "A Reformed Work in Israel," accessed October 2015, http://hagefen.org.il/hagefencwi-history/.

[8] Ibid.

[9] Gartenhaus, *Famous Hebrew Christians*, 156.

[10] A. Zeidman, *Good and Faithful Servant*, 17.

CHAPTER 4: THE SOUP KITCHEN YEARS

[1] M. Zeidman, "The 'Soup Kitchen,'" *Presbyterian Good New and Good Will to the Jews* II (February 1930): 2.

[2] Ibid.

[3] A. Zeidman, *Good and Faithful Servant*, 22. This story is part of the original lore of the Mission, but it also indirectly points to the friendly relationship that Morris had developed with the press.

[4] Ibid., 11.

[5] "Church Again Feeds The Hungry," *Toronto Telegram*, November 3, 1931, 3.

[6] Ibid., 22.

[7] *Toronto Telegram*, April 12, 1938.

[8] Acts and Proceedings of the General Assembly of the Presbyterian Church in Canada 1937, 32.

[9] All poems by Annie Aitken Zeidman are taken from *The Love and the Gift* (Toronto: The Scott Mission, 1986). In this collection her poems often have no title except for the calendar year when they were first published. The calendar years have been placed in parentheses. Used with permission.

CHAPTER 5: THAT JEWISH GENTLEMAN

1 A. Zeidman, *Good and Faithful Servant*, 26–27.
2 Kathleen Bennett, "Letters to the Editor," *Toronto Telegram*, January 13, 1936.
3 "Lawson Protests In House Against Censor's Slashing Rev. M. Zeidman Sermon," *Toronto Telegram*, April 7, 1937.
4 "Presbytery To Consider Censorship of Pastor," *Toronto Telegram*, February 2, 1937.
5 *Toronto Telegram*, March 3, 1937.
6 Abella and Troper, *None Is Too Many*, 284.
7 *The Presbyterian Record*, February 1938, 39.
8 Alan Davies and Marilyn F. Nevsky, *How Silent Were the Churches? Canadian Protestantism and the Jewish Plight during the Nazi Era* (Waterloo: Wilfred Laurier University Press, 1997), 67–68.
9 "Swastika Feud Battles in Toronto," *Globe and Mail*, August 17, 1933, 1.
10 *Toronto Star*, August 17, 1933, 1.
11 Abella and Troper, *None Is Too Many*, 282.
12 A. Zeidman, *Good and Faithful Servant*, 21. (Quote from *Good News and Good Will to the Jews*, April 1935.)
13 Abella and Troper, *None Is Too Many*, 286-87.

CHAPTER 6: THE SCOTT—AND THE ZEIDMANS—CARRY ON

1 Morris Zeidman, "The Relationship of the Jewish Convert to the Christian Church," *Christians and Jews: A Report of the Conference on the Christian Approach to the Jews, Atlantic City, 1931* (New York: International Missionary Council, 1931), 87–92. In this important essay Morris gives his reasons for establishing indigenous Hebrew Christian churches, a movement that wouldn't appear until the rise of Messianic Judaism in the 1970s. One of his reasons is anti-Semitism in the church, and he notes here the embarrassing incident of Christians refusing to take communion with Hebrew Christians, including his sister.
2 Rev. M. Zeidman, "Letters to the Editor," *Toronto Daily Star*, December 23, 1942, 6.
3 Houston, Zeidman, v. Robertson, [1944] 3 Dominion Law Reports 377.

CHAPTER 7: THE LORD WILL PROVIDE

[1] A. Zeidman, *Good and Faithful Servant*, 38.

[2] Elaine affirmed that Morris had made this statement. Later reports suggested that the elderly Mrs. Carmichael was expecting to move out of the home.

[3] A. Zeidman, *Good and Faithful Servant*, 39.

CHAPTER 8: CONFRONTING THE HOLOCAUST

[1] "Will Study South America as a Haven for Refugees," *Toronto Telegram*, August 15, 1939.

[2] M. Zeidman, "Jews in Poland Today," 1946, 1 (one of several essays in the Scott Mission Archives that appeared in *The Scott Mission Review* or other Christian publications).

[3] A. Zeidman, *Good and Faithful Servant*, 34.

[4] Ibid., 35.

[5] M. Zeidman, "Jews in Poland Today," 2.

[6] Ibid., 2–3.

[7] Ibid., 2.

[8] A. Zeidman, *Good and Faithful Servant*, 43.

[9] M. Zeidman, "Jews in Poland Today," 3.

[10] Ibid., 4.

[11] Ibid., 5.

[12] Ibid., 7.

[13] Ibid., 13.

[14] Ibid., 7.

[15] Ibid., 9.

[16] Ibid., 10.

[17] M. Zeidman, "A Small Remnant Survived," 1947, 2 (essay from the Mission archives).

[18] M. Zeidman, "Jews in Poland Today," 12.

[19] Ibid., 13.

[20] M. Zeidman, "A Small Remnant Survived," 13.

[21] A. Zeidman, *Good and Faithful Servant*, 44.

CHAPTER 9: THE GOOD SAMARITAN OF "CZENSTOCHOVA"

[1] A. Zeidman, *Good and Faithful Servant*, 46.
[2] J. B. Salsberg, "The Scott Mission and the Jews in Toronto," *The Canadian Jewish News*, December 23, 1982, 5.
[3] M. Zeidman, "To the Bride of Christ," 1946 (essay in the Scott Mission archives, as above).
[4] J. B. Salsberg, "The tug-of-war between Rev. Morris Zeidman and Moyshe Tarnovky's Chenstochover Society," *Canadian Jewish News*, December 30, 1982, 5.
[5] Ibid.
[6] A. Zeidman, *Good and Faithful Servant*, 45–47.
[7] Ibid., 36.

CHAPTER 10: GROWING PAINS

[1] Alfreda Hall, *Per Adua: The Story of Moulton College 1888–1954* (no publisher, Moulton College Alumnae Association, 1982), 65–66.

CHAPTER 12: PUBLIC CHOICES—PRIVATE STRUGGLES, PART 1

[1] A. Zeidman, *Good and Faithful Servant*, 46.

CHAPTER 13: PUBLIC CHOICES—PRIVATE STRUGGLES, PART 2

[1] Dr. Nelles Silverthorne was for many years the honorary consulting physician at Toronto's Hospital for Sick Children. He succeeded Dr. James Hunter as the second chairman of the board of directors at the Mission, holding the position from 1966 to 1986. Dr. Silverthorne was a leading teacher and pioneering practitioner of paediatric medicine in Canada.

CHAPTER 14: "THE MIRACLE ON SPADINA AVENUE"

[1] "The Miracle on Spadina Avenue," Samuel Campbell, *Toronto Star*, December 20, 1958, 9.
[2] *Toronto Star* online, May 5, 2010.
[3] *Toronto Star* online, October 16, 1986.

CHAPTER 15: ONE MORE VISION

[1] A. Zeidman, *Good and Faithful Servant*, 40.
[2] Ibid., 48.

CHAPTER 16: "SEE YOU IN THE MORNING"

[1] Ibid., 7.

[2] *The Globe and Mail*, October 30, 1964.

[3] Editorial page, *Toronto Telegram*, October 30, 1964.

CHAPTER 17: THE GOOD SAMARITAN WEARS HORN-RIMMED GLASSES

[1] *Presbyterian Record*, June 1969, 8–11.

[2] Rev. Alex Zeidman, "Miraculous way starving Biafran children revive when fed amazes Toronto minister," *Toronto Daily Star*, March 1, 1969, 69.

[3] "Tour of relief duty: Biafra hospitals bombed," *Globe and Mail*, April 21, 1969, 5.

[4] "'Little Hope for Biafra,' Missionary Says," *Toronto Daily Star*, April 21, 1969, 32.

CHAPTER 20: LOSING ALEX

[1] Alex Zeidman, "Fliedner's Remarkable Ministry," *The Presbyterian Record*, October 1976, 16–17.

[2] Don Page, acknowledgements in *Effective Team Leadership* (Nairobi: Evangel Publishing House, 2008).

[3] "Our History," Citizens for Public Justice, includes numerous articles on Gerald Vandezande, CM, accessed May 2015, http://www.cpj.ca/our-history.

[4] Paul Bilodeau, "Scott Mission director dies after his boat capsizes in lake," *Toronto Star*, October 6, 1986, A3.

[5] "Alexander Zeidman Director of Scott Mission aided Sudan relief work," Obituaries, *Globe and Mail*, October 2, 1986, D14.

[6] Bilodeau, "Scott Mission director dies."

[7] Kelly Toughill, "Rich and poor gather to remember Zeidman," *Toronto Star*, October 9, 1986, A16.

[8] Bilodeau, "Scott Mission director dies."

CHAPTER 21: AN UNEXPECTED TURN

[1] Jim Foster, "Director of Scott Mission forced out over 'personality conflict,'" *Toronto Star*, April 5, 1988, A6.

CHAPTER 22: PRAYING THROUGH

[1] "A. Zeidman helped run Mission," *Toronto Star*, April 2, 1992, A8.
[2] "Zeidman, Annie Aitken," Deaths, *Globe and Mail*, April 3, 1992, A14.

CHAPTER 23: THE GRACIOUS HAND OF THE LORD

[1] "Manson, Gertrude," *Toronto Star*, September 8, 1999, B7.

INDEX OF POETRY SELECTIONS

WORKS CITED

Abella, Irving, and Harold Troper. *None Is Too Many: Canada and the Jews of Europe 1933–1948*. Toronto: University of Toronto Press, 1983.

Davies, Alan, and Marilyn F. Nevsky. *How Silent Were the Churches? Canadian Protestantism and the Jewish Plight during the Nazi Era*. Waterloo: Wilfred Laurier University Press, 1997.

Gartenhaus, Jacob. *Famous Hebrew Christians*. Grand Rapids: Baker Book House, 1979.

Hall, Alfreda. *Per Ardua: The Story of Moulton College 1888–1954*. Toronto: Moulton College Alumnae Association, 1982.

Homel, Gene. "Spadina Avenue: The Cosmic Spine." *Outlook* (May/June 2007).

Karon, Jan. *At Home in Mitford*. New York: Penguin Books, 1996.

Nessim, Daniel. "Jewish Missions in Canada—A History." *LCJE Bulletin* 76 (May 2004).

Rohold, Sabati B. *Missions to the Jews*. Toronto: Christian Synagogue, 1918.

Rohold, Sabati B. *The War and the Jew: A Bird's Eye View of the World's Situation and the Jews' Place in It*. Toronto: Macmillan, 1915.

Zeidman, Alex. *Good and Faithful Servant: The Biography of Morris Zeidman*. Burlington: Crown Publications, 1990.

———. "The Christian and Social Action—What happened to the Deacon?" Toronto: The Scott Mission, 1971.

———. "Fliedner's Remarkable Ministry." *The Presbyterian Record* (October 1976): 16–17.

Zeidman, Annie A. *Fifteen Original Bible Songs with Lesson References*. Toronto: Jarman Publications Ltd.

———. *The Love and the Gift*. Toronto: The Scott Mission, 1986.

Zeidman, Morris. "The Relationship of the Jewish Convert to the Christian Church." In *Christians and Jews: A Report of the Conference on the Christian Approach to the Jews*, Atlantic City, 1931. New York: International Missionary Council, 1931.